Children's rights and child protection

Critical times, critical issues in Ireland

Edited by
Deborah Lynch and Kenneth Burns

Manchester University Press
Manchester and New York

distributed in the United States exclusively
by Palgrave Macmillan

Published by Manchester University Press
Oxford Road, Manchester M13 9NR, UK
and Room 400, 175 Fifth Avenue, New York, NY 10010, USA
www.manchesteruniversitypress.co.uk

Distributed in the United States exclusively by
Palgrave Macmillan, 175 Fifth Avenue,
New York, NY 10010, USA

Distributed in Canada exclusively by
UBC Press, University of British Columbia, 2029 West Mall,
Vancouver, BC, Canada V6T 1Z2

British Library Cataloguing-in-Publication Data is available

Library of Congress Cataloging-in-Publication Data is available

ISBN 978 0 7190 9085 1 paperback

First published by Manchester University Press in hardback 2012

This paperback edition first published 2013

Printed by Lightning Source

Children's rights and
child protection

MANCHESTER
1824

Manchester University Press

Contents

Figures and tables

Figures

Tables

Notes on contributors

Helen Buckley is a senior lecturer in the School of Social Work and Social Policy, Trinity College Dublin. Her research interests are in child protection policy and practice, service user perspectives, inter-agency cooperation and knowledge transfer. She was recently appointed Chair of the national panel for the Review of Serious Incidents including Deaths of Children in Care. Recent publications include 'Compliance with guidelines: A case study of child protection in schools', *Irish Journal of Family Law*, Spring 2010 (co-authored with Kathryn McGarry), 'Like walking on eggshells: services users' views and expectations of the child protection system', *Child and Family Social Work*, 2010, and '*Report of an Audit of Child Protection Research in Ireland 1990–2009*' co-authored with Carmel Corrigan and Liz Kerrins, published by the Children Act Advisory Board, 2010.

Kenneth Burns is a college lecturer and Deputy Director of the Master of Social Work course at University College Cork. He has worked as a social worker and social work team leader in child protection and welfare, and his main teaching and research interests are in this area. Recent publications include: *Child Protection and Welfare Social Work: Contemporary Themes and Practice Perspectives* (co-edited with Deborah Lynch, 2008) and '*Career Preference', 'Transients' and 'Converts': A Study of Social Workers' Retention in Child Protection and Welfare* (Burns, 2011). Kenneth is a research associate with the Institute for Social Sciences in the 21st century (ISS21). He is also a member of the UCC Science Shop research group, who are participating in a European Commission Seventh Framework Programme project called *Public Engagement with Research and Research Engagement with Society* (PERARES). He is a founding member of both the Social Work Development Unit (http://swdu.ucc.ie) and the inter-agency Child Protection and Welfare Conference and Research group (http://swconf.ucc.ie).

Alastair Christie is Professor of Applied Social Studies at University College Cork. He worked as a social worker and social work manager in England and Canada before starting his academic career at the University of Lancaster and gaining a PhD in social policy at the University of Manchester. His research interests include: globalisation, migration and social work; social justice and social welfare; and social work as a professional identity. He is the Joint Course Director of the Doctor of Social Science Programme at University College Cork.

Mary Louise Corr is a PhD candidate at the School of Social Work and Social Policy, Trinity College Dublin. Her PhD is a qualitative study investigating the onset and history of offending among young people in contact with criminal justice agencies in Dublin. Previously, Mary Louise was a research intern at the Children's Research Centre, graduated from Trinity College Dublin in 2003 with LLB and completed an MSc criminology at the University of Edinburgh in 2005. She also works as a teaching assistant in Housing Policy and Introduction to Social Policy courses for undergraduate students at Trinity College Dublin.

John Devaney is a lecturer in social work at Queen's University Belfast. Prior to this he worked as a practitioner and manager in children's social services in the statutory sector for twenty years in Northern Ireland. His research interests include familial violence, the impact of adversity in childhood on later adult outcomes, and non-accidental child deaths. He is chair of the Northern Ireland Branch of the British Association for the Study and Prevention of Child Abuse and Neglect, and a member of the North South Ministerial Council Child Protection Research Sub-group. He has published extensively in the area of child protection and domestic violence.

Ann Doyle is a principal social worker with the Health Service Executive South working in the area of aftercare with children and young adults. Ann moved to this post having worked for 13 years as a social worker and manager in child protection and welfare in Cork, London, Sarajevo and Boston. In her present post she has been responsible for developing and standardising the provision of aftercare services and is a member of the national working group developing national policy and procedures in the area of aftercare. Her reports include: *A Proposal for the Development of an Aftercare Service for the Southern Health Board* (2001) and *Policy and Procedures Manual for an Aftercare Service* (Health Service Executive South, 2007).

Ian Elliott is a graduate of Trinity College and the University of Ulster, and also has a Master of Business Administration from the Open University Business School. He was appointed director of NSPCC in June 2001, which involved responsibility for leading services, influencing and campaigning for child protection policies within Northern Ireland. In September 2005 he was seconded to the DHSSPS (Department of Health, Social Services and Public Services) to the role of lead child protection adviser. This role was further expanded by the minister to design and implement a major reform programme for child protection services within the region. He was appointed Chief Executive Officer to the National Board for Safeguarding Children in the Catholic Church in Ireland in July 2007.

Harry Ferguson is Professor of Social Work at the University of Nottingham. After training and working as a social worker, he completed his PhD at the University of Cambridge and then worked in his native Ireland, at Trinity College Dublin, University College Cork, and latterly at University College Dublin, and moved to University of West England in 2001. He has researched and published widely in the areas of child abuse/protection, domestic violence, fatherhood and masculinities, and social theory and social work. His books include *Keeping Children Safe: Child Abuse, Child Protection and the Promotion of Welfare* (with Máire O'Reilly) (A. & A. Farmar, 2001); *Protecting Children in Time: Child Abuse, Child Protection and the Consequences of Modernity* (Palgrave, 2004); and *Best Practice in Social Work: Critical Perspectives* (with Karen Jones and Barry Cooper) (Palgrave, 2008).

Martin Geoghegan is a lecturer in the School of Applied Social Studies, University College Cork. His primary research and teaching interests are in civil society, social movements, governance and youth policy. He is co-Principal Investigator with Fred Powell on the research project *Civil Society, Youth and Youth Policy in Modern Ireland*, which is funded by the Irish Research Council for the Humanities and Social Sciences. His publications include *The Politics of Community Development* (with Powell) and *The Politics of Youth: Youth Policy, Civil Society and the Modern Irish State* (with Powell and Swirak, 2011).

Mary Hargaden has worked in children's social services since the late 1970s. She holds qualifications in both social work and health services management. She has worked in statutory and voluntary social services as practitioner and manager in areas such as child protection and welfare, family support, community development, foster care and intellectual disability. She has worked in the Department of Health as adviser on the setting up of a number of family support initiatives and in the development of policy. She has also served on boards of management of many voluntary and statutory bodies and has been a member of the National Social Work Qualifications Board since 2000. She is currently working as Child Care Manager with the Health Service Executive in PCCC in Local Health Office North Dublin.

Pat Kelleher is a senior social work practitioner within the Health Services Executive and is based in South Lee Social Work Department, Cork. Pat works on the duty section of the social work team in a role that involves the assessment and intervention in respect of new child protection and welfare referrals. Pat qualified a social worker in 2001 having completed the Masters Degree at University College Cork and initially worked in South Lee Social Work Department as an area social worker, managing a long-term caseload. Pat has a particular interest in the area of social work assessment in cases of suspected non-accidental injury and physical abuse.

Ursula Kilkelly is a senior lecturer and Co-Director of the Centre for Criminal Justice and Human Rights, Faculty of Law, University College Cork. Ursula has published widely on children's rights in the *Child and Family Law Quarterly*, the *Human Rights Quarterly* and *Youth Justice: An International Journal*, and the *Irish Journal of Family Law*. She has undertaken funded research for the Ombudsman for Children and the Office of the Minister for Children and Youth Affairs. Her books include *Children's Rights in Ireland: Law, Policy and Practice* (Tottel, 2008); *Youth Justice in Ireland* (IAP, 2006) and *The Child and the ECHR* (Ashgate, 1999). She is currently guest editor of a special issue of *Irish Educational Studies* on education and the law.

Deborah Lynch is a senior lecturer in the School of Social Work and Human Services at the University of Queensland. Previously she was Director of the Master of Social Work course in the School of Applied Social Studies at the University College Cork. She has practised as a social worker in South Africa and Australia, and her main teaching and research interests are child protection and welfare; community work; and social work education. Her most recent publications include: *Child Protection and Welfare Social Work: Contemporary Themes and Practice Perspectives* (co-edited with Kenneth Burns) (A. & A. Farmar, 2008) and *Young People's Views on Youth-Friendly Facilities in East Cork*, a publication on a consultative process with young people (co-authored with Mary McGrath) (ECAD, 2007). Deborah is a research associate with the Institute for Social Sciences in the 21st Century (ISS21) and a founding member of the Social Work Development Unit (University College Cork).

Eilidh MacNab has over 23 years experience of working in the Statutory Children and Family Services in Scotland and Ireland. She holds a Diploma in Social Work/NQSW, MSc in Social Work, Mental Health and Child Protection Qualification. She was a generic social worker for Strathclyde region, Scotland from 1986 and developed an interest in child protection work and became a member of Scotland's First Joint Police/Social Work Unit in 1990, investigating/assessing all claims of child abuse with Central Scotland. Eilidh moved to HSE Dublin North in 1999 as Duty/Intake Team Leader and became Principal Social Worker in 2003. Eilidh is committed to public service and working to promote strengths within children and families that she and her team provide services to within Dublin North.

Paula Mayock is a lecturer and senior researcher at the School of Social Work and Social Policy and Children's Research Centre, Trinity College Dublin. Her research focuses primarily on the lives and experiences of marginalised youth, covering areas including homelessness, drug use, sexuality and mental health. She is a NIDA (National Institute on Drug Abuse, USA) INVEST fellow (2006) and an IRCHSS (Irish Council for the Humanities and Social Sciences) research fellow (2009), and the author of numerous articles, book chapters and research reports.

The Honourable Mrs Justice Catherine McGuinness is President of the Law Reform Commission and former Justice of the Supreme Court, was born in Belfast and educated in Belfast and Dublin (Alexandra College, TCD and the King's Inns). Catherine was called to the Irish bar in 1977. In 1989 she was called to the Inner Bar, and called to the Bar of New South Wales in 1993. In addition to her judicial career, Catherine has served on An Bord Uchtála (the Adoption Board), the Voluntary Health Insurance Board, the National Economic and Social Council, the Second Commission on the Status of Women, and has chaired the National Social Services Board, the Board of National College of Art and Design, the Employment Equality Agency, the Kilkenny Incest Investigation and the Forum for Peace and Reconciliation.

Carl O'Brien is Chief Reporter for *The Irish Times*. He previously held the position of Social Affairs Correspondent (2004–2009) for the newspaper, writing regularly on social care issues. He has also worked for *The Irish Examiner* newspaper as a political correspondent and news reporter.

Eoin O'Sullivan is senior lecturer in Social Policy in the School of Social Work and Social Policy, Trinity College, Dublin and Fellow of Trinity College. He is lead editor of the *European Journal of Homelessness*. Recent collaborative publications include *Young People's Homeless Pathways* (2008), *Lives in Crisis: Homeless Young People in Dublin* (The Liffey Press, 2007); *Crime and Punishment in Ireland 1922 to 2003: A Statistical Sourcebook* (Institute of Public Administration (IPA), 2005), *Crime, Punishment and the Search for Order in Ireland* (IPA, 2004), *Crime Control in Ireland: The Politics of Intolerance* (CUP, 2001) and *Suffer the Little Children: The Inside Story of Ireland's Industrial Schools* (Continuum, 2001).

Fred W. Powell is Professor of Social Policy, Dean of Social Science, and Head of the School of Applied Social Studies at University College, Cork, since 1990. Born in Dublin, he holds degrees from Trinity College, Dublin, the University of Edinburgh and University College Dublin. Previously he lectured at the University of Ulster. He has been an instructor on the Extension Programme of the University of California, San Diego, and has lectured in the United Kingdom, Italy, Portugal and France.

Colin Reid is a social worker by professional training and is Policy and Public Affairs Manager for NSPCC – a post he has held for 10 years. Colin has had extensive involvement in a range of child protection policy issues in Northern Ireland, including cross-border developments, and has worked at a national United Kingdom level on the new vetting and barring arrangements following Soham with the Safeguarding Vulnerable Groups Act. He represents NSPCC on the Board of Public Protection Arrangements in Northern Ireland (PPANI). and outside of NSPCC is Board member of the Regulation and Quality Improvement Authority, the independent health and social care regulator for Northern Ireland. During a part-time secondment to the Office of the First and Deputy First Minister, Colin coco-ordinated the NI Executive statement on safeguarding children. He is a member of the North South Ministerial Council Child Protection Research Sub-group.

Margaret Scanlon is a research officer at the School of Applied Social Studies University College Cork (UCC). Over the last decade she has worked on a range of projects concerned with formal and informal education, both at UCC and at the University of London. She co-authored *Changing Sites of Learning* (with David Buckingham) and several journal articles on out-of-school learning. More recently, she co-authored *The Politics of Youth: Youth Policy, Civil Society and the Modern Irish State* (with Powell, Geoghegan and Swirak, 2011). Her current research interests include: youth work, youth policy, informal learning, and continuing professional development.

Katharina Swirak is a PhD student at the School of Applied Social Studies, University College Cork (UCC). From 2008 to 2010 she worked as a researcher at UCC on the youth policy project *Civil Society, Youth and Youth Policy in Modern Ireland*. She co-authored *The Politics of Youth: Youth Policy, Civil Society and the Modern Irish State* (with Powell, Geoghegan and Scanlon, 2011). Her current research interests include: social policy analysis of preventative interventions aimed at 'youth at risk', youth culture and children's spaces.

Sadhbh Whelan is a researcher whose interests are mainly in child protection and welfare, domestic violence, service-user perspectives, refugees and asylum seekers and children in hospital. She was employed in the Children's Research Centre at TCD from 2002 to 2009. She was co-author of the *Framework for the Assessment of Vulnerable Children and Their Families* (with Buckley and Howarth, 2008) and *Listen to Me! Children's Experiences of Domestic Violence* (with Buckley and Holt, 2006) and *Service Users' Perceptions of the Irish Child Protection System* (with Buckley, Carr and Murphy, 2008).

Mark Yalloway is the project manager for the DRM pilot in Dublin North. Mark is a professionally qualified social worker who has worked as a child protection social worker and team leader in Meath. Mark has also worked as project manager for the development of the Family Welfare Conferencing Service in the former North Eastern Health Board and as senior manager for Children and Family Services in the office of the Lead Local Health Manager for Children and Family Services in Dublin North East since 2007.

Editors' acknowledgements

It takes the labour of many, and the patience and support of others, to complete a book like this. This is particularly true of this edited text, which brings together a wide range of practitioners, academics, service managers and policy makers with knowledge and expertise on critical issues in child protection and welfare. Therefore, we would like to thank the chapter authors for contributing their time, expertise and energy to this book, over and above their myriad family and professional responsibilities.

We would like to acknowledge the dedication and hard work of the Child Protection and Welfare Social Work committee, and for their continued support for these books. The genesis of most of the chapters in this book is the last conference in this series – 'Keeping Children Safe'.

In particular, we would like to pay tribute to the career of Sylda Langford, formerly Director General of the Office of the Minister for Children and Youth Affairs, and we are grateful to Sylda for supporting the conference and book series. Thanks also to Colette Ryan and Rebecca Long for their attention to detail and patience in formatting the reference lists. We are grateful to Tony Mason and staff at Manchester University Press for their advice and support.

We would also like to acknowledge the financial support of the Children Act Advisory Board, the Office of the Minister for Children and Youth Affairs, the School of Applied Social Studies at University College Cork and the College of Arts, Celtic Studies and Social Sciences Research Publication Fund.

As we compiled this book, we were struck by the extraordinary contribution made in the last decade by individuals, civil society organisations, professional groups, children's advocates and survivor groups, on behalf of children. Their work endures and brings us forward; we can never go back.

Finally, family always seem to bear the burden of a project such as this. To Denise and Finbarr, thank you for your continued support and we will try not to say 'this is the last edition' any more. To Kiran, Ella and Leah, we hope this book makes a positive contribution to your experiences of childhood.

Kenneth Burns and Deborah Lynch
Social Work Development Unit,
University College Cork, Ireland.

1

Politics, democracy and protecting children

Kenneth Burns and Deborah Lynch

It shall be the first duty of the Government of the Republic to make provision for the physical, mental and spiritual well-being of the children, to secure that no child shall suffer hunger or cold from lack of food, clothing, or shelter, but that all shall be provided with the means and facilities requisite for their proper education and training as Citizens of a Free and Gaelic Ireland. (Dáil Éireann, 1919)

Introduction

This extract taken from the *Democratic Programme* presented at the first meeting of the first Irish Dáil (Parliament) clearly articulates the primary duty of a democratic republic: to address *all* children's needs as citizens and ensure their well-being. This programme, based on principles of social justice, was considered 'too radical' by some members of the first Dáil, particularly in its earliest drafts (RTÉ, 1969), and was never implemented. Given the levels of poverty at the time, implementation would have possibly been beyond the economic resources of the emerging nation state. However, despite the economic reality of the period, if the principles of this programme had permeated the political, cultural and social milieu through their adoption in the 1937 Irish Constitution, would Ireland's children have been located differently in terms of their position and status within society?

This question has stimulated us to reflect upon lost opportunities as a nation to locate children centrally as citizens where their rights are actualised and enacted within a democracy. After a long gestation period, the Irish nation is positioned to hold a referendum on affording children (some) rights within the Constitution (see Chapters 3 and 4;

Joint Committee on the Constitutional Amendment on Children, 2010). The themes of suppression and denial in relation to social issues such as the 'poor', one-parent families, and the abuse of children within the family and the industrial school system, reoccur through contemporary Irish history (Ferriter, 2004). We are beginning to confront the reality of lost generations of children through society's construction of children as objects, sources of labour, and in need of 'control', rather that the valued and active citizens envisaged in the *Democratic Programme* (Dáil Éireann, 1919). The legacy of the state and the Catholic Church's systemic failure to protect children has been devastating: 'lost' children through an industrial school system characterised by abuse, neglect and cruelty (see Chapter 2; Raftery and O'Sullivan, 1999; Ryan, 2009); mothers and children 'confined' to Magdalen laundries;[1] the sexual abuse and neglect of children within the private 'safe' domain of the family (see, for example, McKay, 1998; Donnellan, 2009), and the clerical sexual abuse of children (see Chapter 5; Moore, 1995; Murphy *et al.*, 2009; Murphy *et al.* 2010; Ryan, 2009).

The enmeshed nature of the relationship between church and state and Irish society's dissonant values regarding children, sustained a culture of suppression and denial in relation to the realities of children's lives within the family and in the care of institutions. The preservation of systems and institutions (and individuals within them) frequently took precedence over the protection of children. One of many examples was the state's failure to pursue reports of physical beatings and humiliations in the industrial school system (see Raftery and O'Sullivan, 1999; Ferriter, 2004). A further example involved the Catholic Church's shielding of individual clergy members, against whom allegations were made of sexual abuse (see Murphy *et al.*, 2009; Murphy *et al.* 2010; Ryan, 2009). The church authorities' modus operandi was to protect the church as an institution over *all* other considerations (Goode *et al.*, 2003), and in denying the reality of severe abuses by its members, it failed children and failed to prevent further abuse. The issue of clerical child abuse is not uniquely Irish, and has emerged in other countries such as the United States of America, Canada, Germany, Belgium, Austria and Australia, among others (see Chapter 5). In Ireland, it is only in recent years, largely through the work of survivor groups, civil society organisations, and the *Commission to Inquire into Child Abuse* inquiry and redress process for persons who were abused in institutions, that we are emerging from this 'hidden' past. Hearing and validating these critical voices has been central in this process. We can no longer use denial. We must confront the need for fundamental change to protect children and ensure their well-being.

This chapter brings together politics, democracy and children's rights to set the context for the chapters that follow. Rather than provide a summary of each chapter in this book, we set out to discuss the broad political context for child protection and welfare in a democratic state. We begin by critiquing the slow road to constitutional and systemic reform in child protection and welfare in Ireland. We identify critical issues, which we argue, are implicated in inhibiting the implementation of fundamental reforms in the area of children's services – reforms that will be outlined and argued for in the following chapters. The purpose of this approach is to examine how democratic political systems and its processes are fundamental to promoting change. The theme of moving from a socio-political culture of suppression and denial towards a more open, accountable and transparent model, will frame our discussions. Finally, we outline why we believe this is a particularly critical time for child protection and welfare in Ireland, and our analysis emphasises the need for a reorientation towards a politics of recognition and action. The chapter concludes with a summary of the structure of the book.

Politics: the slow road to constitutional and systemic reform

The state's child care and protection services were particularly under-developed until the mid-1990s (see, for example, Ferguson and O'Reilly, 2001; Buckley, 2003; Skehill, 2004). Since then there have been many significant positive developments in policy, legislation and services for children (see Burns, 2007; Lynch and Burns, 2008). Many of these developments were instigated during the Celtic Tiger years, which was a period of unprecedented growth and economic prosperity in the Republic of Ireland. Nevertheless, reform in child care and protection services has been ad hoc and incident driven, often prompted by moral panic arising from abuse inquiries, and pressure for reform from civil society organisations, professional associations, the Ombudsman for Children and the United Nations (see, for example, Committee on the Rights of the Child, 2006; Barnardos, 2010; Children's Rights Alliance, 2010; Irish Association of Social Workers, 2010; Ombudsman for Children, 2010).

However, a characteristic of the Irish state has been a repeated failure to implement fundamental recommended reforms; recommendations that are often repeated in successive reports. We question why our democratic political system has not proactively led change, and comprehensively implemented its vision for children as articulated in documents such the *National Children's Strategy* (Government of Ireland, 2000) and *The Agenda for Children's Services: A Policy Handbook* (Office of the Minister for Children, 2007), and fully enacted successive recommendations for the reform of children's services (see, for example, Government of Ireland, 1980; McGuinness, 1993; Office of the Minister for Children and Youth Affairs, 2009).

Notwithstanding the goals of the *National Children's Strategy*, there has never been a national strategic plan that has been collaboratively developed, negotiated and agreed by all stakeholders, and which provides a comprehensive framework for a resourced integrated systems approach to child protection and welfare. These issues are not unique to Ireland, and developing a modern, effective and integrated child protection system has also presented considerable challenges to other nation states (Svevo-Cianci *et al.*, 2010). However, a particular issue in Ireland in protecting children has been the primacy placed on parental autonomy and the privacy of the family, and the lack of an explicit statement of children's rights, within the Constitution. This, we believe, is central to the state's passive orientation towards children rather than the active role indicated in *Democratic Programme*. The failure of successive Irish governments to implement constitutional reform in relation to children's rights, has been implicated in the state's and society's failure to protect and promote the welfare of children (McGuinness, 1993; Murphy *et al.*, 2005). We now outline a number of political and organisational factors, which it appears to us, are implicated in inhibiting the reform process and the full implementation of policy.

Political and organisational factors

We question whether the state has been slow to pursue constitutional reform regarding children's rights because it is concerned about the potential political consequences of conflict with parents regarding further intrusion into the family and regulating parenting. For example, a potential source of conflict may be contained in a recent survey on parenting style and disciplines in Ireland which found that nearly 60 per cent of parents interviewed believed that 'parents should have the right to smack their children if they so wish' (Halpenny *et al.*, 2009, p. 10). This is in conflict with the position of external bodies such as the Committee on the Rights of the Child (2006) and the *European Social Charter (Revised)* (Council of Europe, 1996).[2] Additionally, the state may have taken the 'slow road' to change in an attempt to limit its own liability from individuals and groups seeking to effect their rights. Greater openness and transparency may expose and increase the risk of litigation to the state. Many of the chapters in this book raise questions about our stance towards and treatment of children, and as King (1997, p. 3) argues, 'there are issues of principles and values at stake, which need to be resolved by society, before policies can be drafted and decisions made'. Social and political engagement is fundamental in order to promote the rights of children. However, certain characteristics of the Irish political system may hinder such engagement and leadership.

TDs (Parliamentarians) are immersed in local politics through a brokerage[3] system (Collins and O'Shea, 2003). The democratic political system, primarily focused on individual needs and local issues that could be addressed by local elected councillors, takes TDs' and ministerial time and energy away from their key role of developing policies, enacting legislation and providing leadership on issues of national interest. The pace of political processes to implement policy changes is often drawn out and therefore at variance with the immediacy of children's needs and well-being, particularly those children who are in high-risk situations. Critically, children and young people do not have a vote, and families at risk are marginalised politically as they are not organised or 'powerful' enough to influence political agendas.

The establishment of the Health Service Executive (HSE) in 2005 to centrally manage health, social and personal services in the Republic of Ireland, resulted in government ministers being distanced from front-line service delivery responsibilities. Ministers for Children and Youth Affairs were often appointed to the brief without any prior knowledge of, or expertise in, the area. Therefore, it takes a considerable period of time for a minister to become sufficiently acquainted with this complex brief, while at the same time devoting considerable energy reactively responding to high-profile crises as they arise. Furthermore, in the Republic of Ireland, the Minister for Children and Youth Affairs has, until 2011, been a junior minister with no voting rights at cabinet table.

The HSE, a vast and complex bureaucratic organisation with an annual budget of over €15 billion, often finds itself devoting much of its management and financial resources to the hospital sector. Therefore, social services such as those to children, older adults and persons with a disability are often relegated to minority positions and are largely 'invisible' within the HSE structure. An example of this is contained in Finlay's (2010) analysis of the agendas of the Board of the HSE since its inception, where he found that hospital management issues dominated, whereas the topic of children at risk had only *once*, in 2010, been an agenda item. There have been widespread criticisms from opposition political parties and others of the monolithic organisational structure of the HSE, its governance and its efficacy in delivering services (see, for example, O'Moráin, 2009; Health Information and Quality Authority, 2010c; O'Brien and Taylor, 2010). Had the HSE become 'too big to fail', whereby dismantling it would have been an acknowledgment of political failure? There has been some debate regarding the optimal location of children's services, possibly outside the HSE, in a separate organisation with dedicated management and resources. This new organisation could facilitate and coordinate a shift in policy towards a model of reform being examined in countries such as Canada, United States of America, Australia and New Zealand, which emphasises a '"whole of government" approach where statutory responsibility to address child protection issues is allocated to all government departments providing child and family services' (Buckley, 2010, p. 17). There have been some developments in this regard, which are outlined later in the chapter.

Moving from a culture of suppression and denial: a change in politics?

The beginning of a cultural shift from suppression and denial, to acknowledgement and assuming collective responsibility for past failures and future responsibilities to protect children was marked on 11 May 1999 by An Taoiseach's (Prime Minister's) apology to the survivors of child abuse when he said:

> On behalf of the State and of all citizens of the State, the Government wishes to make a sincere and long overdue apology to the victims of childhood abuse for our collective failure to intervene, to detect their pain, to come to their rescue. (Ahern, 1999, p. 1)

This apology laid the groundwork for the decade-long work of *The Commission to Inquire into Child Abuse* (2000–2009) (see Chapter 2) whose primary functions, later added to in 2005, were to:

- to hear evidence of abuse from persons who allege they suffered abuse in childhood, in institutions, during the period from 1940 or earlier, to the present day;
- to conduct an inquiry into abuse of children in institutions during that period and, where satisfied that abuse occurred, to determine the causes, nature, circumstances and extent of such abuse; and

- to prepare and publish reports on the results of the inquiry and on its recommendations in relation to dealing with the effects of such abuse.

The testimonies and key findings contained in the final *Commission to Inquire into Child Abuse Report* (Ryan, 2009) demonstrate how harmful a culture of secrecy and suppression is for children. However, despite the acknowledgement of systemic failures, and the professed learning from Ryan and other inquiry reports, we question whether these lessons have translated into a culture of greater transparency and openness within government and state organisations. There is some evidence for concern in this regard.

The HSE, the body charged with the care and protection of children, and its minister, are implicated in perpetuating a culture of secrecy. The Ombudsman, in describing how difficult it was for her to access HSE records to pursue complaints from the public, said that:

> I think there is a huge issue around the excessive secrecy and legalism of the HSE and it strikes me that it is a cultural thing ... it is redolent of a body that looks not to the public interest ... and seeks at times to protect its own interests (quoted in Donnellan, 2010, p. 6).

The HSE initially declined, much to the chagrin of the Minister for Children and Youth Affairs (its overseeing minister), to share case records with a review body established by this minister to investigate the deaths of children in its care (see Nelligan, 2010; Office of the Minister for Children and Youth Affairs, 2010). Furthermore, O'Brien writing in this volume (see Chapter 8), compared the content of published HSE 'section 8' reports[4] (see, for example, Health Service Executive, 2009b) with preliminary reports from its own employees. He noted that the final published 'section 8' report often suppressed critical comments from front-line staff, which indicated an under-resourcing of essential services, and critical problems in service delivery such as children at risk on waiting lists for assessment; and in direct contravention of policy, a significant number of children in care were without an allocated social worker. Since we wrote about these issues previously (see Lynch and Burns, 2008) it appears that many of these matters remain unaddressed (see, for example, Health Information and Quality Authority, 2011). As a society we continue to learn more about the under-resourcing of services to children and families, which emphasises the heavy burden on social workers and other professionals working with children and their families (see Chapters 7 and 8; Health Information and Quality Authority, 2010a, b, c). However, it should be acknowledged that in a time of severe economic crisis, the state has created 250+ new social work posts in child protection and welfare to address criticisms arising from the Ryan Report.

Is there an inherent problem in the socio-political process that inhibits openness and transparency, which also permeates state institutions? In her analysis of the politics of states' reporting to the United Nations Committee on the Rights of the Child, Friedner Parrat (2010) argues that a state's level of openness is linked to the perceived consequences and gains of disclosure regarding its approach to children and their rights. In her model, based on Rawl's theoretical work, she developed four ideal types of state in relation to their reporting on children's rights to the Committee on the Rights of the Child. In the best-case scenario, a liberal democracy,[5] where New Zealand was cited as an exemplar, 'will tell the truth, provide all available information and point out existing problems' (p. 472). This is in contrast to the least ideal scenario where a state provides insufficient information and there is a lack of transparency in their reporting. In her study she found that 'the reported improvements in children's rights depend not only on state party's economic means, but also on its will to report truthfully' (p. 472).

As outlined above, there have been issues with Ireland's approach to openness and transparency regarding children. Until the HSE and politicians acknowledge the degree to which child protection and welfare services are under-resourced, which would require investment in research and comprehensive information systems, only then can we begin to implement fundamental changes throughout the child protection system. The development of the new – and curiously named – *HSE Child Welfare and Protection Social Work Departments Business Processes. Report of the NCCIS Business Process Standardisation Project* (Health Service Executive, 2009a), may be one step in addressing information deficits in this area. The incessant partial disclosure of information concerning systemic issues only serves to weaken confidence in the services, and undermine staff morale. The benefits of a more open, accountable and transparent model is that this information will inform the development of services of the future and improve the lives of children and lead to a more just society as envisaged by Rawls in a liberal democracy.

Politicians and state organisations want to be perceived as effective: they are concerned about being tainted by negative disclosures and it is unsurprising that they fear being transparent about 'failures'. Additionally, hiding 'failures', or at least not pro-actively indentifying issues of concern, is mirrored in the 'overtly legalistic and defensive' (O'Brien, 2010, p. 15) approach by the HSE in responding to children's issues, and reflects a unwillingness to assume accountability because it may lead to redress, legal or otherwise. In this regard, the Department of Justice and Law Reform has indicated a concern that the constitutional change regarding children's rights will lead to more family law cases, which would have significant cost implications for the state (O'Brien and McCarthy, 2010). A further concern regarding a culture of secrecy was the attempted dilution by the last Fianna Fáil-led government of the democratically agreed text for a referendum on children's rights (see Chapter 4 for copy of the full amentment text; Joint Committee on the Constitutional Amendment on Children, 2010). The 2010 text had been debated and agreed in an inclusive and transparent democratic process. The dilution of the 2010 text was shrouded in secrecy and a leaked version of the Bill raises serious questions about the Irish state's commitment to children's rights (see O'Mahony, 2011) and its move towards a politics of recognition and action.

Critical times, critical issues: towards a politics of recognition and action

We are conscious that our portrayal of child protection on the island of Ireland in this and following chapters, may lead to unease and discouragement. However, the subtitle of this volume – *Critical times, critical issues* – is chosen to reflect both urgency and opportunity for change. While there have been other critical times for child protection and welfare, this time, we argue, is a particularly significant one. The publication of the Ryan Report and the subsequent public debate and critiques of the current system, allied to the proposed referendum on constitutional change in the area of children's rights, will provide new impetus for more fundamental reform and improvements than previously.

We see this as a critical time to draw to a close the era of denial, secrecy and suppression in relation to the care and protection of children. If we are committed to the ideals of a liberal democracy, then we must move towards greater openness and transparency. We can no longer claim ignorance, particularly in light of the recommendations of the Ryan Report and its implementation plan.

A change in government in Ireland in 2011 has brought new hope for reform. The new Labour/Fine Gael government established for the first time a Department of Children and Youth Affairs with its own full cabinet minister. Within a few days of coming into office this new government also announced a new child protection and welfare agency independent of the HSE (Smyth, 2011). Hopefully, these developments will drive the reorganisation of children's services and the development of an integrated approach to policy and service delivery for children and young people across all government agencies. Key issues will be the referendum on children's rights and the full implementation of the Ryan Report implementation plan. Significant also is the commitment in the new programme for government to abolish the HSE (over a period of time), which will result in the control of this essential part of the public sector coming back under the political realm of the Minister for Health, thereby increasing political accountability. While these commitments are potentially progressive, time will tell whether these changes will result in meaningful change to the quality of life of all children in Ireland.

In ten years from the publication of Ryan, we hope to write about a democratic society within which children's citizenship is embedded and those children who most need care and protection are supported by a progressive, resourced and integrated child protection and welfare system. There is much energy, interest, enthusiasm and professional skills to be harnessed in this endeavour. What we do now is critical.

Structure of the book

This chapter has questioned how effective the democratic process has been in improving the lives of those children most at risk and their families. This volume examines the contemporary position of children on the island of Ireland, and critiques how the socio-political, legal, organisational and cultural domains impact on children's lives. The book is about how structures, practices, policy and systems can be improved and better integrated to improve children's well-being. The individual chapters had their genesis in a child protection and welfare conference, which has contributed to some limitations in the scope of this book and the range of contributors. For example, it is a limitation that service-user contributions are not included; and social action and community approaches do not get sufficient coverage. However, it is our belief, that the analysis of the Republic of Ireland experience presented here will make a valuable contribution to international debates in child protection and welfare. The range of contributors and wide variety of topics covered in this edited book brings a diversity, richness and depth, which, we believe, parallels the multi-faceted nature of the field of child protection and welfare. This book was completed just prior to the publication of the *Commission of Investigation. Report into the Catholic Diocese of Cloyne* (Murphy *et al.*, 2010), an inquiry completed in 2010 but not published until mid-2011. Therefore, this inquiry report and surrounding debates concerning issues such as mandatory reporting, are not specifically addressed in this book. We have chosen not to group and theme the chapters, and the book can be read sequentially or by dipping into chapters of interest.

Acknowledgements

The authors would like to thank Fred Powell for his advice on earlier drafts of this chapter. We would also like to acknowledge Fintan O'Toole for pointing us in the direction of the 1919 Democratic Programme.

Notes

1 The Magdalen laundries were penitential institutions run by Catholic nuns whose role it was to reform 'fallen' girls (women involved in prostitution and women who became pregnant outside marriage). Some women and children lived significant periods of their lives in these laundries performing labour that provided an income for the religious order, and they were often purposefully deprived of an education (Ferriter, 2004; Smith, 2007).
2 Irish law permits parents to use 'reasonable chastisement' (physical punishment such as slapping) on a child. For further information, see Chapter 3.
3 Brokerage is a form of political 'clientelism' where politicians 'broker' access to state bureaucracies on behalf of citizens in return for pledges of electoral support.
4 The Health Service Executive, under a provision in the Child Care Act 1991, must publish an annual report on the adequacy of child and family services. These reports are known as the 'section 8' reports.
5 Rawls defined a liberal democracy as one where people 'agree on the most just society they can possibly construct' (Rawls, 1971 cited in Friedner Parrat, 2010, p. 473).

References

Ahern, B. (1999) *Taoiseach's Apology – May 1999* (online), National Office for Victims of Abuse for Adults who have Experienced Abuse. Available from: www.nova.ie/TaoiseachsApology/ (accessed 16 June 2008).

Barnardos (2010) *Our Campaigns* (Online), Dublin, Barnardos Ireland. Available from: www.barnardos.ie/policies_and_campaigns/our-campaigns.html (accessed 15 June 2010).

Buckley, H. (2003) *Child Protection Work: Beyond the Rhetoric*, London, Jessica Kingsley Publishers.

Buckley, H. (2010) 'More social workers will not keep children safe', *The Irish Times*, Dublin, The Irish Times.

Burns, K. (2007) 'Child protection and welfare work: The impact of social service delivery on employee welfare', in Herrmann, P. and Herrenbrueck, S. (eds), *Changing Administration – Changing Society. Challenges for Current Social Policy*, New York, Nova Science.

Children's Rights Alliance (2010) *Saving Childhood Ryan – Eight Organisations Fighting for Children Together* (online), Dublin, Children's Rights Alliance. Available from: www.childrensrights.ie/index .php?q=knowledgebase/child-protection/saving-childhood-ryan-eight -organisations-fighting-children-together (accessed 15 June 2010).

Collins, N. and O'Shea, M. (2003) 'Clientelism: facilitating rights and favours', in Adshead, M. and Millar, M. (eds) *Public Administration and Public Policy in Ireland*, London, Routledge.

Committee on the Rights of the Child (2006) *Consideration of Reports Submitted by States Parties Under Article 44 of the Convention on the Rights of the Child. Concluding Observations: Ireland* (online), Geneva, United Nations. Available from: www.childrensrights.ie/pubs/IRLCON COBS.pdf (accessed 17 February 2008).

Council of Europe (1996) *European Social Charter (Revised)*, Strasbourg, Editions du Conseil de l'Europe.

Dáil Éireann (1919) *Democratic Programme, Dáil Éireann – Volume 1 – 21 January, 1919*, Dublin, Houses of the Oireachtas.

Donnellan, E. (2009) 'Roscommon inquiry team will establish facts, says Harney', *The Irish Times*, Dublin.

Donnellan, E. (2010) 'Ombudsman accuses HSE of having a culture of secrecy and legalism', *The Irish Times*, Dublin.

Ferguson, H. and O'Reilly, M. (2001) *Keeping Children Safe: Child Abuse, Child Protection and the Promotion of Welfare*, Dublin, A. & A. Farmar.

Ferriter, D. (2004) *The Transformation of Ireland, 1900–2000*, London, Profile Books.

Finlay, F. (2010) 'The Current Crisis and the Role of Education', *Vice-President For Teaching and Learning Seminar*, University College Cork.

Friedner Parrat, C. (2010) 'The politics of reporting: A study of states' strategies for reporting to the UN Committee on the Rights of the Child', *Political Studies*, 58, pp. 472–496.

Goode, H., McGee, H. and O'Boyle, C. (2003) *Time to Listen: Confronting Child Sexual Abuse by Catholic Clergy in Ireland*, Dublin, The Liffey Press.

Government of Ireland (1980) *Task Force on Child Care Services: Final Report to the Minister for Health*, Dublin, Stationery Office.

Government of Ireland (2000) *The National Children's Strategy. Our Children – Their Lives*, Dublin, Stationery Office.

Halpenny, A. M., Nixon, E. and Watson, D. (2009) *Parenting Styles and Discipline: Parents' and Children's Perspectives. Summary Report, The National Children's Strategy Research Series*, Dublin, Office of the Minister for Children and Youth Affairs.

Health Information and Quality Authority (2011) *Report on a follow-up inspection of the Health Service Executive fostering service in HSE Dublin North Central Area,* Cork HIQA. Health Information and Quality Authority (2010a) *Inspection of the HSE Fostering Service in HSE Dublin North Area* (online), Cork, HIQA. Available from: www.hiqa.ie/publications.asp (accessed 14 July 2010).

Health Information and Quality Authority (2010b) *Inspection of the HSE Fostering Service in HSE Dublin North Central Area* (online), Cork, HIQA. Available from: www.hiqa.ie/publications.asp (accessed 14 July 2010).

Health Information and Quality Authority (2010c) *Inspection of the HSE Fostering Service in HSE Dublin North West Area* (online), Cork, HIQA. Available from: www.hiqa.ie/publications.asp (accessed 14 July 2010).

Health Service Executive (2009a) *HSE Child Welfare and Protection Social Work Departments Business Processes. Report of the NCCIS Business Process Standardisation Project October 2009,* Dublin, Health Service Executive.

Health Service Executive (2009b) *Review of Adequacy of Services for Children & Families 2007* (online), Dublin, Health Service Executive. Available from: www.hse.ie/eng/services/Publications/services/Children/2007section8.pdf (accessed 29 January 2010).

Irish Association of Social Workers (2010) *Publications and Press Releases* (online), Dublin, Irish Association of Social Workers. Available from: www.iasw.ie/index.php/press-releases (accessed 15 June 2010).

Joint Committee on the Constitutional Amendment on Children (2010) *Twenty-Eighth Amendment of the Constitution Bill 2007 Proposal for a Constitutional Amendment to Strengthen Children's Rights. Final Report,* Dublin, Houses of the Oireachtas.

King, M. (1997) *A Better World for Children: Explorations in Morality and Authority,* London, Routledge.

Lynch, D. and Burns, K. (2008) 'Contexts, themes and future directions in Irish child protection and welfare social work', in Burns, K. and Lynch, D. (eds) *Child Protection and Welfare Social Work: Contemporary Themes and Practice Perspectives,* Dublin, A. & A. Farmar.

McGuinness, C. (1993) *Kilkenny Incest Investigation: Report Presented to Mr. Brendan Howlin T.D. Minister for Health,* Dublin, Stationery Office.

McKay, S. (1998) *Sophia's Story,* Dublin, Gill & Macmillan.

Moore, C. (1995) *Betrayal of Trust: The Father Brendan Smyth Affair and the Catholic Church,* Dublin, Marino Books.

Murphy, F. D., Buckley, H. and Joyce, L. (2005) *The Ferns Report: Presented to the Minister for Health and Children,* Dublin, Stationery Office.

Murphy, Y., Mangan, I. and O'Neill, H. (2009) *Commission of Investigation. Report into the Catholic Archdiocese of Dublin* (online), Dublin, Commission of Investigation, Dublin Archdiocese, Catholic Diocese of Cloyne. Available from: www.dacoi.ie/ (accessed 1 December 2009).

Murphy, Y., Mangan, I. and O'Neill, H. (2010) *Commission of Investigation.*

Report into the Catholic Diocese of Cloyne, Dublin, Department of Justice and Equality.

Nelligan, M. (2010) 'Feeble attempts to keep us in the dark are futile', *The Irish Times*, Dublin.

O'Brien, C. (2010) 'Children lost in a system of failures and secrecy', *The Irish Times*, Dublin.

O'Brien, C. and Taylor, C. (2010) 'Child protection concerns ignored by a service in crisis, says watchdog', *The Irish Times*, Dublin.

O'Brien, S. and McCarthy, J. (2010) 'Children's rights set for vote delay', *The Sunday Times*, London.

O'Mahony, C. (2011) 'Children deserve better protection', *The Irish Examiner*, Cork.

O'Moráin, P. (2009) 'Time to remove child protection from the Health Service Executive', *Irish Social Worker* (Autumn), p. 12.

Office of the Minister for Children (2007) *The Agenda for Children's Service: A Policy Handbook*, Dublin, Stationery Office.

Office of the Minister for Children and Youth Affairs (2009) *Report of the Commission to Inquire into Child Abuse, 2009. Implementation Plan*, Dublin, Department of Health and Children.

Office of the Minister for Children and Youth Affairs (2010) *Group Appointed by Minister Outline Intentions for Child Death Reviews* (online), Dublin, Department of Health and Children. Available from: www.omc.gov.ie/viewdoc.asp?Docid=1258&CatID=11&mn=&StartDate=1+January+2010 (accessed 6 July 2010).

Ombudsman for Children (2010) *A Report Based on an Investigation Into The Implementation of Children First: National Guidelines For The Protection And Welfare Of Children*, Dublin, Ombudsman for Children's Office.

Raftery, M. and O'Sullivan, E. (1999) *Suffer Little Children: The Inside Story of Ireland's Industrial Schools*, Dublin, New Island.

RTÉ (1969) *Democratic Programme: The First Dáil* (online), Dublin, RTÉ Archive. Available from: www.rte.ie/laweb/ll/ll_t15_main.html (accessed 16 June 2010).

Ryan, S. (2009) *Commission to Inquire into Child Abuse Report (Volumes I–V)*, Dublin, Stationery Office.

Skehill, C. (2004) *History of the Present of Child Protection and Welfare Social Work in Ireland*, New York, Edwin Mellen Press.

Smith, J. M. (2007) *Ireland's Magdalen Laundries and the Nation's Architecture of Containment*, Notre Dame, University of Notre Dame Press.

Smyth, J. (2011) 'HSE to lose child protection role', *The Irish Times* (11 March).

Svevo-Cianci, K., Hart, S. N. and Rubinson, C. (2010) 'Protecting children from violence and maltreatment: A qualitative comparative analysis assessing the implementation of U.N. CRC Article 19', *Child Abuse and Neglect*, 34, pp. 34–56.

2

Child outcasts: The Ryan Report into industrial and reformatory schools

Fred Powell, Martin Geoghegan, Margaret Scanlon and Katharina Swirak

> In its detail and horror, the Ryan Report often read like a cross between an anthropological study and a novel by the Marquis de Sade. Images – for example, the Christian Brother who played ceili music loudly on the radio to drown out the screams of the child he was torturing – burned themselves into the brains of those who read it. (Fintan O'Toole, *The Irish Times*, 28 December 2009)

The Report of the *Commission to Inquire into Child Abuse* (2009) (Ryan Report) has shocked the world. It was foreshadowed by Mary Raftery and Eoin O'Sullivan in their revelatory book *Suffer Little Children*, published a decade earlier in 1999 and Mary Raftery's television documentary *States of Fear* (1999). The common focus was on the hidden history of the institutional care of children where the clergy managed harsh and punitive regimes. What is distinctive about the Ryan Report is its unrelenting objectivity in exposing the truth, with a cold, unemotional logic. It chillingly, through survivor testimony, reveals a culture of fear and violence in Irish industrial and reformatory schools, which constitute very serious human rights violations by any international standard. Both Church and State are exposed by the Ryan Report as agents and accomplices in these human rights violations. Irish civil society is also challenged by what Fintan O'Toole (2009b) calls a cultural propensity to have 'known unknowns – things that are known to be true but treated as if they were outlandish fictions'. Drawing on the work of Barnes (1989), Ferguson (2007) and official sources, in this chapter we explore the narrative of Irish industrial and reformatory schools, as a system designed on the principles of social exclusion, which dehumanised an 'outcast' child population. The 'known unknown' of Irish child care policy, we contend, was that it was based on, what Raftery and O'Sullivan (1999, pp. 12–17) have identified as a series of myths that protected the Irish public from having to acknowledge the truth regarding child abuse. The Ryan Report (2009) has confronted these myths with facts in the pursuit of truth and reconciliation, albeit that the names of the alleged perpetrators (both living and dead) have been anonymised in a compromise with the religious congregations. It was the product of nearly a decade of investigation involving 1,500 witnesses and two committees: investigatory (contested evidence) and confidential (uncontested evidence). Between 2,000 and 3,000 children were placed in reformatory schools and 170,000 in industrial schools between 1936 and 1952 (Ryan, 2009, Volume 1, paras 3.01–3.04). About 1.2 per cent of the age cohort were placed in industrial schools during this period.

Discipline and punishment

Discipline in industrial and reformatory schools was ruthlessly enforced. As Barnes (1989, p. 101) puts it, 'Although corporal punishment was cast in as favourable light as possible, strong evidence exists that some schools featured frequent and severe beatings [of children].' She based this conclusion on an analysis of inspectors' reports, which 'while inspectors reported on the one hand a low incidence of corporal punishment, on the other they felt obliged to censure some managers for excessive use of the cane' (ibid.). Once again we are confronted by contradictory behaviour by the state, raising fundamental issues about the social construction of the industrial school inmate as victim, criminal and outcast. There was a further issue regarding the exploitation of child labour. Raftery and O'Sullivan (1999, p. 155) note 'many of the industrial schools were in fact little more than forced labour camps for children'. Children as young as seven years were forced to work in what inmates called 'Little Auschwitz' (ibid., p. 46). Punishment and forced labour were inextricably linked. At the insistence of Irish politicians, there was no factory inspection system for Irish reformatories and industrial schools (*Irish Times*, 23 July 1901). These outcast children, in Ferguson's (2007, p. 123) phrase were treated as 'moral dirt'.

The Cussen Report (1936) and the Derrig Rules (1933): child care in a free state

The establishment of the Irish Free State appears to have led to an absence of state regulation over industrial schools. In Britain, the system was reformed to constrain the use of corporal punishment. In Ireland, the Derrig Rules in 1933 had the opposite effect. Arnold (2009, p. 32) comments that, 'In Ireland there seemed under Tomás Derrig [Minister for Education] to be a deliberate attempt to turn the country away from these reforms, to give broader license to the [Religious] orders running the [industrial and reformatory] institutions and to ignore lapses when these came to public attention.' Public concern did lead to the establishment of the Cussen Commission. The Cussen Report (1936) was essentially a reaffirmation of the system (apart from a recommendation for a name change) that served to dampen public criticism. All records of the Cussen Committee have disappeared (Raftery and O'Sullivan 1999, p. 78). The Cussen Report was published on 17 August 1936 and received a muted public and political reaction. Perhaps that was inevitable, given its endorsement of the status quo. But at a deeper level one senses that it was the product of a cover-up. While the Cussen Report envisaged changes in nomenclature (which were officially ignored) and more informality (for example, less legalism) in a judicial structure that was oblivious to children's human rights, as well as better education and training in a system (which relentlessly exploited child labour and neglected educational development), it offered no convincing critique of the system of industrial and reformatory schools. Ireland was about to adopt a new constitution in 1937 that was both in theory and practice as theocratic as it was democratic. The social power of the Catholic Church was, in 1936, at its apogee; its authority unchallengeable. The Cussen Report bore testament to the dominance of the Church over State, but also to collusion by the State in a violently oppressive system of institutional child care.

The Kennedy Report (1970): reform and 'cover-up'

During the second half of the twentieth century, Ireland began to slowly transform itself from a penal social state based upon the coercive confinement of citizens with welfare needs, including children, unmarried mothers, the mentally ill and intellectually disabled. For these social groups exclusion was extreme. They were simply rejected by society and confined in institutions, where many were seriously abused. In the post-war world the human rights of people detained in institutions became an international public policy issue. Ireland joined the United Nations in 1955 and the European Union in 1973, submitting itself to international law and human rights standards, and the architecture of confinement had to be dismantled. Deinstitutionalisation slowly led to a policy of community care. New initiatives in child protection very gradually changed the direction of public policy, but the old legacy of institutionalisation, particularly the spectre of child abuse continued to haunt Irish society, leaving many unresolved issues, including the constitutional rights of children (see Chapters 3 and 4). The Kennedy Report (1970, pp. 6–7), which was established to investigate the reformatory and industrial school system, made thirteen recommendations, which included the immediate closure of the boys' reformatory at Daingean and Marlborough House Remand Home and the replacement of the system of industrial and reformatory schools by 'modern special schools'. Institutional care was to be a last resort with a new focus on community care.

While the Kennedy Report was regarded as a watershed in terms of social policy reform, there was no published evidence of inquiry into the abuses of the system. There was a virtual absence of discussion of the context of the committee's decision to recommend the immediate closure of Daingean Reformatory School and Marlborough House Remand Home. The recommendations simply suggest that the physical conditions within these institutions were unsuitable for purpose and the training of staff (or lack of it) a cause for concern. Furthermore, the Kennedy Report did not recommend closure of St Patrick's Institution, which it acknowledged was a children's prison. As a result, St Patrick's Institution remains open for boys to the present day. Its position was, therefore, somewhat contradictory.

The failure of the Kennedy committee to address the issues of child abuse in general and the use of corporal punishment in particular (see analysis of legal basis for corporal punishment in Ireland in Chapter 3), is undoubtedly a grave indictment of its report. It failed to reveal the endemic abuse that characterised the industrial and reformatory school system. It was not that the Kennedy Report was unaware of the abusive regimes within Daingean and Marlborough House. The record shows that it was. The full committee visited Daingean on 28 February 1968. In subsequent correspondence it emerged that it was aware of the poor physical conditions of the building, the dirty and grubby state of the children, but also the use of corporal punishment, involving beating children on their naked buttocks (Ryan Report,

2009, Volume I, paras 15.202–15.227). However, despite the reservations of one member of the Kennedy Committee, it was decided that to make any reference, however, oblique to this particular method of punishment in Daingean would be likely to lead to a disclosure of child abuse and would have caused 'a grave public scandal' (Ryan Report, 2009, Volume I, 15.216). The Kennedy Committee would also have been aware of the history of riots at Daingean in 1956 and 1958 and an arson attempt in 1968, as indicators of the level of dissatisfaction among the children incarcerated in this institution (Ryan Report, 2009, Volume 1, paras 15.228–15.252). Remarkably, none of this history of unrest was commented upon by the Kennedy Committee. The chair of the committee Justice Eileen Kennedy was, as a Dublin-based judge, clearly aware of physical abuse at Marlborough House, Dublin (Ryan Report, 2009, Volume I, paras 16.114, 16.127–130). These deficiencies in the report have led to serious criticism of its shortcomings. Bruce Arnold (2009, pp. 69–70) has characterised the Kennedy Committee as a 'cover up' and a 'whitewash'. Manifestly, the Kennedy Committee preferred not to challenge cultural myths or the social power of the Catholic Church by revealing the truth about human rights abuses within the Irish industrial and reformatory school system. That task was left to the *Commission to Inquire into Child Abuse*, established in 2000.

The Ryan Report (2009): truth without reconciliation

The Commission to Inquire into Child Abuse, established in 2000, was a landmark in terms of exposing the dark secrets of institutional care in Ireland over a century. It consisted of two committees: the Investigation Committee and the Confidential Committee. *The Commission to Inquire into Child Abuse* was chaired by Justice Mary Laffoy until 2004 and from 2004–2009 by Justice Sean Ryan. *The Commission to Inquire into Child Abuse* heard evidence from 18 religious orders and congregations, and 857 reports of child abuse involving 474 males and 383 female survivors. Originally, it was envisaged that it would operate on the principles of truth and reconciliation based on the experience of post-apartheid South Africa. It quickly became evident that its ability to operate as a truth and reconciliation commission was highly constrained, owing to an unwillingness on the part of most religious orders to accept responsibility for their alleged deeds. Justice Sean Ryan, who succeeded Justice Mary Laffoy as Chair of the Commission in 2004, worked out a compromise that granted anonymity to the accused, both living and dead. While this compromise can be criticised for perpetuating the culture of secrecy outlined by Burns and Lynch in Chapter 1, it did allow the *Commission to Inquire into Child Abuse* to carry out its investigation and issue a final report.[1]

A key element in the campaign of truth-telling has been the role of the campaign group *One in Four*. Arnold (2009, p. 227) notes that 'the *One in Four* group became quite outspoken on behalf of the abused generally at this time and countered what it called an attempt to rewrite the history of sexual abuse'. Under the dynamic leadership of Colm O'Gorman, *One in Four* began to transform Irish public consciousness regarding the significance of child abuse in Irish society. There were many other survivor groups who became instrumental in unlocking their own narratives including: *Irish SOCA* (Survivors of Child Abuse); *SOCA* (United Kingdom); *The Irish Deaf Society*; *Right to Peace, Right to Place*; *Alliance Victim Support*; *Irish Survivors of Institutional Abuse International*; the *Aislinn Centre*; and the *London Irish Women's Group* (Ryan Report, 2009, Volume 2, para. 1.149). All of these organisations began to provide a survivors' perspective on the growing public scandal of institutional child abuse that challenged the Church to account for its actions and the State for a serious failure of regulation in human rights terms. Through their social agency, survivors' groups became a moral voice that could not be ignored. Truth was beginning to assert itself. But reparation remained a contested reality, because of the serious institutional financial implications. This made reconciliation impossible because the Church contested the veracity of the survivors' testimony.

The Residential Institutional Redress Act 2002 established the Residential Institutions Redress Board. Its purpose is to provide compensation for survivors of 123 institutions, who have experienced abuse. Its establishment was accompanied by what has been called 'The Secret Deal', which indemnified the Catholic Church for its involvement and cooperation in the redress scheme (Arnold, 2009, p. 206). The terms of the agreement between Church and State limited the liability of the Church to approximately €128 million. This has generated considerable controversy since critics argue that the Church should bear equal responsibility with the State for compensating survivors of institutional abuse, which is estimated to cost the Irish State at least €1 billion in compensation payments. Further criticism has arisen in relation to the willingness of the religious orders to fully apologise for the violations of human rights in the institutions, which they managed. The publication of the *Report of the Commission to Inquire into Child Abuse*, in May 2009 was to intensify pressure on the Church to address these issues. A review audit of the assets of the religious orders and congregations was initiated by the State during 2009 in response to growing public anger regarding the Church's position on compensation to the survivors. The Church continues to have difficulties in relation to atonement because it believes that it is being unfairly scapegoated by the media (Flannery, 2009).

The publication of the Ryan Report during 2009 was a seminal event in the process of disclosure and truth-telling. The report ran to 2,600 pages, composed of five volumes. Its revelations are thorough and deeply shocking, identifying over 200 institutions. Most of the abusers were members of the clergy. These are the stark facts that underpin the powerful testimony of the survivors of abuse regimes during most of the twentieth century. The Ryan Report reveals that over a 35-year period child abuse was 'endemic' in the industrial and reformatory school system in Ireland. Its revelations have been reported around the world, exposing the failure of Ireland's human rights record in relation to children to critical international scrutiny. The crimes against children described in the Ryan Report are on a systemic scale and involve a degree of sadistic cruelty that is difficult to comprehend. Public reaction has been one of shock and horror. An editorial in the *Irish Times* (21 May 2009) poignantly captured the full import of the Ryan Report in a remarkable summation:

> The Report of the Commission to Inquire into Child Abuse is the map of an Irish hell. It defines the contours of a dark hinterland of the State, a parallel country whose existence we have long known but never fully acknowledged. It is a land of pain and shame, of savage cruelty and callous indifference. The instinct to turn away from it, repelled by its profoundly unsettling ugliness, is almost irresistible. We owe it, though, to those who have suffered there to acknowledge from now on that it is an inescapable part of Irish reality. We have to deal with the now-established fact that, alongside the warmth and intimacy, the kindness and generosity of Irish life, there was, for most of the history of the State, a deliberately maintained structure of vile and vicious abuse. Mr. Justice Ryan's report does not suggest that this abuse was as bad as most of us suspected. It shows that it was worse. It may indeed have been even worse than the report actually finds – there are indications that 'the level of sexual abuse in boys' institutions was much higher than was revealed by the records or could be discovered by this investigation.

Volume 3 of the Ryan Report (2009) provides statistical and verbatim analysis of survivors' evidence given by witnesses to the Confidential Committee, regarding the nature and scale of child abuse in Irish institutional care up to 1989. There were, as already noted, 857 reports of child abuse, involving 474 males and 383 female survivors given to the Confidential Committee. This evidence is corroborated by testimony from 493 survivors given to the Investigation Committee, summarised in Volume 4 of the Ryan Report (2009, paras 5.01–5.142). The mandate of the Confidential Committee was to hear evidence 'of those survivors of childhood institutional abuse who wished to report their experiences in a confidential setting ... to be conducted in an atmosphere that was informal and as sympathetic to, and understanding of the witnesses as was possible in the circumstances' (Ryan Report, Volume 1, 2009, para. 1.09). It exposes a catalogue of physical, emotional and sexual abuse, in tandem with neglect that cannot be explained by unique historical or cultural circumstances. While most of the reported abuse occurred prior to the Kennedy Report (1970), which recommended the closure of the system, complaints continued until 1989, the end date for the statistical evidence. The clergy emerge as the primary agents of child abuse in both statistical and oral evidence, which would seem to be incontrovertible, and could not be considered normal in any culture at any time.

With regard to the 'scapegoating' of the clergy argument put forward in their defence by contributors to *Responding to the Ryan Report (2009)* (edited by Fr Tony Flannery), the burden of evidence contained in the Confidential Committee's report, both statistical and oral, clearly indicates that the Catholic clergy were the main perpetrators of child abuse within the Irish institutional care system. The Ryan Report (Volume 3, 2009, paras 7.90–7.91 and 9.55–9.58) demonstrates statistically that: (i) in relation to physical abuse in male industrial and reformatory schools, 71 per cent (394) named as physical abusers were male religious and a further 10 per cent (39) were female religious; and (ii) in relation to female industrial and reformatory schools 69 per cent (241) religious sisters and other members of the clergy were named as physically abusive, out of the 347 named. Furthermore, with reference to sexual abuse in male industrial and reformatory schools, 65 per cent (151), the majority of those named were religious staff (139 Brothers and 12 Priests) (Volume 3, 2009, para. 7.139). However, in female industrial and reformatory schools the majority 144 (77%) of those identified as sexual abusers were mainly lay non-staff members (Volume 3, 2009, paras 9.94–9.95).

Apart from sexual abuse in female industrial and reformatory schools, members of the Catholic clergy were clearly and overwhelmingly the perpetrators of child abuse. Detailed content analysis of survivor testimony strongly supports this conclusion, in relation to the overall context of child abuse. Furthermore, the sexualised nature of child physical abuse (which often occurred simultaneously with sexual abuse) makes differentiation between established categories of child abuse problematic and artificial. These were care regimes where child abuse was multi-dimensional and pervasive. Child abuse became an expression of the abuse of total institutional power – a phenomenon described in Erving Goffman's celebrated sociological study, *Asylums* (1961). While the analysis is based on the survivor evidence given to the Confidential Committee (Volume 3 of the Ryan Report), it is notable that the Investigation Committee interviewed 250 male survivors in an adversarial context and concluded that 'the principal complaints of male interviews was physical abuse' (Ryan Report, Volume 4, 2009, para. 5.04). Contextually, physical abuse meant the exploitation of the body as a site of punishment and domination. What we constantly need to bear in mind is that the survivors' narrative of institutional child abuse is experientially and morally on a par with survivors of penal regimes in totalitarian societies, whereby there is a common thread of an absence of a human right to bodily integrity associated with democratic societies. Power was total and exercised without restraint. This disadvantaged youth population had no protection. The fact that they were minors makes these human rights violations even more serious.

The Ryan Report (2009, para. 7.06) defines physical abuse as: 'The wilful, reckless or negligent infliction of physical injury on, or a failure to prevent such injury to, the child'. There were 474 reports of physical abuse involving 26 reformatory and industrial schools given in evidence to the Confidential Committee by 403 male witnesses, some of whom had been admitted to more than one school (Ryan Report, Volume 3, 2009, para. 7.08). Similarly, the Confidential Committee received 383 reports of physical abuse from 374 female witnesses (99%) in 39 schools (Ryan Report, Volume 3, 2009, para. 9.06). In total, calculating all reports from male and female witnesses there were 857 reports of physical abuse.

The Ryan Report (Volume 3, 2009, para. 7.16) records a wide variety of forms of physical punishment from the male witness statements, including:

> punching, flogging, assault and bodily attacks, hitting with the hand, kicking, ear pulling, hair pulling, head shaving, beating on the soles of the feet, burning, scalding, stabbing, severe beatings with or without clothes, being made to kneel and stand in fixed positions for lengthy periods, made to sleep outside overnight, being forced into cold or excessively hot baths and showers, hosed down with cold water before being beaten, beaten while hanging from hooks on the wall, being set

upon by dogs, being restrained in order to be beaten, physical assaults
by more than one person, and having objects thrown at them.

The locations, according to the witnesses' statements encompassed:
classrooms, offices, cloakrooms, dormitories, showers, infirmaries,
refectories, the bedroom of staff members, churches, work areas and
trade shops, fields, farmyards, play/sports areas and outdoor sheds
(Ryan Report, Volume 3, 2009, para. 7.17). Male survivors in their
witness statements gave chilling examples of the diversity of locations,
the use of corporal punishment as public theatre and for initiation
rights in a macabre atmosphere of *manqué* religiosity: 'I had a hiding
in the boot room, you had to take your shirt off, you were completely
naked and he ... (Br. X) ... beat me with a strap and a hurley stick on
the behind and the legs and that.'

The Ryan Report (Volume 3, 2009, paras 7.20–7.27) recorded
evidence from male witnesses in relation to the implements used in
physical abuse that the 'leather' (strap) was most commonly used
instrument (381 witnesses) but that there were a further 232 witness
accounts of being hit by sticks (including: canes, ash plants, blackthorn sticks, hurleys, broom handles, hand brushes, wooden spoons,
pointers, batons, chair rungs, yard brushes, hoes, hay forks, pikes and
pieces of wood with leather tongs attached) as the following examples
illustrate:

> They used the leather for the least excuse. It was heavy, stitched and
> with waxed ends. It was very painful, you would scream in pain. As
> convent boys we didn't have a chance. The other boys, the city kids who
> were tough, and the Brothers, all picked on us. We stuck together which
> wasn't a good idea.

> Some of the Brothers had different leathers, I know because I made
> them when I was 14, in the boot room, some of them had little tiny leads
> in them, some had coins, some were straight. They weren't soft, they
> were hard.

> I'll never forget the cat-o'-nine-tails, 10 tongs ... (thongs) ... it used to
> have knots across the bottom. Observing other boys stripped and the
> blood running down as they were being flogged across the body, it was
> terrible. There must have been a new rule by the Government at some
> stage because it happened no more. (Ryan Report, 2009, Volume 3,
> paras. 7.20 and 7.22)

Females were also subjected to severe physical abuse in the industrial
school system, in which they traditionally constituted, by far, the larger
gender group. The survivors reported high levels of violence by staff,

with 166 female witnesses testifying to being beaten with various objects including wooden sticks; blackthorn sticks, rulers, pointers, window poles, wooden spoons, chair legs, wooden crutches, hurley sticks, cricket bats, coat hangers, towel rollers and sally rods. In addition, 77 witnesses reported being beaten with bamboo canes and 99 with leather straps (Ryan Report, 2009, Volume 3, para. 9.14).

Apart from the infliction of severe beatings, female survivor witness statements record other serious forms of physical abuse, including: being hit, slapped, kicked, pushed, pinched, burned, bitten, shaken violently, physically restrained and force fed. This physical abuse ranged from being slapped on the hand to being beaten naked in public. The female witnesses also reported having their heads knocked against walls, desks and window ledges, being beaten on the soles of their feet, the backs of their hands, around their hands and ears, having their hair pulled, being swung off the ground by their hair, and made to perform tasks that they believed put them at risk of harm or danger (Ryan Report, Volume 3, para. 9.11). The following testimony from female witnesses is illustrative:

> (We were) ... beaten everywhere, bang your head of the wall, pinch your cheeks, beat you with a cane ... She ... (Sr. X) ... would grab you and hit you.
>
> I remember once I got a big yellow blister on my hand, it was really painful ... Normally when you got a beating from someone you had to hold your hand out for a *slap like that* ... (demonstrated outstretched palm) ... not always of course, some of them would hit you anywhere on the legs or anywhere ... She ... (Sr. X) ... said Why are you holding your hand out like that? Give me the other hand ...You have to have 10 on that hand and 10 on the other. I couldn't part with this hand, it was yellow and throbbing it was, and she forced it open and slapped it. The blister burst, I'll never forget the pain. (ibid.)

What can we conclude from this survivor evidence relating to the physical abuse of children in care in Ireland over most of the twentieth century? First, that institutionalisation was totally unsuitable for these children's needs. Second, that the disciplinary regime of the clergy administering these institutions constituted as the Ryan Commission concluded, endemic violence. Third, that the absence of human rights in the form of adequate child care legislation in line with modern child care practice left these children open to abuse on a mass scale. Children have no rights in the Irish Constitution (see Chapters 3 and 4). There have been two referenda on the rights of the unborn child but we still await a referendum on the rights of the born child. Religion rather than human rights has set the agenda. Fourth, 'the charity myth' perpetuated by church and state and supported by large and powerful elements within Irish civil society, allowed this human rights tragedy to occur. While we have concentrated on evidence of physical abuse, it was compounded by and cannot be disaggregated from neglect, emotional abuse and sexual abuse. The evidence offered from survivor testimony clearly indicates that physical abuse was linked by an overall strategy of dehumanisation to other forms of abuse in institutions where food was in short supply and hunger the norm. The assaults on children's bodily integrity demonstrate a serious neglect of their physical well-being. The culture of fear supported by ritualistic beatings and other forms of physical punishment calibrated to instil maximum fear and anxiety, demonstrate an atmosphere of emotional abuse that would be difficult to surpass. Finally, the survivors' testimony regarding the administrating of corporal punishment, strongly suggests that it was carried out in a highly sexualised way. The use of corporal punishment in Ireland's industrial and reformatory school system was frequently, and beyond doubt, also a form of sexual abuse coupled with sadistic physical abuse and informed by a policy of dehumanisation. This constitutes a profound cultural contradiction in a society that proclaimed its religious virtue and outsourced the care of children to the Catholic Church – the charity myth. The darkest secret of all was that industrial and reformatory schools in Ireland were based on a policy of social genetics (Barnes, 1989).

Conclusion

In this chapter we have sought to critically examine 'the charity myth' upon which the Irish reformatory and industrial school system was constructed during the nineteenth century, and which lasted until the late twentieth century. The Ryan Report (2009) has formed the backdrop to our analysis. During the twenty-first century Ireland has been haunted by a legacy of institutional child abuse, revealed in the Ryan Report (2009), which has shocked public opinion across the world. By any historical and cultural standards the cruelty visited upon destitute Irish children, in the name of charity, stands out as a major human rights issue. The ethos of the Church-run institutions promoted a culture of dehumanisation. This, it has been argued, stemmed from the outcast status of children from poor backgrounds. They were viewed not only as destitute but as a threat to public health and the gene pool. A policy of social genetics sought to cleanse the Irish population of their unwanted children. Within the reformatory and industrial schools the regime was based upon dehumanisation. It was administered through a policy of intense and pervasive physical abuse, which demarcated the children's status as an ostracised 'sub-human other'. They were without the basic human rights that define citizenship within a democratic society.

The Irish State simply handed these children over to the Catholic Church without any effective system of accountability or safeguards. The tragic consequences for 170,000 children form the content of the Ryan Report (2009) that bears testimony to some of the most serious human rights violations against children in recorded human history. The conclusions we can draw from this historical tragedy is that:

1 Children's right are fundamental to public policy in any society that wishes to be regarded as part of the civilised world.
2 Faith-based charities (with their ideological agendas) are not suited to the care of children.

With searing logic, the Ryan Report (2009) has exposed 'the charity myth' upon which the Irish industrial and reformatory school system was constructed. Sadly, the resistance of the Catholic Church in coming to grips with this historic legacy and its underlying moral stands in the way of reconciliation. Acceptance of responsibility is the basis of atonement. The survivors' narratives form the background to the factual structure of the Ryan Report (2009), which also draws upon detailed research and investigation of the evidence. These elements constitute the 'known knowns' of the abusive legacy of Irish child care institutions. Irish civil society is still struggling with the 'unknown knowns' of child care policy. An expected constitutional referendum on children's rights during 2012 will finally test public reaction to the Ryan Report and possibly change the course of Irish history.

Note

1 See the *Commission to Inquire into Child Abuse* website for complete text of all five volumes of the Commission's report: www.childabusecommission .com/rpt/pdfs/.

References

Arnold, B. (2009) *The Irish Gulag*, Dublin, Gill & Macmillan.
Barnes, J. (1989) *Irish Industrial Schools 1868–1908: Origins and Development*,

Dublin, Irish Academic Press.

Commission into the Reformatory and Industrial School System (1936) *Report of Commission into the Reformatory and Industrial School System (Cussen Report)*, Dublin, Stationery Office.

Commission of Inquiry into the Reformatory and Industrial School System (1970) *Report of the Commission of Inquiry into the Reformatory and Industrial School System (Kennedy Report)*, Dublin, Government Publications Office.

Commission to Inquire into Child Abuse (2009) *Report of Commission to Inquire into Child Abuse Volumes I–V (Ryan Report)*, Government Publications Office, Dublin.

Ferguson, H. (2007) 'Abused and looked after children as "moral dirt"', *Journal of Social Policy*, 36(1), pp. 123–139.

Flannery, T. (ed.) (2009) *Responding to the Ryan Report*, Dublin, Columba Press.

Goffman, E. (1961) *Asylums*, London, Penguin.

Inter-departmental Committee on Child Care (1896) *Report of the Inter-departmental Committee on Child Care (Mundella Report)*, London, Local Government Board.

The Irish Times (2009), 'Editorial' (21 May).

O'Toole, F. (2009) 'Law and anarchy, cruelty of care', *The Irish Times* (23 May).

O'Toole, F. (2009b) 'On Ryan Report', *The Irish Times*, 28 December.

Raftery, M. and O'Sullivan, E. (1999) *Suffer the Little Children: The Inside Story of Ireland's Industrial Schools*, Dublin, New Island Books.

Report of the Reformatories and Industrial Schools Commissioners, H.C. 1884, c3876 XLV. 1.

3

Children's rights in child protection: Identifying the bottom line in critical times

Ursula Kilkelly

Introduction

This is an important time to reflect on the practical challenges associated with the delivery of child protection services in Ireland. For children and their families, and for those who provide services to them, these are critical times; the budget deficit means that available resources arc falling, and will continue to do so, and that those working to deliver those services will continually be expected to do more for less. This may lead to less intervention in the family to protect children, or intervention only in the most serious cases. But how are these decisions to be made and what factors should inform the process? The aim of this chapter is to consider the legal framework within which these decisions are made in so far as it defines the role of the state in protecting children from harm. When is state intervention in the family legitimate, and what level of intervention in the family is required in order to ensure children are adequately protected? The classic dilemma of child protection is how to strike the appropriate balance between a state service that operates somewhere between an unwanted level of authoritarian interference (that is in no one's interests) and a passive assumption that parents' treatment of their children is their (and only their) concern. This is a universal dilemma that plays out in legal systems all over the world. As Fortin notes with respect to the UK, for example,

> the law over the last century has reflected an underlying uncertainty experienced by policy-makers over finding an appropriate compromise between obliging the state to find and protect every child who is being abused and maintaining family privacy. (Fortin, 2009, p. 552)

It is arguably impossible to have a system that guarantees the most appropriate and timely response in every case and there will always be high profile cases which will highlight that the balance has been wrongly struck (see, for example, the Kilkenny case, McGuinness, 1993; the West of Ireland farmer case, North Western Health Board, 1998; and the Monageer case, Brosnan, 2009). It is critical, however, that the legal system strikes this balance appropriately, thereby giving every chance to those who implement the law to do likewise. This chapter considers where the balance is struck in law in the Republic of Ireland between child protection and family integrity and this analysis is set against the backdrop of Ireland's international children's rights obligations.

Convention on the Rights of the Child

The United Nations Convention on the Rights of the Child (CRC) is the most important international instrument on the treatment of children (United Nations, 1989). It enjoys almost universal application and it has recently celebrated its twentieth anniversary. Ireland ratified the CRC in 1992, thereby committing (under Article 4) to take 'all appropriate legislative, administrative and other measures' to implement the Convention. Many CRC provisions are directly relevant to child protection where Articles 3, 19 and 39 are the most important. Article 3(1) provides that:

> In all actions concerning children, whether undertaken by public or private social welfare institutions, courts of law, administrative authorities or legislative bodies, the best interests of the child shall be a primary consideration.

Under Article 3(2), states undertake to:

> ensure the child such protection and care as is necessary for his or her well-being, taking into account the rights and duties of the child's parents and shall take all appropriate legislative and administrative measures to this end.

It is also pertinent that under Article 3(3):

> states must ensure that the institutions, services and facilities responsible for the care or protection of children shall conform with the standards established by competent authorities, particularly in the areas of safety, health, in the number and suitability of their staff, as well as competent supervision.

These Articles set down a clear, but minimum marker, about the right of the child to care and protection. More specifically, they call for a quality-proofing of children's services with particular reference to keeping children safe and providing them with the support of professionally trained staff.

The second important provision in the CRC is Article 19, paragraph 1, which requires states to take:

> all appropriate legislative, administrative, social and educational measures to protect the child from all forms of physical or mental violence, injury or abuse, neglect or negligent treatment, maltreatment or exploitation, including sexual abuse, while in the care of parent(s), legal guardian(s) or any other person who has the care of the child.

Article 19 is significant because it recognises that children need protection from harm caused in the care of family, such as abuse or neglect inflicted by parents. In this way, it expands on traditional human rights obligations, which stress the need to protect citizens from the state (Kilkelly, 2008b). It is also important that 'harm' is broadly defined to include physical and mental injury, intentional harm as well as injury caused through neglect or negligence. Article 19(1) lists the obligations on the state to protect children from harm, and Article 19(2) goes on to require the adoption both of preventive measures, as well as measures that identify, report, refer, investigate, treat and follow up instances of child maltreatment. Article 39 of the CRC requires that states take all appropriate measures to promote physical and psychological recovery and social reintegration of a child victim of any form of neglect, exploitation, or abuse. According to the CRC, such recovery and reintegration shall take place in an environment which fosters the health, self-respect and dignity of the child.

So, the CRC makes robust provision for the child's right to protection from harm and places extensive obligations on the state as to how this provision should be implemented. Before looking at what the Republic of Ireland has done in this regard, it is worth highlighting the extensive provision made for the family in the CRC. As well as recognising in the Preamble that the best place for children to grow up is with their family, other provisions dealing with the child's rights in this area include Article 5 on parents' responsibility to provide direction to children in the exercise of their rights in line with the child's evolving capacity; Article 7 on the right of the child to know and be cared for by his/her parents; Article 9 concerning the child's right to contact with his/her parents, and Article 18 concerning parental responsibility and parents' right to state support in such functions. These provisions are an important recognition of how important the child is to the family and vice versa, thereby making explicitly clear how integral the family is to the child's protection (Kilkelly, 2008a).

Compliance with the CRC

In addition to the work undertaken by scholars, statutory and non-governmental organisations to monitor the implementation of children's rights in Ireland (Children's Rights Alliance, 2006; Kilkelly, 2007 and 2008b; Ombudsman for Children, 2006a), international bodies are also charged with monitoring standards at national level. The most important of these is the United Nations Committee on the Rights of the Child, which examined Ireland's compliance with the CRC in 1998 and 2006. In 1998, its findings addressed its substantial concerns about the absence of respect for the rights of children, a welfare – rather than rights – approach to children's issues, and the absence of coherent strategy and coordinated service provision relating to children (Committee on the Rights of the Child, 1998). Other concerns included the failure to adopt legislation prohibiting corporal punishment within the family, the prevalence of child abuse and violence within the family and the lack of mandatory reporting mechanisms for cases of child abuse (see Shannon, 2010 for most recent commentary regarding mandatory reporting and child protection). In response to these concerns, the Committee made a number of recommendations on the issue of child protection. In particular it considered that:

- all measures are taken to ensure families in need receive necessary resources and supports;
- co-ordinating structures be put in place to deliver children's services;
- Ireland systematically promote and facilitate children's participation and respect for their views in decisions and policies affecting them;
- all appropriate measures, including of a legislative nature, be taken to prohibit and eliminate the use of corporal punishment within the family;
- an awareness-raising campaign be conducted to ensure that alternative forms of discipline are administered in conformity with the Convention;
- Cases of abuse and ill-treatment of children should be properly

investigated, sanctions applied to perpetrators and publicity given to decisions taken, with due regard to the principle of respect for the child's privacy. (Committee on the Rights of the Child, 1998)

Significantly, also, the Committee recommended that Ireland 'take further steps to ensure that the Convention is fully incorporated as part of the domestic law, taking due account of its general principles as defined in Article 2 (non-discrimination), Article 3 (best interests of the child), Article 6 (right to life, survival and development) and Article 12 (respect for the views of the child)' (Committee on the Rights of the Child, 1998, p. 4).

While some positive developments took place before Ireland's record was examined again (for example, the Office of the Ombudsman for Children was established; the National Children's Strategy was adopted; and the Children Act 2001 was enacted reforming youth justice), little was done to implement the Committee's specific recommendations on child protection in 1998. Accordingly, in 2006, the government was criticised further on these issues and in particular, the Committee highlighted as a significant problem the absence of a comprehensive national strategy for the prevention of child abuse and the continuing delays in accessing support services in this area (Committee on the Rights of the Child, 2006). It recommended that *Children First, the National Guidelines for the Protection and Welfare of Children* (Department of Health and Children, 1999) be placed on a statutory basis, that Ireland take measures to ensure that all reported cases of abuse and neglect are adequately investigated and prosecuted, and that victims of abuse and neglect have access to counselling and assistance with physical recovery and social reintegration (Committee on the Rights of the Child, 2006). It also recommended the development of a comprehensive child abuse prevention strategy, including the development of adequate responses to abuse, neglect and domestic violence, the need to facilitate local, national and regional coordination, and to conduct sensitisation, awareness-raising and educational activities in this area. Furthermore, it recommended that government ensure that the evaluation of all employees and volunteers working with children is undertaken prior to recruitment and that adequate support and training is provided for the duration of their employment (Committee on the Rights of the Child, 2006).

The Committee also expressed its 'deep concern' that punishment of children by their parents is still not prohibited by law. Reiterating its earlier recommendation, it urged the government to explicitly prohibit all forms of corporal punishment in the family and take measures to sensitise and educate parents and the general public about the unacceptability of corporal punishment (Committee on the Rights of the Child, 2006). This recommendation was supported by the Council of Europe Commissioner for Human Rights, Mr Thomas Hammarberg, following his visit to Ireland in November 2007 (Council of Europe, 2008).

In the context of family support, the Committee on the Rights of the Child noted the absence of child-specific and focused services for families, and that responsibilities are divided between several government departments. With regard to the rights of children at risk, it recommended that the government undertake an extensive review of the support services provided under the different governmental departments in order to assess the quality and outreach of these services and to identify and address possible shortcomings. It also, crucially, recommended the extension of social work services provided to families and children at risk to ensure a seven day, 24-hour service (Committee on the Rights of the Child, 2006). However, little progress has been made to implement this decision. This item is addressed in recommendation number 93 of the Ryan Report implementation plan (Office of the Minister for Children and Youth Affairs 2009b, p. 74), but interestingly it only refers to a pilot in two areas of the country and no specific implementation timeframe is provided.

European Convention on Human Rights

While not child-specific, the European Convention on Human Rights (ECHR) contains a number of provisions of relevance to the child's right to protection from harm (Kilkelly, 2004 and 2008b). It is also part of Irish law by virtue of the ECHR Act 2003 (Kilkelly, 2009). From the child's perspective, Article 3, which prohibits torture, inhuman and degrading treatment or punishment has been shown to offer considerable scope for protecting children from harm. The sections that now follow outline the principal case-law of the European Court of Human Rights (ECtHR), against which Irish law and practice will then be measured.

Corporal punishment

According to Article 3 of the ECHR, children, like adults, have the right to be free from inhuman and degrading treatment or punishment; crucially, they have the right to an effective legal response to such harm when it occurs. While the ECtHR has held that only ill-treatment that reaches a minimum level of severity will fall within the scope of the provision, it has established that this is a relative assessment which depends on all the circumstances of the case, including the effects of the treatment and the age of the victim.[1] The application of this standard to children's cases means that the ECHR provides a remedy to children who have experienced abuse and ill-treatment where that ill-treatment meets the Article 3 threshold. Child applicants have had some success in this regard. In *Warwick* v *UK*, for example, the (former) European Commission of Human Rights found that one stroke of a cane given to a 16-year-old girl constituted degrading punishment, in violation of Article 3.[2] However, in 1993, in *Costello-Roberts* v *UK*, the ECtHR rejected that the punishment received by a 7-year-old boy who was given three 'whacks' on the bottom with a gym shoe by his headmaster was severe enough to reach the Article 3 standard. The Court's conclusion enjoyed the support of only five members of the nine-judge Court and even the majority expressed reservations about the appropriateness of the punishment used.[3]

The reach into the family

The *Costello-Roberts* case made it clear that ECHR obligations cannot be delegated to private institutions such as schools. Building on this, in *A* v *UK*, the scope of protection offered by Article 3 was extended further to include physical punishment and abuse within the family (Smith, 1999).[4] Here, the caning of a 9-year-old boy by his stepfather was found to be severe enough to constitute degrading treatment within the meaning of Article 3. At national level, the injuries were considered to be sufficiently serious to merit the initiation of criminal proceedings against the stepfather but he was acquitted on the defence that the punishment amounted to 'moderate and reasonable chastisement'. This fact led the ECtHR to conclude not that the punishment itself violated the Convention, but rather that the law and its application did not provide the boy with effective protection from ill-treatment. Accordingly, it was the way in which the legal framework was organised that was problematic and because this is something for which the state is responsible, this gave rise to a violation of Article 3.

The *A* case was a victory for children's rights because it confirmed that parents could not be excused for beating their children even where it was disguised as the application of discipline for misbehaviour. At the same time, *A* reinforces that only physical punishment which causes injury of a particular severity will fall within the scope of Article 3. Comments made by the ECHR suggest that there is – or was at the time at least – no support for the view that punishment of a mild nature, such as slapping, will reach the level required to breach that provision. That is not an immutable position, however, and it is now arguable that as increasing numbers of Council of Europe states ban all forms of physical punishment against children this position will establish itself as the norm, thereby exposing the Republic of Ireland to further criticism (Arthur, 1999; Hamilton, 2005). This is supported by the fact that 18 Council of Europe states have now prohibited the corporal punishment of children.[5] Moreover, it is also relevant that Ireland has been found in breach of the Council of Europe Revised Social Charter for failing to prohibit physical punishment of children.[6] A similar finding against Portugal in 2007 gave rise to its legal ban in this area in 2008.[7] These factors will undoubtedly be persuasive in future cases before the European Court, which will also be likely to take into account the concerns and recommendations of the United Nations Committee on the Rights of the Child, as outlined above.

The broader duty of child protection

The severity of ill-treatment aside, the case law of the ECtHR makes it clear that its potential extends to protecting children in the private, as well as the public sphere. The particular vulnerability of children means that they must have state protection against any treatment which constitutes a serious breach of personal integrity. Article 1 of the ECHR, which guarantees Convention rights to everyone, taken together with Article 3, thus requires states to take effective measures designed to ensure that children are not subject to inhuman or degrading treatment, including where it is inflicted by private individuals.

The scope of this positive obligation was clarified by the Court in *Z and Others* v *UK* in 2001.[8] The applicants in this case were four children who suffered appalling abuse and neglect at the hands of their parents over a period of several years. They claimed that the local authority had failed to take effective steps to bring it to an end, giving rise to a violation of their right to protection under Article 3. Having found that their neglect and injury reached the level of severity required to bring it within the scope of Article 3, the ECtHR then went on to note that the local authority was aware of this treatment and had both a statutory duty and a range of powers available to them to protect the children. Despite the sensitive and difficult decisions facing social services and the important countervailing principle of respecting and preserving family life, therefore, the Court concluded that the system had failed to protect the children from serious, long-term neglect and abuse in violation of Article 3.[9] The ECtHR also found that, because there was no mechanism available to the applicants for establishing the liability of the state for acts or omissions involving the breach of their Convention rights, there was also a violation of Article 13, which guarantees the right to an effective domestic remedy.

Z and Others offers the first child-focused analysis under the Convention of where the balance should be struck between respecting the integrity of the family and protecting children from abuse. Here, the local authority got the balance wrong: although it was initially justified in taking steps to maintain the family as a unit by giving support to the parents, the gravity of the conditions and problems suffered by the children required that effective and practical steps be taken to safeguard their welfare when the situation at home failed to show a significant and timely improvement. Apart from the familiarity of the facts, this case also has legal relevance, given that the ECHR now has effect in Irish law. Under section 3 of the ECHR Act 2003, every organ of the state shall perform its functions in a manner compatible with the state's obligations under the Convention. Accordingly, the Health Service Executive (HSE) is required to comply with Convention obligations as set out by the European Court and where it fails in this regard, section 3(2) of the Act offers a remedy to those who have suffered injury, loss or damage as a result (Kilkelly, 2009).

The facts of *Z and Others* are not unfamiliar in the Irish context, as high profile cases like the so-called West of Ireland farmer's case (North Western Health Board, 1998), the Kilkenny incest case (McGuinness, 1993) and the more recent tragedies associated with Roscommon and Monageer (Brosnan, 2009), make clear. Of course, no two cases are alike and a range of factors may combine to produce the tragic fate of the children involved. While these have been examined in the respective inquiries, the role played by law and policy has not often been critically analysed.

The Child Care Act 1991

The principal statutory instrument governing child protection services in Ireland is the Child Care Act 1991. Importantly, section 16 of the Child Care Act places a duty on the Health Service Executive

(HSE) to institute care proceedings where a child is in need of care and protection which he or she is unlikely to receive unless either a care or a supervision order is made. This supplements the duty of the HSE under section 3 of the Act (i.e. to promote the welfare of children not receiving adequate care and protection). Significantly, the HSE must regard the welfare of the child as the first and paramount consideration while also giving due consideration to the child's wishes, with due regard to the rights of the child's parents under the Constitution and otherwise. The HSE must also have regard to the principle set out in section 3(2)(c) of the 1991 Act, that it is generally in the best interests of a child to be brought up in his or her own family.

The constitutional perspective

The express reference to parents' constitutional rights in section 3 of the 1991 Act makes it clear that although the child's interests are paramount, they are not the sole consideration in decisions taken by the HSE in this area. The weight of the constitutional perspective is also clear from an analysis of the relevant constitutional case law. The strong constitutional position of the family (defined by the courts as the family based on marriage)[10] is clear from Article 41 of the Constitution, which defines it as 'the natural primary and fundamental unit group of Society', and as a 'moral institution possessing inalienable and imprescriptible rights, antecedent and superior to all positive law'. The idea, enshrined in subsection 3(2) of the 1991 Act, and developed by case law, therefore, is that there is a sphere of family autonomy over which the state has no authority and that this is both in the family and in society's interests. This sphere includes the education and upbringing of children, as reflected in the terms of Article 42.1, in which the state 'acknowledges that the primary and natural educator of the child is the Family and guarantees to respect the inalienable right and duty of parents to provide, according to their means, for the religious and moral, intellectual, physical and social education of their children'. However, this authority is not completely without bounds and in this regard, Article 42.5 provides that:

> In exceptional cases, where the parents for physical or moral reasons fail in their duty towards their children, the State as guardian of the common good, by appropriate means shall endeavour to supply the place of the parents, but always with due regard for the natural and imprescriptible rights of the child.

This clause has been interpreted by the courts in a number of high profile cases in which the courts have established a very high threshold for state involvement in the otherwise private environment of the family. The dominant jurisprudence here was set out first in *Re JH (an infant)*, and followed in the more recent cases of *North Western Health Board* v *HW* (the PKU case) and *N* v *HSE* (the Baby Ann case).[11] What is clear from these cases is that notwithstanding the paramountcy of the child's best interests – as required by statute – this principle must be:

> construed as involving a constitutional presumption that the welfare of the child ... is to be found within the family, unless the Court is satisfied on the evidence that there are compelling reasons why this cannot be achieved, or unless the Court is satisfied that the evidence establishes an exceptional case where the parents have failed to provide education for the child and continue to fail to provide education for the child for moral or physical reasons.[12]

Thus, notwithstanding that Article 42.5 refers explicitly to the 'rights of the child', and the legislation requires that the best interests of the child be considered as a paramount consideration, constitutional interpretation and application of these provisions has led to those rights being ignored or underplayed in preference to the rights of the family. While this has been subjected to much academic analysis (see, for example, Carolan, 2007; Conneely, 2003; Enright, 2008; Kilkelly and O'Mahony, 2007), it is also an issue of clear practical importance too. In the case *of Comerford* v *Minister for Education*, a case not unlike the *Z and Others* case highlighted above, the facts caused McGuinness J to remark that the Health Board (as it then was) might have moved earlier to take the applicant and the other children into care 'given the level of neglect and lack of supervision by the parents which has caused immense problems to all of the children'.[13] This was notwithstanding that the Health Board had to bear in mind 'the extremely strong rights given to parents and the family in the Constitution and the comparative lack of express constitutional rights for the child as against the parents'. In another capacity, Ms Justice Catherine McGuinness, then Senior Counsel and Chairperson of the Kilkenny Incest Investigation, noted the inferior constitutional position of the child forcefully in her report on the failure of the authorities to take steps to protect the children concerned from abuse suffered within the family (McGuinness, 1993, p. 56). More recently, research has shown that the interpretation of Article 42.5 by the courts has cast a long shadow over the treatment of children by the state, suggesting that a 'chilling effect' against formal intervention in the family prevails in child protection services in some areas (Kilkelly, 2007). Thus, although it is true that a child protection system that sanctions intervention in the family without adequate justification or necessary safeguards causes problems of a different kind, there is nonetheless, ample evidence that the balance has not been accurately struck in Irish law.

Operationalising Section 3

So how do practitioners implement section 3 in practice? According to Buckley, operationalising of the section 3 duty requires professionals who work with children and families to understand 'the causes, signs and effects of child abuse and neglect' (2002, p. 43). Guidance is crucial to understanding but it appears to be scant here. In particular, although section 3 requires the HSE to identify children who are 'not receiving adequate care and protection' the legislation does not define the phrase, or articulate where the 'adequate' standard should lie. The terms 'adequate care and protection' suggest a broad rather than a narrow duty, ranging from children suffering serious harm and ill-treatment to parents who are unable, for whatever reason, to provide children with a sufficient level of care.[14] But where should priority be placed where resources are scant and time-limited? In terms of understanding child abuse and neglect, *The National Guidelines for the Protection and Welfare of Children*, revised in 2009, assist here by providing detailed definitions of neglect, harm and emotional, physical and sexual abuse (Office of the Minister for Children and Youth Affairs, 2009a, pp. 11–13). In terms of implementing statutory duties, the *Guidelines* also set out the principles of inter-agency working and coordination, which must form part of the state's response to reports of child abuse and neglect, while providing specific guidance for the management of concerns by the HSE and the Gardai (police) in this area. However, significant doubt has been cast on the state's resourcing of these functions (see, for example, Burns and Lynch, 2008; O'Brien, 2009).

Despite numerous recommendations to this effect, the *Guidelines* have not yet been given a statutory basis, although this was announced in 2011, and so remain guidance only (Kilkelly, 2008a, pp. 284–285). Submissions made to the review of the *Children First Guidelines* in 2008 noted substantial problems with their implementation including regional variation, operational difficulties, difficulties arising from the absence of a mandatory basis and the absence of a monitoring or evaluation process in relation to their implementation (Office of the Minister for Children and Youth Affairs, 2008, p. 58). Significantly, the revised *Guidelines* contain greater detail on the systems to be put in place to respond effectively to reports of child abuse, but it remains to be seen whether they are sufficient to address the concerns documented by Buckley (2007) and the Ombudsman for Children (2006b) with regard to the lack of a systematic approach within the HSE to complaints of abuse. Buckley has also raised concerns about the imbalance in the attention and resources focused on child abuse, rather than on neglect, which is arguably more widespread, as resources are allocated in line with perceptions of the seriousness of the concerns presented (Buckley, 2005, p. 2). The fact that resources for child protection services are likely to be reduced overall in line with cuts to public spending across the board means that very serious challenges will continue to prevail both for social workers and, most importantly, for children and families who need their assistance. This challenge awaits the new Department of Children and Youth Affairs.

Bridging the gap

The above analysis suggests that law and policy may not be sufficiently robust to ensure that children are protected effectively from serious harm as required by the provisions of the Convention on the Rights of the Child and the case-law of the European Court of Human Rights. It is perhaps of note, in this context, that the government has recently made it clear that it deems the child protection legislative and policy framework to be adequate at this time, although it considers that 'awareness of and adherence to these provisions is inconsistent and in places unimplemented' (Office of the Minister for Children and Youth Affairs, 2009b, p. 30). Significantly, in response to the Ryan Report, the government has given a commitment to the development of a new National Children's Strategy (2011–2020) and an ongoing process of benchmarking Irish law and policy against policy in other jurisdictions and ensuring compliance with the Convention on the Rights of the Child (ibid., p. 31).

From a practical perspective it is also very welcome that a range of measures are to be taken to improve accountability and the quality of services provided to children. Significant is the recent recruitment of 260 additional social worker positions targeting the area of child protec tion (Office of the Minister for Children and Youth Affairs, 2009b, pp. 46–47). These are all important measures that have the potential to ensure that children have effective protection from abuse and neglect.

These will have minimal impact, however, if the constitutional framework which currently downplays or ignores the rights of children and shows undue deference to the inalienable rights and integrity of the family goes unchanged. In this regard, the report of the Joint Oireachtas Committee on the Constitutional Amendment on Children on revised proposals to amend the Constitution is very welcome (Oireachtas Committee on the Constitutional Amendment, 2010). In short, the Committee appears to have taken on board the broad-ranging criticism directed at the 2007 proposals (see, for example, Kilkelly and O'Mahony, 2007; Carolan, 2007) and has instead proposed a form of words that, if inserted into the Constitution, would provide enormous potential for robust and relatively radical change to the status and treatment of children in Irish law and practice. The 2010 proposals are lengthy and complicated and worthy of very serious consideration (see, for example, Kilkelly and O'Mahony, forthcoming).

However, its critical elements are as follows. First, it recognises the natural and imprescriptible rights of all children, including their right to have their welfare regarded as a primary consideration, and undertakes to protect and vindicate those rights. Second, it provides that 'in the resolution of all disputes concerning the guardianship, adoption, custody, care or upbringing of a child, the welfare and best interests of the child shall be the first and paramount consideration'. Third, it provides a state guarantee to vindicate the 'rights of all children as individuals', including the right to such protection and care as is necessary for the child's safety and welfare, the right to an education and the right of the child's voice to be heard in any judicial and administrative proceedings affecting the child, having regard to the child's age and maturity. Finally, it proposes to amend the existing Article 42.5 (see above) to ensure that any intervention in the family designed to protect the rights of children is proportionate and regulated by law. It also makes certain other changes necessary to ensure adoption operates in a manner that is fair and consistent with the best interests of the child.

In brief, the proposal is a principled and careful attempt to resolve many of the current difficulties with the Constitution from a children's rights perspective, and its delicate wording underpins the potential it offers to bring about meaningful change in the protection of children's rights in Ireland. If passed, the core principles of the CRC – that decision making concerning children be informed by their best interests and that children have the right to be heard with regard to their age and maturity – would form part of the fundamental law of the state. Children would be recognised in the Constitution as autonomous bearers of rights, rather than simply members of the family unit, and the child's right to protection and care would be specifically enumerated in the Constitution for the first time. All of this occurs in the context of recognition that a child's parents remain the primary protectors of the child's welfare and that state intervention will only be permissible where parents fail in that responsibility; even then, intervention must be shown to be proportionate before it can be justified, involving a recalibration of the delicate balancing exercise that must underline all decisions in this area. In this way, the primacy of parents and families is recognised and protected, the risk of excessive intervention is mitigated, and an effective and workable mechanism is provided to allow legitimate state intervention in those cases where it is genuinely necessary in the best interests of children. Although it remains to be seen whether the proposals are put to the people in this form, or at all, and if they are, whether the people choose to accept them, it is clear that the proposals have the potential to radically reshape the way in which children are perceived and treated in Irish law, policy and practice. Its impact would be felt across the range of children's services, but it would arguably be felt most acutely in the area of child protection.

Conclusion

This chapter has highlighted the standards set by international instruments and best practice that require effective state mechanisms to be put in place to protect children from neglect and abuse, and respond effectively when it is identified. It has drawn attention to the fact that although guidance is available in the legislative and policy framework – notably the Child Care Act 1991 and the *Children First – National Guidance for the Protection and Welfare of Children* – these developments are overshadowed by a constitutional position which downplays the rights of children in favour of the integrity of the family. This has had an apparent 'chilling effect' on the way in which social services are resourced and managed, and the political priority that the child's right to protection from harm within the family (as opposed to the risk posed to children from those outside the family) has been afforded. The government is committed to amending the Constitution and the proposals published in 2010 have been warmly welcomed by many groups working with, and for, children. The aftermath of the Ryan Report, and the ongoing public disquiet with the way in which child protection has been ignored and underplayed (see, for example, O'Brien, 2009; Smyth, 2010) mean that there is now an important and perhaps unique opportunity to reform our Constitution with permanent, positive results. Every effort must be made to ensure that only the highest standards prevail.

Notes

1 *Ireland* v *UK*, no 5310/81, Series A no 25, 2 EHRR 25, para. 162.
2 No 9471/81 *Warwick* v *UK*, Comm Rep, 18.7.86, DR 60, p. 5, paras 86–88.
3 *Costello-Roberts* v *UK*, no 13134/87, Series A no 247–C, 19 EHRR 112.
4 *A* v *UK*, no 25599/94, Reports 1998–VI no 90, para 21.
5 These include Austria, Bulgaria, Croatia, Cyprus, Denmark, Finland, Germany, Greece, Hungary, Iceland, Latvia, Netherlands, Norway, Portugal, Romania, Spain, Sweden, Ukraine. See www.coe.int/children.
6 Resolution ResChS(2005)9. Complaint No 18/2003 by the World Organisation against Torture against Ireland.
7 Resolution CM/ResChS(2008)4 Complaint No 34/2006 by the World Organisation against Torture (OMCT) against Portugal. Available at www.coe.int.
8 *Z and Others* v *UK*, no 29392/95, Reports 2001–V.
9 Ibid., paras 69–75.
10 See, in particular, *State (Nicolaou)* v *An Bord Uchtála* [1966] I.R. 567.
11 *Re JH* [1985] I.R. 375; *North Western Health Board* v *HW* [2001] 3 I.R. 635 and *N* v *Health Services Executive* [2006] I.E.S.C. 60.
12 *Re JH* [1985] I.R. 375 at 395.
13 *Comerford v Minister for Education* [1997] 2 I.L.R.M. 134.
14 See further section 8(2) of the 1991 Act which also assists.

References

Arthur, R. (1999) 'The European Court of Human Rights and the abolition of corporal punishment in Ireland', *Irish Journal of Family Law*, 4 IJFL 10, pp. 10–14.

Brosnan, K. (2009) *Monageer Inquiry*, Dublin, Department of Health and Children.

Buckley, H. (2005) 'Reviewing Children First: Some considerations', *Irish Journal of Family Law*, 3, pp. 2–8.

Buckley, H. (2007) 'Differential responses to child protection reports', *Irish Journal of Family Law*, 1, pp. 1–7.

Burns, K. and Lynch, D. (eds) (2008) *Child Protection and Welfare Social Work: Contemporary Themes and Practice Perspectives*, Dublin, A. & A. Farmar.

Carolan, E. (2007) 'The constitutional consequences of reform: Best interests after the amendment', *Irish Journal of Family Law*, 3, pp. 9–13.

Children's Rights Alliance (2006) *From Rhetoric to Rights. Second Shadow Report to the United Nations Committee on the Rights of the Child*, Dublin, Children's Rights Alliance.

Committee on the Rights of the Child (1998) *Consideration of Reports Submitted by States Parties Under Article 44 of the Convention. Concluding observations of the committee on the rights of the child* [Online], United Nations. Available from: www.hri.ca/fortherecord1998/documentation/tbodies /crc-c-15–add85.htm (accessed 15 July 2005).

Committee on the Rights of the Child (2006), *Concluding Observations: Ireland* CRC/C/IRL/CO2 29.

Conneely, E. (2003) 'Children's rights in irish constitutional law', *Irish Journal of Family Law*, 2(10), pp. 2–5.

Council of Europe (2008) *Report by the Commissioner for Human Rights Mr Thomas Hammarberg on his Visit to Ireland 26–30 November 2007* (online), CommDH (2008) 9. Available from: www.coe.int (accessed 10 January 2010).

Department of Health and Children (1999) *Children First: National Guidelines for the Protection and Welfare of Children*, Stationery Office, Dublin.

Enright, M. (2008) 'Interrogating the natural order: Hierarchies of rights in Irish child law', *Irish Journal of Family Law*, 1, pp. 3–7.

Fortin, J. (2009) *Children's Rights and the Developing Law* (3rd edn), Cambridge, Cambridge University Press.

Hamilton, C. (2005) 'Child abuse, the United Nations Convention on the Rights of the Child and the criminal law', *Irish Law Times*, 23(6), pp. 90–96.

Kilkelly, U. (2004) 'Children's rights: A European perspective', *Judicial Studies Institute Journal*, 4(2), pp. 68–95.

Kilkelly, U. (2007) *Barriers to the Realisation of Children's Rights in Ireland*, Dublin, OCO.

Kilkelly, U. (2008a) 'Children's rights and the family: Myth or reality?', *Studies: An Irish Quarterly Review*, 97, pp. 7–14.

Kilkelly, U. (2008b) *Children's Rights in Ireland: Law, Policy and Practice*, Dublin, Bloomsbury.

Kilkelly, U. (ed.) (2009) *ECHR and Irish Law* (2nd edn), Bristol, Jordans.

Kilkelly, U. and O'Mahony, C. (forthcoming) 'Measuring progress: The treatment of the child in Irish law', in Smith, J. and Luddy, M. (eds) *Children, Childhood and Irish Society*, University of Notre Dame Press.

McGuinness, C. (1993) *Kilkenny Incest Investigation: Report presented to Mr Brendan Howlin TD, Minister for Health by South Eastern Health Board*, Dublin, The Stationery Office.

Miles, J. (2001) Case Commentary, '*Z and Others v UK; TP and KM v UK*: Human rights and child protection', *Child and Family Law Quarterly*, 13(4), pp. 431.

North Western Health Board (1998) *West of Ireland Farmer Case*, Manorhamilton, North Western Health Board.

O'Brien, C. (2009) 'Case studies reveal State fails to protect children adequately – Long waiting lists for childcare "dangerous"', *The Irish Times*, 10 October 2009.

Office of the Minister for Children and Youth Affairs (2008) *National Review of Compliance with Children First: National Guidelines for the Protection and Welfare of Children*, Dublin, The Stationery Office.

Office of the Minister for Children and Youth Affairs (2009a) *The National Guidelines for the Protection and Welfare of Children* (2nd edn), Dublin, The Stationery Office.

Office of the Minister for Children and Youth Affairs (2009b) *Report of the Commission to Inquire into Child Abuse 2009 Implementation Plan*, Dublin, Department of Health and Children.

Ombudsman for Children (2006a) *Report of the Ombudsman for Children to the UN Committee on the Rights of the Child*, Dublin, Ombudsman for Children.

Ombudsman for Children (2006b) *Report of the Ombudsman for Children to the Oireachtas Joint Committee on Health and Children on Complaints Received About Child Protection in Ireland*, Dublin, Ombudsman for Children.

Oireachtas Committee on the Constitutional Amendment (2010) *Proposal for a Constitutional Amendment to Strengthen Children's Rights – Final Report*, Dublin, Houses of the Oireachtas.

Shannon, G. (2010) *Third Report of the Special Rapporteur on Child Protection. A Report Submitted to the Oireachtas 2009*, Dublin, Office of the Minister for Children and Youth Affairs.

Smith, R. (1999) 'To smack or not to smack? A review of A v UK in an international and European context and its potential impact on parental physical chastisement' (online), *Web Journal of Current Legal Issues*. Available from: http://webjcli.ncl.ac.uk/1999/issue1/smith1 .html (accessed 1 February 2010).

Smyth, J. (2010) 'Abused, then failed by the State: How a girl met a tragic end', *The Irish Times*, 4 March 2010.

United Nations (1989) *Convention on the Rights of the Child*, Geneva, United Nations.

4

It is a long way from Kilkenny to here: Reflections on legal and policy developments before and since the publication of the *Kilkenny Incest Investigation*

Catherine McGuinness

The general theme for this chapter is a historical perspective on developments in child protection and welfare in Ireland, drawing on my experience and involvement with child abuse inquiries, with particular reference to the recommendations arising from these processes. In accordance with this theme I draw directly on my experience of the legal aspects of childcare and protection issues and in particular with my involvement in the *Kilkenny Incest Investigation* (McGuinness, 1993). I was the Chairperson of the *Kilkenny Incest Investigation* team, which was one of the first seminal inquires of this type in the Republic of Ireland. The focus of the chapter then shifts to current developments. The Joint Committee on the Constitutional Amendment on Children (2010) has published its third and final Report proposing an agreed text for an amendment to Article 42 of Bunreacht na hÉireann concerning the rights of children as individuals. This is an event of great importance and I examine the Committee's proposed amendement and discuss its potential to reform the Irish's state's approach to child care and protection. It has been a long way from Kilkenny to here.

Others (Kilkelly, 2008) have dealt in some detail with the history of child protection and care in Ireland, and with the influence of Articles 41 (The Family) and Article 42 (Education) of the Constitution (see Chapters 1, 4 and Burns and Lynch, 2008; Kilkelly, 2008). It seems necessary to me, however, to provide a brief historical and statutory background to my discussion of the *Kilkenny Incest Investigation* and of later developments concerning both child protection and the rights of children.

Historical and statutory background of child protection in Ireland prior to the Kilkenny Investigation

Prior to the nineteenth century there was little or nothing in the way of formal or institutional provision for the protection of children. It was only during the latter part of the nineteenth century that the first institutions were established with the aim of sheltering and protecting children who were seen to be at physical and, more especially, at moral risk. These early moves to protect vulnerable children were, in the main, inspired by Church authorities, both Catholic and Protestant. As far as the Roman Catholic Church was concerned a strong influence was that of Cardinal Cullen, who held office from 1849 to 1878. At that time, many children were housed (as were their parents) in very poor conditions in local workhouses, and it was sought to rescue children from these circumstances. Children also often came before the courts charged with petty offences, and it was felt that there was a need for a system to deal with such children.

A parallel situation applied in England and the first Reformatory Schools Act was passed in 1854 in that jurisdiction. It was not, however, extended to Ireland, owing to fear of proselytism. The English Industrial Schools Act 1857 was, however, extended to Ireland, and it was under this Act that the institutions were set up that later became the subject of the Commission to Investigate Child Abuse (CICA) and the Ryan Report (see Chapter 2 and Ryan, 2009). The Prevention of Cruelty and Protection of Children Act was passed in 1889, and the same period saw the establishment of the Society for the Prevention of Cruelty to Children. By 1899 seventy-one industrial schools had been established in Ireland, with 8,422 inmates; but 5,988 children still remained in workhouses. The history of this period is excellently covered in Joseph Robins' (1980) work *The Lost Children: A Study of Charity Children in Ireland 1700–1900*.

The most important development, in a sense the culmination of the nineteenth century concern for children at risk, came with the Children Act 1908. At the time of its introduction this was seen as a progressive and enlightened measure, and was known as the Children's Charter. Given the social and statutory context, this was undoubtedly the case, as was acknowledged by O'Flaherty J in the Supreme Court case of *MF* v *Superintendent of Ballymun Gárda Station*

[1991] 1IR 189. What was less praiseworthy was that, subsequent to the 1908 Act, all enthusiasm for reform of the law concerning children seemed to fade. For the best part of a century, and from the foundation of the independent Irish State in 1922 until the middle of the 1990s, the 1908 Children Act remained the central statutory basis both for the criminal law concerning child offenders and for the protection of deprived and vulnerable children. With the development of child care aspects of the work of the health boards, particularly from 1970 onwards, considerable legal ingenuity was brought to bear in using marginally relevant sections of the 1908 Act, which permitted a 'petty session court' to place children in the care of 'a relative or other fit person', to base applications to take children into care. Unfortunately for the health boards, the Supreme Court in the 1989 case of *State (D & D)* v *G* [1990] ILRM 10 held that the health boards had no statutory power to act as 'fit persons' under the 1908 Act. This gave rise to immediate reactive legislation in the Children Act 1989, which regularised the existing situation; but no doubt this episode gave ammunition to those groups, including social workers and family lawyers, who had for years campaigned for modern child care legislation. Two years later the Child Care Act 1991 was passed by the Oireachtas (Irish Parliament). The major parts of that Act, concerning in particular taking children into care, were not brought into immediate effect. This was the background, as far as public law on child care was concerned, against which the Kilkenny Incest Investigation began.

Brief reference should also be made to other developments concerning the general rights of children as opposed to a right to care and protection outside that provided in the normal way by the family. I have already mentioned the provisions of Articles 41 and 42 of the Constitution, which will be discussed further in the context of the current recommendations of the Oireachtas Joint Committee. Provision was made for the legal adoption of children in the Adoption Act 1952, subsequently amended on a number of occasions. Until 1988, however, adoption was limited to the children of unmarried parents, owing to the view taken of the constitutional protection of the rights of the married family. A number of high court cases between birth mothers and prospective adopters gave rise, on appeal, to influential dicta by the Supreme Court on the respective rights of children, parents and the family. In the first of these major cases, *G* v *An Bord Uchtála* [1980] IR 32, the rights of the child were set out by O'Higgins CJ as follows:

> The child also has natural rights. Normally these will be safe under the care and protection of its mother. Having been born, the child has the

right to be fed and to live, to be reared and educated, to have the opportunity of working and of realising his or her full personality and dignity as a human being. These rights of the child (and others which I have not enumerated) must equally be protected and vindicated by the State.

In the same cases, the rights of the natural mother (birth mother) were also explained as arising under Article 40, since she as an unmarried parent was not endowed with the inalienable and imprescriptible rights ascribed to the family under Article 41. The father of a child placed for adoption had virtually no rights, and certainly no constitutional rights, but that is a discussion for another day (see, for example, the Law Reform Commission's Consultation Paper, *Legal Aspects of Family Relationships LRC CP55–2009*).

Under the Adoption Act 1988 a strictly limited possibility of adoption was granted to children of married parents, but only in the exceptional case of virtually total abandonment and failure of duty by the married parents, in accordance with Article 42.5 as strictly interpreted by the Supreme Court.

The Guardianship of Infants Act 1964 had placed the welfare of the child as the 'first and paramount consideration' in any dispute concerning a child, but from time to time doubts were expressed as to whether this, if literally interpreted, was fully in accordance with the family and parental rights set out in the Constitution. For example, in *G* v *An Bord Uchtála*, Walsh J had stressed that 'first and paramount' did not mean that the child's welfare was the only consideration. In the important 1985 case of *In Re JH (An Infant)* [1985] IR 375/390, where the dispute was between established prospective adopters and the very recently married parents of the child in question, the high court granted custody of the child, on welfare grounds, to the adoptive parents. The Supreme Court held, however, that the court had applied the wrong test. The child had rights under the Constitution as a member of a family:

> to belong to a unit group possessing inalienable and imprescriptible rights antecedent and superior to all positive law, to protection by the State of the family to which it belongs and to be educated by the family and to be provided by its parents with religious, moral, intellectual, physical and social education.

In this context it must, of course, be recalled that following the 1966 Supreme Court decision in *Nicolaou* v *An Bord Uchtála* [1966] IR 567, the legally married family alone benefits from these inalienable and imprescriptible rights as set out in Article 41 and 42. The child in question on that test was returned to the birth parents.

This authoritative statement of the inter-related rights of the family and the child has been particularly influential on later judgments where, as stated by Geoffrey Shannon (2005, p. 1): 'the Supreme Court has veered away from enumerating children's rights by holding that the project of articulating the rights of children was a matter for the Government'. It is, however, notable, that the decision in *In Re JH* was closely followed by the Supreme Court in *N and Anor* v *Health Service Executive and Ors* [2006] IESC 60 (the 'Baby Ann' case) – again a case where the dispute for custody of a child was between prospective adopters of two years standing and the very recently married birth parents.

The position of the children of unmarried parents (illegitimate children) and the overt legal discrimination against such children remained unsolved until 1987. In 1982 the Law Reform Commission had published their *Report on Illegitimacy (LRC4–1982)* which recommended the enactment of legislation removing all such discrimination. After some considerable controversy the Status of Children Act 1987 removed the distinction between the rights of children of unmarried parents and those of married parents, though the Act held back from granting equal guardianship rights to unmarried fathers, an equality issue which is still unresolved.

Progress on promoting children's rights since the *Kilkenny Incest Investigation*

Before discussing the *Kilkenny Incest Investigation* itself I want to stress that both the Investigation and its Report were the work not of an individual but of a team, and I wish to pay tribute to the three other members of that team, Brid Clarke, then Head Social Worker, Eastern Health Board, Martin Hynes, then Programme Manager, Community Care Department, South Eastern Health Board, and Dr Sheelagh Ryan, then Director of Community Care and Medical Officer of Health, Midland Health Board. All the analysis and recommendations are the joint work of the team, and are built on their joint knowledge and experience of the child care system that applies throughout Ireland.

The basic facts of the Kilkenny case are set out in Chapter 1 of the Report:

> On March 1st 1993, at the Central Criminal Court, a forty-eight year old County Kilkenny father of two was given a seven year jail sentence, having pleaded guilty at an earlier court hearing to six charges of rape,

incest and assault from a total of fifty-six charges covering the period
1976 to 1991.

The sentence attracted considerable media coverage as details
became public of a history of physical and sexual abuse which had been
ongoing for a fifteen year period.

At the court hearing on 1ˢᵗ March, it emerged that the victim had had
a number of hospital admissions over the years for treatment of serious
physical injuries and had been in contact with health professionals
including general practitioners, social workers and public health
nurses. (McGuinness, 1993, p. 9)

The terms of reference of the Investigation, which was established
by the then Minister for Health, Brendan Howlin, TD, were as follows:

- to carry out an investigation, insofar as the health services are
  concerned, of the circumstances surrounding the abuse
  referred to in the case heard in the Central Criminal Court on
  1 March 1993, and in particular to establish why action to halt
  the abuse was not taken earlier, and
- to make recommendations for the future investigation and
  management by the health services of case of suspected child
  abuse. (p. 11)

Since 1993 there have been a number of investigations of one kind or
another into cases of serious neglect and abuse of children (see, for
example, Western Health Board, 1996; Murphy et al., 2005; Brosnan,
2009). It has, perhaps, become a regular feature of these investigations for blame to be put on 'the system', or on 'systemic failure'. It is
understandable that, in reaction to these repeated findings, commentators, including Fergus Finlay CEO of Barnardos Ireland, should call
for acceptance of individual responsibility for failings in individual
cases. I sympathise with this point of view. In the Kilkenny case,
however, I consider that the major fault indeed lay in the system, or
rather lack of system, rather than with the individuals involved, each
of whom did what they believed was the best they could for the girl at
the centre of the story.

The findings of the investigation are relatively well known, certainly
among social workers and others who are involved in the child welfare
and protection system. A basic problem was the failure of communication between the individuals involved, and between the various
sectors of the health service; also between them and others, such as
members of the Gárda Síochána and the hospital doctors and general
practitioners who treated the girl. There was little or no consistent

record-keeping or exchange of information, and individual doctors had widely differing interpretations of the duty of patient confidentiality. The statute law was more than 80 years out of date and there were inherent difficulties in the interpretation of the constitutional rights of children.

Our recommendations mirrored these findings. We stressed the immediate need to implement the remaining sections of the Child Care Act 1991 and to provide the necessary resources to do so. We recommended the provision of new statutory guidelines on the identification, investigation and management of child abuse. We emphasised the need for inter-agency cooperation and the increased use of multi-disciplinary and well managed case conferences. Other recommendations dealt with the recording of information, the clarification and improved dissemination of medical guidelines on confidentiality, with the prevention of abuse and with the treatment of victims. And we also stated:

> We feel that the very high emphasis on the rights of the family in the Constitution may consciously or unconsciously be interpreted as giving a higher value to the rights of parents than to the rights of children. We believe that the Constitution should contain a specific and overt declaration of the rights of born children. We therefore recommend that consideration be given by the Government to the amendment of Articles 41 and 42 of the Constitution so as to include a statement of the constitutional rights of children.

This particular recommendation drew much public attention at the time, and it would be fair to say that it has been referred to at frequent intervals since 1993. I would, again, like to point out that this was not my personal recommendation, but the unanimous recommendation of the members of the team, drawn from our joint experience in the field of child care and protection.

Almost 17 years later, the Final Report of the Joint Oireachtas Committee (2010) is, in a sense, a response. Much has changed in the meantime both in Ireland and on the international scene. The 1991 Act was fully brought into effect (though whether sufficient resources have ever been provided is open to question) and the enactment of the Children Act 2001 has brought the hope of reform in the way in which our criminal justice system deals with young offenders. In 1992, Ireland had already made a formal legal commitment accepting the obligations of the United Nations Convention on the Rights of the Child and undertaking to implement its provisions. There is no doubt that there is an increasing public awareness of the rights set out in the

UN Convention. References to Convention rights have begun to appear in the judgments of the high court, particularly in connection with the requirement in Article 12 of the Convention that the voice of the child be heard in judicial and administrative proceedings affecting the child. This position has been strengthened by the mandatory terms of the Brussels 2 Revised Council Regulation (Council Regulation 2201/2003 EC of 27 November 2003), which is, of course, now part of domestic law. It is perhaps disappointing, however, that in his recent judgment in the case of *McD* v *L* [2007] IESC 81, delivered on 10 December 2009, the Chief Justice, in correctly emphasising that the UN Convention was not a part of Irish domestic law, should have given a somewhat dismissive impression in his references to the Convention.

The Children's Ombudsman was appointed under the Ombudsman for Children Act 2002; she and her office have proved to be articulate, effective and courageous in upholding the rights of children. Voluntary bodies such as the Children's Rights Alliance and Barnardo's have added their voices to the debate, as have individual legal writers such as Dr Ursula Kilkelly of University College Cork and Geoffrey Shannon of the Law Society.

The Joint Oireachtas Committee has itself, in its Report, set out a most competent statement of the historic context and the present legal position. It is also an important factor that the Committee has put forward an agreed proposal for amendment. Tribute should be paid to the qualities of Mary O'Rourke TD as chairperson, who must have shown a remarkable combination of leadership and consensus building.

The joint Committee considered and, in effect, rejected the original amendment proposed by the government in February 2007 in the Twenty-Eighth Amendment of the Constitution Bill 2007. In my view they were entirely correct in so doing. The proposed Article 42(A) was overly concentrated on the relatively narrow question of the possible adoption of the child of married parents, and the text regarding actual children's rights could only be described as minimalist. The Joint Committee also points out that absent from that text was any explicit obligation to guarantee the protection of those rights.

It is interesting that the Committee appears not to have given much attention to the recommendations for amendment of Articles 41 and 42 made by the Constitutional Review Group in their weighty (in every sense) report of 1996. This was not, of course, included in the Committee's orders of reference. On rereading the comprehensive discussion and recommendations of the Constitutional Review Group (a very highly qualified and distinguished body) I was in admiration of their diligence and learning. My instant reaction, however, was to feel how much things had moved on since 1996.

The present Joint Committee does not suggest any amendment of Article 41, which deals with the family. The Review Group had suggested the introduction of at least some gender equality into Article 41.2, the somewhat notorious reference to the life of woman in the home,[1] but of course recommendations in this area fall outside the remit of the present Committee, which was to deal solely with children's rights issues.

The Joint Committee proposes what is virtually a new Article 42, the full text of which is reproduced at the end of this chapter. There can be no doubt that the Committee has made a notable effort to rebalance the rights of children, parents and the family and to under-write the constitutional rights of children as individuals. I believe that to a large extent they have succeeded. What strikes one at once is that, whereas the present Article 42 begins and continues with parents and 'the family', leaving only a passing reference to children to the final paragraph (Article 42.5), the Committee's proposed new Article 42 puts the rights of children and their vindication right at the beginning. In the proposed Article 42.2, in enumerating the rights of children as individuals, the wording clearly reflects that of the UN Convention on the Rights of the Child. In particular this includes, at 42.2.iii:

> the right of the child's voice to be heard in any judicial and administra-tive proceedings affecting the child, having regard to the child's age and maturity.

As was pointed out by the Chief Justice in his judgment in *McD* v *L*, the UN Convention envisages that States would ensure 'that their national law or administrative practices provide protection for the rights specified in the Convention'. Ireland has ratified the Convention and one must presume that by this ratification, and by its interaction with the Committee on the Rights of the Child, the government, on behalf of the country (in effect of us all) accepted the aims and obligations for the Convention. It would not, therefore, be surprising to find the Convention reflected in the text of Ireland's Constitution in the Article dealing with the rights of children.

In the proposed Article 42.3, firm support is given to the role of parents as the primary and natural carers, educators and protectors of their children. This is accepted by the vast majority of Irish people and it is right that it be given acknowledgement and support in the

Constitution. The Committee's Report provides an extensive survey of the various submissions received, and I could find no opinion expressed in any of these submissions other than that, in the normal and ordinary way, the best place for a child is in the care of its parents. There was no sign of any eagerness to displace parents rather than support them.

In the discussion which has followed the publication of the Report a number of spokespersons have issued dire warnings that the proposed amendment is a charter for 'the State' to snatch children away from parents on the slightest excuse. Given the text of the proposed amendment in 42.3 and 42.4, and the reference to 'proportionate means', this expressed fear seems to me to be a deliberate distortion of both the intention and the wording of the Committee. It is somewhat strange to find that among those who appear most opposed to an enhancement of children's rights are the same spokespersons who on other occasions are the most vocal upholders of the rights of another class of children – the unborn.

The proposed amendment goes on to deal with current problems regarding the adoption of the children of married parents in certain situations. These problems stem from the current terms of Article 42.5 and their strict interpretation by the Supreme Court.

While I welcome the Committee's suggested amendment of Article 42, I believe that problems may possibly arise in the future interaction of Article 41 and 42, on account of the actual wording of Article 41.1, and arising from the Supreme Court's firmly established dicta that the family to which Article 41 refers is the family based on legal marriage and none other (for example, *Nicolaou* v *An Bord Uchtála*, reinforced in *McD* v *L*).

The wording of Article 41.1 and its guarantee to protect the family is extremely strong. As the judgments in *In Re JH* and the 'Baby Ann' case make clear, this wording, taken together with the present Article 42, establishes a powerful presumption that a child of married parents can be left in the custody of another party only in the most exceptional cases. The bar is set extremely high, and the presumption, which is of course itself predictive, has been held to trump even strong predictive contrary evidence as to the future welfare of the child. Will the proposed changes in Article 42 change this situation, and if so to what extent? Only time, and possible future Supreme Court decisions, will tell.

But it is important to remember that the Article 41 guarantees belong only to the *married* family. In a situation where the parties were not a married couple, and there was therefore no constitutional family, it was perfectly acceptable for Fennelly J to state (again in *McD v L*):

> Some basic points are not, however, and could not be in dispute. First among these is that the welfare of the child must at every point be the overwhelming and governing consideration.

and to state that Section 3 of the Guardianship of Infants Act expressed in statutory form a universal human value that nobody could contest.

Does this mean that in a situation where parents are married it is 'family first' in a dispute concerning a child's welfare, but 'child first' where the parents are unmarried? Is the child of unmarried parents in a stronger constitutional position?

In all fairness to the Committee, these questions were not strictly speaking part of their remit. One might well feel that they had a hard enough task without having to tackle the knotty question of how the State should define the family, and what rights should be given to unmarried parents, in particular fathers. As I write, it is reported that the German Constitutional court has directed the German government to provide custody rights for unmarried fathers, while the degree to which the unmarried family is recognised differs from state to state within the EU. It must be noted, of course, that there is a wide degree of recognition of differing family groups in the jurisprudence of the European Court of Human Rights, while the Supreme Court has recently referred a question regarding the position of an unmarried father to the European Court of Justice. This story is far from an end.

Conclusion

Members of the government have repeatedly confirmed the government's commitment to a referendum on children's rights. The Joint Committee has put forward a reasoned recommendation, but there is as yet no sign of a possible date for such a referendum. A suggestion that the delay was due to a wish to postpone outstanding by-elections was indignantly rejected by Barry Andrews, the then Minister for Children and Youth Affairs, who suggested that unspecified difficulties have been put forward by a number of government departments. It is, of course, normal practice for any proposed legislation to be circulated at an early stage to government departments for comment, and one presumes that departments are most likely to comment where a proposed change may affect that department's functioning, or more crucially its expenditure (see Chapter 1).

The Joint Oireachtas Committee has provided us, as citizens, with a considered Report, which sets out the present law and discusses the relevant issues fully and in clear language, easily to be understood by members of the public. The Committee has put forward an agreed proposal in a situation where there has been widespread public demand for change. It is now time for the Government to state clearly:

1 whether they now maintain their previous commitment to a referendum on children's rights;
2 whether they accept, at least in general terms, the Committee's recommendations;
3 if they have objections to the Committee's proposals, the nature of these objections and their alternative proposals; and
4 what is the firm proposed date for any proposed referendum.

Joint Committee on the Constitutional Amendment on Children (2010): Proposed text for Article 42

1. 1° The State shall cherish all the children of the State equally.
    2° The State recognises and acknowledges the natural and imprescriptible rights of all children including their right to have their welfare regarded as a primary consideration and shall, as far as practicable, protect and vindicate those rights.
    3° In the resolution of all disputes concerning the guardianship, adoption, custody, care or upbringing of a child, the welfare and best interests of the child shall be the first and paramount consideration.
2. The State guarantees in its laws to recognise and vindicate the rights of all children as individuals including:
    i   the right of the child to such protection and care as is necessary for his or her safety and welfare;
    ii   the right of the child to an education;
    iii the right of the child's voice to be heard in any judicial and administrative proceedings affecting the child, having regard to the child's age and maturity.
3. The State acknowledges that the primary and natural carers, educators and protectors of the welfare of a child are the child's parents and guarantees to respect the right and responsibility of parents to provide according to their means for the physical, emotional, intellectual, religious, moral and social education and welfare of their children.
4. Where the parents of any child fail in their responsibility

towards such child, the State as guardian of the common good shall, by proportionate means, as shall be regulated by law, endeavour to supply or supplement the place of the parents, regardless of their marital status.

5. Provision may be made by law for the adoption of any child where the parents have failed for such a period of time as may be prescribed by law in their responsibility towards the child and where the best interests of the child so require.

6. Provision may be made by law for the voluntary placement for adoption and the adoption of any child and any such law shall respect the child's right to continuity in its care and upbringing.

7. 1° The State shall not oblige parents in violation of their conscience and lawful preference to send their children to schools established by the State, or to any particular type of school designated by the State.

   2° The State shall, however, as guardian of the common good, require in view of actual conditions that the children receive a certain minimum education, moral, intellectual and social.

   3° Parents shall be free to provide education in their homes or in private schools or in schools recognised or established by the State.

8. The State shall provide for free primary education and shall endeavour to supplement and give reasonable aid to private and corporate educational initiative, and, when the public good requires it, provide other educational facilities or institutions with due regard, however, for the rights of parents, especially in the matter of religious and moral formation. (Joint Committee on the Constitutional Amendment on Children, 2010, pp. 15–17)

Note

[1]   41.2.1° In particular, the State recognises that by her life within the home, woman gives to the State a support without which the common good cannot be achieved.
41.2.2° The State shall, therefore, endeavour to ensure that mothers shall not be obliged by economic necessity to engage in labour to the neglect of their duties in the home.

References

Brosnan, K. (2009) *Monageer Inquiry*, Dublin, Department of Health and Children.

Burns, K. and Lynch, D. (eds) (2008) *Child Protection and Welfare Social Work: Contemporary Themes and Practice Perspectives*, Dublin, A. & A. Farmar.

Joint Committee on the Constitutional Amendment on Children (2010) *Twenty-Eighth Amendment of the Constitution Bill 2007 Proposal for a Constitutional Amendment to Strengthen Children's Rights. Final Report*, Dublin, Houses of the Oireachtas.

Kilkelly, U. (2008) *Children's Rights in Ireland: Law, Policy and Practice*, Sussex, Tottel Publishing.

Law Reform Commission (1982) *Report on Illegitimacy* (online), Dublin, Law Reform Commission. Available from: www.lawreform.ie /Family_Law_PL/Default.267.html (accessed 31 July 2010).

Law Reform Commission (2009) *Legal Aspects of Family Relationships LRC CP55–2009* (online), Dublin, Law Reform Commission. Available from: www.lawreform.ie/Consultation_Papers_Published/Default.134.html (accessed 30 July 2010).

McGuinness, C. (1993) *Kilkenny Incest Investigation: Report Presented to Mr. Brendan Howlin T.D. Minister for Health*, Dublin, Stationery Office.

Murphy, F. D., Buckley, H. and Joyce, L. (2005) *The Ferns Report: Presented to the Minister for Health and Children*, Dublin, Stationery Office.

Robins, J. (1980) *The Lost Children: A Study of Charity Children in Ireland 1700–1900*, Dublin, Institute of Public Administration.

Ryan, S. (2009) *Commission to Inquire into Child Abuse Report (Volumes I–V)*, Dublin, Stationery Office.

Shannon, G. (2005) *Child Law*, Dublin, Thomson Round Hall.

Western Health Board (1996) *Kelly: A Child is Dead. Interim Report of the Joint Committee on the Family*, Dublin, Government Publications Office.

5

Safeguarding children in the Catholic Church in critical times: Some reflections on the Irish experience

Ian Elliott

The Catholic Church on the island of Ireland occupies a prominent position in most people's thinking when considering the subject of keeping children safe. However, in many cases, this is for the wrong reasons. No other body in Ireland has been the subject of such sustained criticism, nor has been damaged so severely by its failure to act to prevent harm to children, than the Catholic Church (hereafter, Church). That the Church has been the subject of several government inquiries in recent years within the Republic of Ireland testifies to that fact. Inquiries have been held into the management of child abuse in the Diocese of Ferns, the Archdiocese of Dublin, the Diocese of Cloyne, and the abuse of children within residential units and industrial schools run by the Church in Ireland (Murphy *et al.*, 2005, 2009; Ryan, 2009). Despite these inquiries and recommendations, problems continue to manifest within the Church regarding child protection. Indeed, in recent times the Catholic Church in other countries such as the United States, Germany, Belgium and Austria has experienced its own crises regarding child protection. These international developments have focused additional media interest on the situation within Ireland. It has also confirmed that the problem is not one that is unique to Ireland but extends across the world.

The recent revelations from survivors of clerical abuse were heartbreaking and when one reads the *Commission to Inquire into Child Abuse Report* (Ryan, 2009), it is hard to escape the conclusion that this society failed a generation of Irish children and abandoned them to a care system that was characterised by neglect, abuse and cruelty. Although it is tempting to see this as a failure on the part of the Church alone, I believe that to do so would be a mistake. Government and its agencies were also guilty of poor practice which ignored the well-being of children (see Chapters 1 and 2 for further background). The inquiry reports describe a list of failures by the Church and State resulting in immense harm to the most vulnerable children within Irish society. These failures endured for years and were tolerated by an apathetic government that abdicated their responsibilities in the face of Church authority (Ferriter, 2004). When considering this fact, one simple question arises: what importance do we place on safeguarding vulnerable children in Ireland today? It is a question that we all have to face and to answer.

It is tempting to rush to the conclusion that vulnerable children are well protected within modern-day Ireland, but where is the evidence that would support this view? A review of the most recent *Review of Adequacy of Services for Children and Families* report suggest that there is much room for improvement (Health Service Executive, 2009). Is our legislation and policy sufficient in the area of child protection? Does the resourcing of our state services communicate a high regard for our children with particular attention being paid to those that are at risk? These are some of the issues that are under examination in this book. I would suggest that, as a society, we are indifferent and reluctant to admit our collective failings in safeguarding and protecting children.

This chapter focuses on the Irish experience of responding to clerical abuse of children within the Church and explores the challenges faced by a new body set up to address the problem. It begins by describing the genesis of this body, the National Board for Safeguarding Children in the Catholic Church in Ireland (NBSCCC), and then reflects on some of the challenges it faces in restructuring the Church's approach to child protection and implementing policies, systems and services to ensure that children's safety and well-being are always put first. The chapter concludes by highlighting some of the essential requirements for guiding the Board's future work in relation to safeguarding children in the Church.

National Board for Safeguarding Children in the Catholic Church in Ireland

In July 2007 I was appointed to the post of Chief Executive Officer (CEO) for the newly created Safeguarding Board with a National Office located in Maynooth on the campus of St Patrick's College in the Republic of Ireland. The Board was given a threefold remit of advising on policy, developing services and auditing practice. It is this latter remit that sets it apart from any other initiatives undertaken by the Church in previous years. The Board is an incorporated, non-profit making body whose membership comprises the four archbishops, four senior religious leaders, and the Bishop of the Diocese of Waterford and Lismore in the South-East of Ireland. The setting up of that body was seen as marking a significant development in the approach that had so far been taken to tackling the problem of clerical abuse within the Church. It appeared to me to signal a critical change in the way in which the hierarchy within the Church intended to respond to the problem. It suggested the emergence of a new determination to create a framework within the Church that would ultimately help transform it from its long-established and acknowledged highly unsatisfactory state in relation to protecting and safeguarding children to one of that would be seen as an exemplar for best practice. To do this, the body needed to be capable of confronting and challenging internal resistances, and of overcoming opposition from those in authority in the Church. Therefore, it was accepted that it would have to be professionally led. It would have to draw members from different, relevant backgrounds (such as the legal profession, academia, policing, business and health) who could together help to create a new way of addressing the problem.

When established, the National Board for Safeguarding Children in the Catholic Church in Ireland took the legal form of a limited company registered under the name of *Coimirce*. The relevance of the name should be noted as it means 'protecting or safeguarding' within the Irish language. Although the budget would be entirely provided by the Church, the organisation was to be given powers that previously would only have been exercised by the religious hierarchy themselves. For the first time, the Church was moving outside its traditional and familiar territory and vesting trust and power into a new and untested body to help it to address the problem of child abuse and the clergy; a body that would be led by lay people and guided by professionals. Critical factors that are implicated in the response of the Church to the issue of safeguarding children are addressed here and I begin by highlighting the complex and fragmented structure of the Church in Ireland and critical issues relating to culture.

Structure of the Roman Catholic Church in Ireland

The Catholic Church represents a substantial part of Irish society. It is the largest membership organisation on the island of Ireland with over four and a quarter million members. There are 1,366 parishes,

2,646 churches, 5,069 priests, 942 brothers and 8,093 sisters (Veritas, 2007). The Church in Ireland is a very substantial organisation; it is not a single body, but rather a number of quite separate – albeit linked – bodies. There are dioceses, religious congregations, orders, missionary societies, prelatures and religious institutions. In all, there are 186 different parts to the Catholic Church in Ireland and each has its own head. Many have their own constitutions and their headquarters are located in Italy, France, the United States, or some other part of the world.

Not being a member of the Church when I took up my post, I had only a very rudimentary understanding of the structure and culture of the Catholic Church on the island of Ireland. Naively, I believed that it was one large but single body with an overall head in charge. I had no appreciation of the complex and fragmented nature of the body that is referred to as the 'Catholic Church' nor did I know very much about the *Code of Canon Law* (Vatican, 1983). By necessity, the NBSCCC and I as its Chief Executive Officer, have had to gain a fuller understanding of canon law and its application to the critical issues associated with safeguarding children and holding those who have harmed children to account within the Church. This has also included an examination of the interface between civil law and canon law and the importance of ensuring that the two systems do not oppose each other as they jointly address their specific areas of relevance.

The issue of ensuring that civil law and canon law are jointly given their place in responding to safeguarding concerns, when they arise, remains challenging. The first issue to address was the need to ensure that both were prioritised. We sought to achieve this by emphasising the sequence with which the systems are employed. Quite simply, civil law is given precedence and when it has been worked through to conclusion, the application of canon law proceeds. This is a generalisation but it emphasises the critical importance of ensuring that the Church response does not interfere with, or inhibit, the state agencies investigation of any concerns.

Although it is described as a single Church, it is more easily understood as a single communion with close to two hundred different constituent elements within the island of Ireland. No one person who is resident on the island of Ireland holds the authority to direct all the various parts of the body to act in a particular way. For example, at the time of writing, Cardinal Brady is the president of the Episcopal Conference but his direct authority within the Church is limited to his own Archdiocese of Armagh. As Ireland's most senior Catholic he is a person of great influence within the Church but he alone cannot direct another bishop to follow a particular course of action. This separateness may in some respects be viewed as a strength but in others, such as the safeguarding of children, it is a hurdle to be continually overcome. In my experience over the last three years as CEO of the NBSCCC, it is the major barrier that impedes progress in the area of safeguarding children. The fact that it is so fragmented makes the adoption of a single, shared approach extremely difficult as it allows each of the heads of the different constituent elements of the Church to exercise their judgement on any proposed development or strategy. This means that advances are achieved on a consensus basis involving all 186 Church authorities. Furthermore, there is no history of close, collaborative working across ecclesial boundaries within the Church. Dioceses, religious orders and congregations tend to work in isolation from each other. This makes the strategic utilisation of scarce resources to combine to achieve a shared aim almost impossible. Add to this the fact that the Church is an organisation that operates in both jurisdictions on the island of Ireland[1] under the same leadership and you start to gain some impression of the difficulties facing the implementation of a shared, consistent response to an issue like child abuse.

Communicating effectively with all the constituent parts is also very difficult. There are formal and informal channels. In most cases the formal channels are slow, hard to access, and very limited. These would include the quarterly episcopal conferences held in the Pontifical University at Maynooth lasting two or three days at a time. Similarly, the Conference of Religious of Ireland has an executive board that meets three or four times a year. Gaining access to these meetings is difficult as there is always a very heavy agenda with many competing issues seeking attention. The informal channels also present their own challenges. Working out how you can communicate effectively to all the constituent parts in a timely way and without the possibility of your communication being distorted, is a constant challenge, particularly as many of the issues that you are looking to communicate are difficult and contentious in nature.

Senator Frances Fitzgerald, who was the leader of the Irish Senate (Seanad Éireann) and who is now Minister for Children and Youth Affairs, delivered an address to the Humbert Summer School entitled *Child Abuse and Neglect cannot be seen as Problems of the Past* (Fitzgerald, 2009). She detailed a number of ways in which she feels children are being failed in Irish society. When faced with coping with an economy in recession, we look to cut the budget for the Ombudsman for Children. What sort of a message does that send out with regard to our priorities and the value that we place on safeguarding our children? I mention this example which Senator Fitzgerald referred to in her address because the Church does not exist in isolation from the rest of society. It is an integral part of Irish society and the attitudes and values that are to be found in society as a whole are also present within the Church.

Quite simply, the starting point for any strategic approach to safeguarding children in society or within the Church is recognising the value of the child and their inherent right to be protected, nurtured and developed at all times. If we lose sight of this simple fact, we run the risk of placing the needs of others or organisations above those of the child. On occasions, this is exactly what the Catholic Church in Ireland has been guilty of when it has placed its own needs and those of the clergy before those of the vulnerable child. Instead of confronting the problem of clerical abuse and dealing with it, it has in many instances, mismanaged its response and lost sight of the critical need to protect the child. It has done this by virtue of the fact that it has emphasised the need to defend itself rather than to protect the child. If you protect the child, you will also protect the Church. However, if you focus on protecting the Church and abandon the child, you will cause major harm to the Church and incalculable damage to children. This simple but vitally important piece of learning can be drawn directly from any objective review of the recent history of the problem of clerical abuse within the Catholic Church in Ireland. The child must always come first.

Putting children first: restructuring the Church's approach to child protection

There is no hiding the fact that the Church has repeatedly failed to protect children and allowed individuals who are a risk to children to occupy positions within its ranks. It is critical also to record the fact that they were aided to some degree in this by a weak and ineffective criminal justice system and a government that deferred to those in authority in the Church. The publication of the inquiry report chaired by Judge Yvonne Murphy confirmed this fact when her Commission of Inquiry examined the management of child abuse cases within the Archdiocese of Dublin (Murphy et al., 2009). Taking a representative sample of cases, they found a catalogue of bad practice, cover-up and incompetence. The implication drawn from these findings is that these deficits are likely to exist elsewhere in the Church but have not yet been exposed as they were within the Dublin Archdiocese. The need for establishing a transparent and credible response to safeguarding issues as they emerge in the Church was further heightened by these concerns. Survivor groups have called for a national inquiry into clerical child sexual abuse and this has received support from Cardinal Sean Brady (Moriarty, 2010).

It would be entirely wrong to view the problem of clerical abuse as a product of the modern era. Moreover, it has been part of the life of the Church for almost as long as the Church itself has existed. The paper trail for this has been recorded and stretches back as far as the Council of Elvira in AD 309 (Doyle *et al.*, 2006). Nor is it purely an Irish problem, although some commentators have tried to portray it as such (Downes, 2009). They highlight the fact that priests of Irish origin who have travelled to other parts of the world have been identified as among the worst serial abusers in those countries.

The crisis in the Catholic Church in the United States had a profound impact on the Irish Church with many priests returning home following the emergence of allegations regarding their involvement in abuse. The arrival of these priests was not overseen by any one body within Ireland and it is unclear how many returned. Many settled in retirement without the relevant bishop being made fully aware of their history. From 2002 to 2004, more than seven hundred priests were removed from active ministry in the American Church on the foot of allegations of abuse. The investigations undertaken by the *Boston Globe* newspaper, along with a number of high level legal actions, served to inform and mobilise public opinion leading eventually to the adoption of a 'zero tolerance' policy within the Catholic Church in the United States (United States Conference of Catholic Bishops, 2002).

Since the 1990s significant advances have been made to confront the problem here and bring it into the public domain. For example, the Church commissioned the research undertaken by the Royal College of Surgeons in 2000, entitled *Time to Listen: Confronting Child Sexual Abuse by Clergy In Ireland* (Goode *et al.*, 2003). This study contained a detailed analysis of the incidence and impact of clerical abuse within the Irish Church. It also contained a number of recommendations in relation to responding to the problem. However, not all of these were ever acted upon, such as the proposal that bishops should receive training in management and leadership. It is tempting to see the failure to fully implement the recommendations as a consequence of apathy and intransigence. I would not agree with this view and see it as being far better explained as a product of the fundamental difficulty facing the Church in trying to effect change on a united front, namely its structure, as highlighted in the previous section. In my view, the most difficult issues for the Church to overcome are those that arise from its structure. The task of organising and motivating the whole Church to adopt and implement a single approach to any issue should not be underestimated. Authority is structured in such a way as to allow independence. No one person in Ireland can direct and require the various constituent parts of the Church to act or to follow one particular course of action. This simple fact helps to explain why it has been so difficult to implement a single strategy in the past or to apply across the whole Church the valuable lessons learned from painful experiences relating to the abuse of children by clerics.

The structure also inhibits the Church's ability to learn from the mistakes that are made by its individual members. This vital process requires an openness and a willingness to share with each other, which is not often evident. To a degree, this has only recently emerged and become a feature of safeguarding practice in the Church. This sharing of experience has been facilitated by the NBSCCC by bringing relevant people together for training and seminars so that people can develop relationships with each other.

New child protection safeguarding standards and guidance for the Catholic Church

In February 2009, the National Board published its guidance *Safeguarding Children: Standards and Guidance for the Catholic Church* (NBSCCC, 2009). The importance of this development is not simply that the content of the guidance was compliant with legislation in the field in both jurisdictions on the island of Ireland, as well as with canon law within the Church. The true value of the document lay in the fact that all the constituent parts of the Church had signed a *Memorandum of Understanding* with the National Board, that they would implement the contents of the guidance fully and would mandate the National Office to audit and review their practice to ensure compliance. For the first time, all 186 constituent parts of the Church had given power to an independent body to monitor their practice. This represents the single most valuable development that has taken place during the short but eventful life of the National Board and for me as its chief officer.

It should be noted that the Church in Ireland had begun this journey back in 1996 when they adopted *Child Sexual Abuse: Framework for a Church Response* (Irish Catholic Bishops' Advisory Committee on Child Sexual Abuse by Priests and Religious, 1996) and added to it with the launch of *Our Children, Our Church* (the Irish Catholic Bishops' Conference, Conference of Religious of Ireland, and the Irish Missionary Union, 2005) at the end of 2005. This was issued following the publication of the report of the government inquiry into the Diocese of Ferns (Murphy *et al.*, 2005). However, neither of these documents included within them any means, or mandate, to monitor practice as it occurred across the Church. The sponsoring bodies of the bishops, and religious assumed that if guidance were brought forward, all parts of the Church would interpret and implement it uniformly. In both respects, experience showed that this has not been the case. Therefore, any new guidance would have to be supported by a tangible and verifiable commitment to adopt and implement it consistently, along with a mandate to monitor implementation. Without these measures, any new initiative would suffer a similar fate and leave children at risk. It is this that sets the new guidance issued in February 2009 apart and brings the Church to a very different place compared to where it has previously been. For the first time, the Church has mandated an independent body to review and monitor its practice. It is this vital fact that sets the new guidance apart from any that has preceded it. As with any guidance, its value will be determined by the extent to which it is implemented and followed.

I strongly believe that it is the actions of people that ultimately protect children, or the failure to act that places children at risk. The existence of policies and procedures, although important, should not be viewed as ends in themselves; they are only a means to an end. The extent to which the *Safeguarding Children* guidance issued in February 2009 is valuable to the Church, will be determined by the extent to which it changes the actions of bishops, religious provincials, or those involved in the safeguarding structure when relating to, or caring for, children. Children are not necessarily safer just because the guidance exists. It has to be acted upon for it to have value.

As well as providing guidance, there is also a need for an effective framework to exist across the Church to deliver services when they are needed. However, the creation of this comprehensive safeguarding structure still seems to be some way off. Safeguarding services that are provided apply to specific areas of the Church only. The Child Protection Service in the Archdiocese of Dublin is a good example of this feature. That service exists to support the priests of the Archdiocese rather than all the members of the Church who reside and minister within its boundary. Within the boundaries of the Archdiocese, there are well over a hundred religious orders, congregations or missionary societies that have personnel in ministry.

Therefore, if an issue arises that relates to a member of any of these bodies within Dublin, that service will look to refer it on to the leadership of the particular group to deal with the matter. In most cases, other Church authorities would not have access to any professional staff to respond to those cases, which must place a question mark over the quality of response that can be made.

This does not appear to me to be the best utilisation of the scarce resources that exist within the Church as a whole to respond to concerns when they arise. This may also be seen as another example of the difficulties that arise through the fragmented structure that exists within the Church. There are too many boundaries and too little willingness within by those in authority to overcome the limitations they cause. Each constituent element looks after its own with insufficient regard to the needs of others, and particularly how this lack of integration may lead to vulnerable children being disadvantaged further by not having access to a professional service.

What is needed is the creation of a single coherent and effective safeguarding structure in the Church. This framework should be independent of dioceses and religious authority structures to enable it to respond to concerns where they arise within the Church as a whole rather than in one particular part of it. Taking this step will require a major change on the part of those in authority in the Church. However, the publication of the *Report into the Catholic Archdiocese of Dublin* (Murphy *et al.*, 2009) has added a new impetus to the call for change. The hierarchy feel themselves to be under scrutiny to an unprecedented degree. The fact that crises have arisen in other countries such as Germany, Belgium and Austria, has added extra pressure and urgency to find a viable solution to the problem of clerical abuse.

In 2010, the Pope took the highly unusual step of sending a pastoral letter to the Irish Church (Pope Benedict XVI, 2010). This event provides further evidence of the concern that the continuing problem of clerical child sexual abuse gives rise to at the highest level within the Church. An apostolic visitation took place in the autumn 2010. Although no details have been released with regard to how this very high-level team undertook their task, it is certain that they scrutinised the way in which the problem has been responded to and managed by those in authority in Ireland. One can speculate as to what resulted from the visit but it is likely that we will see the experiences gained from the crisis that occurred within the American Church in 2002 being applied to the difficulties facing the Irish Church. This may explain the membership of the apostolic team itself, which was largely drawn from the American and Canadian Church.

Despite the many setbacks and crises, the journey the Church has taken since 2009 has been very significant. We should not lose sight of the fact that there are champions for children at all levels of the Church and many are within the hierarchy. A sense of purpose and commitment is increasingly evident. The aim of establishing the Church as an exemplar for best safeguarding practice has gained major support from the clergy, and the lay faithful alike. The Church's hierarchy is becoming more confident and more willing to receive advice, guidance, and also correction. The Church is in a very different place to where it was prior to the establishment of the NBSCCC. Through the NBSCCC it now has an independent advocate for the rights of the vulnerable child. The call for change is building and will result in radical modification in the way that the Church functions. It is unclear what those changes will be, but it is reasonable to speculate that some consideration will be given to addressing the problems created by the complex structure of the Church. Perhaps we will see a move towards a more open and engaging structure that will reach out more to the marginalised and vulnerable in our communities. It would be my hope that whatever change takes place gives consideration to the position of children and seeks to address the obstacles that remain in the way to achieving the effective safeguarding of children within the Church.

This positive momentum commands little attention in the media. Just as a child who receives nothing but criticism finds it hard to believe that it will ever be given recognition for its efforts to improve, so parts of the Church are disbelieving that they will ever get a fair hearing if they try to inform others about what is happening. The fact remains that a great deal that is constructive has taken place already and the Church today is a safer place than previously. If you go into any church across the country you are likely to find displayed within it the contact details for the parish safeguarding representative, the Health Service Executive and the Gardai. However, I do not wish to give the impression that the Church is further down the road than is the case. There is still a great deal for the National Board to do to put in place a properly resourced, independent safeguarding structure that can deliver best practice to all parts of the Church. We believe that there is a commitment and recognition that the problem is capable of being solved if sufficient will exists to achieve it. We can reach our aim of being seen as an exemplar for best practice in the field of safeguarding children, which would be a remarkable achievement, given the history of the problem and the fact that it has been so resistant to change previously. Getting there is still some way off but there is an undeniable and growing sense that it is achievable.

Concluding comments

I conclude by highlighting some of the requirements that I would note for guiding the future work of the National Board, my Office, and for all those with whom we work in safeguarding children in the Church. In relation to structure, resources, services and policy development, the following should be noted. First, the development of a coherent and comprehensive framework for the delivery of safeguarding services across all parts of the Church is fundamental. The present structure is dominated by the large and rich dioceses at the expense of the small and poor dioceses who do not have access to the same resources. As a consequence, creating comprehensive best practice is much more demanding for them. Second, the Church should undertake a recruitment process to employ of a larger number of suitably qualified and experienced professionals who can support the embedding of best safeguarding practice across all parts of the Church. Third, a review of the *Coimirce* initiative should be undertaken, to highlight what has been learned from the first years of its existence. The learning from this review should be disseminated widely within the Church and should be applied to the future life of the safeguarding structure within the Church. The fourth should be to continue to build trust with all the various stakeholders and to seek their continued support for the development of the work. In particular, these would include the survivors of abuse, priests and members of the hierarchy and leaders of the religious, and the faithful within the Church as a whole. Fifth, to ensure that all policy and procedural changes brought forward within the Church comply fully with civil child protection policy and legislation, and reflect best practice in both jurisdictions on the island of Ireland.

We need to move away from a purely reactive response to a much more strategic and proactive approach. To achieve this, the Church has to be prepared to learn from its history and find the courage to seize the opportunity which it now has to reach for a new reality. Consistently putting the safety of the child first before all other considerations is not just optional advice, it is essential. If nothing else, I would believe that this vital lesson has now been accepted by the vast majority of those in authority within the Church.

Note

1   The phrase 'the island of Ireland' is meant to collectively denote the 26 counties of the Republic of Ireland and the six counties of Northern Ireland which are part of the United Kingdom.

References

Downes, J. (2009) 'What turns our Catholic priests into monsters?, *The Sunday Tribune*, 26 July 2009.

Doyle, T., Sipe, A. and Wall, P. (2006) *Sex, Priests and Secret Codes: The Catholic Church's 2000–Year Paper Trail of Sexual Abuse*, Los Angeles, Volt Press.

Ferriter, D. (2004) *The Transformation of Ireland, 1900–2000*, London, Profile Books.

Fitzgerald, F. (2009) *Child Abuse and Neglect Cannot be Seen as Problems of the Past* (online), Fine Gael. Available from: www.finegael.org/news /a/947/article/ (accessed 21 April 2010).

Goode, H., McGee, H. and O'Boyle, C. (2003) *Time to Listen, Confronting Child Sexual Abuse by Catholic Clergy in Ireland*, Dublin, The Liffey Press.

Health Service Executive (2009) *Review of Adequacy of Services for Children and Families 2008*, Dublin, Health Service Executive.

Irish Catholic Bishops' Advisory Committee on Child Sexual Abuse by Priests and Religious (1996) *Child Sexual Abuse: Framework for a Church Response*, Dublin, Veritas Publications. Available from: www .catholicbishops.ie/images/docs/csaframework.pdf (accessed 30 July 2010).

Irish Catholic Bishops' Conference, Conference of Religious of Ireland and the Irish Missionary Union (2005) *Our Children, Our Church: Child Protection Policies and Procedures for the Catholic Church in Ireland*, Dublin, Veritas Publications. Available from: www.catholicbishops.ie/images /stories/cco_publications/safeguarding/our childrenourchurch.pdf (accessed 30 July 2010).

Moriarty, G. (2010) 'Brady expresses support for full abuse inquiry', *The Irish Times* (1 April).

Murphy, F. D., Buckley, H. and Joyce, L. (2005) *The Ferns Report: Presented to the Minister for Health and Children*, Dublin, Stationery Office.

Murphy, Y., Mangan, I. and O'Neill, H. (2009) Commission of Investigation. Report into the Catholic Archdiocese of Dublin (online), Dublin, Commission of Investigation, Dublin Archdiocese, Catholic Diocese of Cloyne. Available from: http://www.dacoi.ie/ (accessed 1 December 2009).

National Board for Safeguarding Children in the Catholic Church (2009) *Safeguarding Children: Standards and Guidance Document for the Catholic Church in Ireland*, Dublin, Veritas Publications. Available from: www.safeguarding.ie (accessed 30 July 2010).

Pope Benedict XVI (19 March 2010) *Pastoral Letter of the Holy Father Pope Benedict XVI to the Catholics of Ireland*, Rome, Libreria Editrice Vaticana. Available from: www.vatican.va/holy_father/benedict_XVI/letters /2010/ (accessed 30 July 2010).

Ryan, S. (2009) *Commission to Inquire into Child Abuse Report (Volumes I–V)*, Dublin, Stationery Office.

United States Conference of Catholic Bishops (2002) *Essential Norms for Diocesan/Eparchial Policies Dealing with the Sexual Abuse of Minors by Priests or Deacons*, Washington, DC, United States Conference of Catholic Bishops. Available from: www.usccb.org/ocyp/norms (accessed 30 July 2010).

Vatican (1983) *Code of Canon Law* (online), Libreria Editrice Vaticana. Available from: www.vatican.va/archive/ENG1104/_INDEX.HTM#fonte (accessed 14 July 2010).

Veritas (2007) *Irish Catholic Directory*, Dublin, Veritas Publications.

6

White *Children First*? Whiteness, child protection policies and the politics of 'race' in Ireland

Alastair Christie

Although Ireland has become an increasingly multi-cultural society since the mid-1990s,[1] there continues to be little attention paid to 'race' or racism in child protection policies. Ireland has always included individuals and groups that were marked as culturally/racially 'different' (Lentin and McVeigh, 2006), but recent immigration has brought a new 'visibility' to Black and minority ethnic groups, and has stimulated debate about the nature of Irish society and about Irish identity. In recent decades a few prominent Irish individuals have been identified as Black, but in many ways this simply reinforces the dominant assumption that to be Irish is to be white. In this chapter, I argue that white Irishness is reproduced by child protection policies and discuss how discourses of white Irishness underpin child protection policies. Such a recognition is a necessary step in developing anti-discriminatory child care/protection policies and practices.

The *National Children's Strategy, Our Children – Their Lives* (Office of the Minister for Health and Children, 2000) notes that 'children from ethnic minority communities, such as refugees and other immigrants, have special needs' (p. 23); the government has failed in the past to address fully issues that affect children such as 'poverty, homelessness and, increasingly, racism' (p. 9); and 'tackling racism and promoting respect for socially and culturally diverse communities will therefore continue to be a key social policy issue' (p. 70). Moreover, *The Agenda for Children's Services Policy Handbook* (Office of the Minister for Children, 2007) requires that a whole child/whole system approach is adopted, which is 'culturally sensitive and anti-discriminatory' (p. 14) and that child care services should promote 'social inclusion, addressing issues of ethnicity, disability and rural/urban communities' (p. 35). In a similar way, the government's *National Action Plan Against Racism 2005–2008* (Department of Justice, Equality and Law reform, 2005) argues for 'a more inclusive intercultural approach to childcare provision' (p. 120).

However, while national strategies, policy handbooks and plans highlight the significance of racism and the need to provide culturally sensitive, anti-discriminatory and socially inclusive intercultural child care services, the revised national guidelines on child protection and welfare, *Children First: National Guidelines for the Protection and Welfare of Children* (Office of the Minister for Children and Youth Affairs, 2010),[2] fail to provide guidance on how 'race' and racism impact on child care and child protection services. *Children First* provides the basic guidelines on child protection and is used on a day-to-day basis by all those professionals and volunteers who provide services to children. Yet this key document fails to provide even the most basic guidance on how the politics of 'race' and practice of racism might impact on child protection and welfare services, and therefore leaves unquestioned the dominance of white Irishness in child care/protection services.

However, awareness of politics of 'race' is not completely absent from all statements made by government employees about child care services. Phil Garland, the Health Service Executive's Assistant National Director for Children and Families acknowledged that the state's child care policies and practices in relation separated migrant children[3] may be potentially 'racist' (Smyth, 2010). The inadequacy of child care services to this group of children is perhaps the most obvious example of institutional racism within the Irish child care system (Christie, 2003). However, in the rest of this chapter, I argue that dominant discourses of white Irishness frame all national child care/protection services in a way that supports institutional racism and obscures the strengths and needs of migrant and/or Black and minority ethnic children living in Ireland. I ask how discourses of white Irishness frame current child protection policies and practices and remain as the dominant norm against which all childhoods and child care practices are judged. In particular, the chapter identifies the absence of any discussion of 'race' or racism in the newly revised *Children First: National Guidelines for the Protection and Welfare of Children.* While major concerns have been identified regarding services for separated children, the revised guidelines exclude discussion of how the politics of 'race' and racism impact on separated children and/or Black and minority ethnic children living in Ireland. Before discussing specific child protection policies and reviews, I briefly discuss the concepts of 'race', racialisation and white Irishness.

'Race', racialisation and white Irishness

'Race' is often placed in inverted commas to indicate that it is a contentious term and that, in reality, there is only one 'race', the human race. If different 'races' do not exist, Miles (1989) recommends that the category 'race' should be discarded by social scientists. However, while 'race' may not have an objective reality it remains one of the 'most persistent and seductive fictions of the twenty-first century' (Nayak, 2005, p. 141). Although a fiction, 'race' has profound social, cultural and economic consequences for us all and is therefore worthy of critique and social analysis (Gilroy, 1987). If 'race' does not exist then it has to be asked why and how does 'race' remain such a common and powerful way in which individuals and groups are categorised through the attachment of specific racial meanings. Not only does this process of racialisation categorise individuals and groups, but racial meanings are also often identified with social 'problems'. Often there is a linkage between the racialisation of 'social problems' and the racialisation of particular groups, so that the latter often become identified as a 'social problem' (see Lentin (2007) for a discussion of 'crisis racism' in Ireland). A linkage can be seen in the way that asylum seekers have come to be defined as a 'social problem' in Ireland. This deflects our attention away from questioning the assumptions underpinning the national migration system and analysing asylum seeking as a by-product of global capitalism and uneven development. Processes of racialisation may have potentially positive outcomes for Black and minority ethic groups, as individuals and groups may use 'Black' strategically as a source of resistance and solidarity. However, more usually, racialisation reproduces dominant racial hierarchies and provides justification for racism (Gray, 2004; Garner, 2006).

Within these processes of racialisation, white individuals and groups largely remain 'invisible', and their racial identities remain unquestioned. However, everybody is racialised, including whites, and at some levels all must 'live', 'perform' and 'do' 'race'. From positions of dominance, whites historically have had the 'luxury of racialising others without necessarily, except strategically, developing or invoking strong racial consciousness' (Lewis, 2004, p. 626). Whiteness is the norm that historically has meant that 'race' was displaced onto the racialised 'other' (Reay, 2008), so that 'race' became 'something to do with blacks' (Mac an Ghaill, 2002, p. 107). By not being named, whiteness is reproduced as the dominant perspective through which all practices and policies are judged and measured (Dyer, 1997). For most whites, their racial identity only becomes 'prominent and self-conscious in the symbolic and actual presence of non-whites' (Lewis, 2004, p. 628). Whites' racialised identities may not be conscious to whites; however, they are present, even if not enacted. Whiteness often becomes more visible to whites when they compete for resources within areas that include Black and minority ethnic groups.

Whiteness as an 'invisibility', is, as Garner (2006) describes it, a 'malevolent absence' which 'is determined by the perspective from which whiteness is *experienced*' (emphasis in original, p. 260). Hence for Black Irish, whiteness may be constantly 'visible', whereas for white Irish, their racial identity may only become 'visible' in particular contexts where the designation of whiteness as 'normal' and racially unmarked is questioned (Hartigan, 2005). However, perhaps paradoxically, this inability (or absence of sensibility) to recognise whiteness does not restrain people who identify themselves as white from speaking on behalf of the whole community. As argued by Dyer (1997, p. 2):

> There is no more powerful position than being "just" human. The claim to power is the claim to speak for the commodity of humanity. Raced people can't do that – they can only speak for their race. But non-raced people can, for they do not represent the interests of race.

Ahmed (2007) develops this argument by stating that if being human is to be white, then to be non-white is to be not/or less than human. Denial of humanity to individuals and groups that are racialised as non-white is the basic 'building block' of racism. Not all whites experience whiteness and/or directly benefit from this racial privilege (McIntosh, 1988), but it is a 'dividend' that is readily available to whites, even if it is regularly contested (Lewis, 2004, p. 634).

In North American literature on whiteness, Garner (2006) identifies three particular ways of conceptualising whiteness: as a set of norms, a contingent hierarchy and a resource. First, as a set of norms, whiteness is linked to values associated with civilisation, technology and force, and is defined as the opposite to savagery, primitiveness and weakness. Second, whiteness is conceptualised as a contingent hierarchy in which various individuals' and groups' abilities to claim degrees of whiteness leads to access to economic, social and cultural capital. Groups were seen as more or less white. In this racialised hierarchy, 'race' and colour are separate, but overlapping criteria enabling Italian, Irish and other European migrants to the USA in the nineteenth and early twentieth centuries to be considered ideologically and culturally 'different and lesser "white races"' (Garner, 2006, p. 264). The positions of individuals and groups in this racial hierarchy and their subsequent access to economic and cultural capital enable Garner to conceptualise whiteness in a third way as a resource. He identifies how research in the USA has shown that whiteness is linked to privileged access to resources such as employment, housing and education. Ireland is a less racially diverse country than the USA, but there is growing evidence that whiteness, and especially Irish whiteness, gives access to forms of economic, social and cultural capital.

While identifying these three ways of using whiteness, Garner (2006) is quick to point out that a focus on whiteness runs the risk of reifying 'white identities'. His main objective in analysing whiteness is to problematise white identities as raced and privilege-holding and to identify how the dominance and operation of whiteness in social structure and relations sustains racism. Like Garner (2006), my focus on whiteness here is not to diminish the importance of other forms of oppression and the way that whiteness intersects with, for example, class, gender, sexuality and (dis)ability, but to consider how these work simultaneously, and in interaction.

Borrowing the title of Ignatiev's book, *How the Irish Became White* (Ignatiev, 1995), in which he describes how the Irish in America distanced themselves from other migrant groups by emphasising their identity as white, Lentin (2007) argues that the Celtic Tiger affluence and new inward migration have resulted in the Irish in Ireland 'becoming white'. From the earliest invasions of Ireland in the twelfth century by the Normans, the Irish have been racialised through characteristics of 'backwardness, nomadism and beggary ... compounded by superstition (later Popery), anarchy and a penchant for violence' (Ní Shuinéar, 2002, p. 179). The Irish were defined by the English as the 'other' and depicted in a similar way to all those who were colonised within the British Empire as being part of the 'white man's burden'. While the majority of the people living in Ireland were visibly white, they were often depicted as 'less than white' and in need of being 'civilised'. Prior to the recent period of immigration to Ireland starting in the mid-1990s, McVeigh (1992) had identified specific forms of racism in Ireland. These were based largely on the importing of racism from other countries, in particular the USA and Britain as well as already existing forms of 'indigenous' racism against members of the Traveller community and other minority ethnic groups. The importing of racism is associated with the return of Irish immigrants and took particular forms when introduced into particular Irish social and cultural contexts. For example, Fanning (2002) identifies how the modern Irish identity is linked to colonialism. Through the history of Irish participation in US and British colonial expansion, and consumption of popular culture that celebrates the exploitation and genocide of indigenous non-white communities, modern white Irish identities have been produced in opposition to notions of 'primitive' Black populations in African and the USA.

This positioning of colonial subjects as 'uncivilised' was reinforced by the role of the Irish Catholic church in sending missionaries to 'morally educate' indigenous communities in many parts of the developing world. As argued by Coogan (2000, p. 508), 'we [people living in Ireland] were brought up believing that Africans as a class were much in need of the civilising influences of the Irish religious as parched earth was to water'. Fanning (2002) goes on to link the Irish missionary movement with the development of Irish nationalism, by identifying how the peak of the activity of the Irish missionary project took place at the same time as the emergence of the Irish nation state in the first half of the twentieth century. For Garner (2006), Irish forms of whiteness are enmeshed within religious affiliation and relationships to Irish language and culture that emerged during the struggles for political independence. With membership of the European Union (EU), Irish forms of whiteness came to be defined within a wider European culture which privileges particular racialised hierarchies (Lentin, 2007). The 'whiteness' of Irish people has always been contingent, with Irish people being 'categorised both as 'white' and 'in-between' during their experiences of colonialisation, emigration and national independence' (Garner, 2004, pp. 28–29). White, Irish immigrants to Europe, Australasia and North America have been privileged for the most part by being categorised as white. For example, Negra (2006, p. 1) argues that Irishness in the USA often has the status of an 'enriched whiteness' in which Irish Americans can gain from being a minority ethnic group, while also celebrating their whiteness. While forms of 'enriched whiteness' may exist for Irish communities in the UK, the postcolonial relationship, class relations and different patterns of migration/integration have resulted in this group occupying an 'in-between' position, between white and Black, in a racialised hierarchy. As such, racialised patterns of identification are complex and contested so that in different contexts Irish people's identification with whiteness is more, or less, assured. For return migrants, Ní Laoire (2008) argues that questioning the white Irish majority's view of an imagined community is not always welcomed. While there are spaces for return migrants to 'challenge hegemonic ideas, and at time of return migrants do so, the close association between belonging and voice means that return migrants can disappear into an imagined white Irish majority, through processes of silencing and invisibility' (p. 44). These powerful processes of silencing and invisibility are evident in the production of child care/protection policies.

The 'presence' and 'absence' of 'race' within the child protection guidelines

Children First: The National Guidelines for the Protection and Welfare of Children (hereafter *Children First* guidelines) were first published in September 1999 and reissued in 2004. While the guidelines do not have the status of a statutory requirement, the Department of Health and Children expects all agencies to apply the guidelines in their work with children. Subsequently, in 2005, the *Ferns Report* (Murphy *et al.*, 2005) investigated the child sexual abuse by Catholic clergy in the Diocese of Ferns and recommended that the child protection guidelines be updated. This report was critical of the guidelines and in 2006, the government initiated a reviewing process that resulted in the publication of three reports on the *Children First Guidelines: Service Users' Perceptions of the Irish Child Protection System* (Buckley *et al.*, 2008); *An Analysis of Submissions made on National Review of Compliance with Children First: National Guidelines for the Protection and Welfare of Children* (Office for the Minister for Children and Youth Affairs, 2008a); and *National Review of Compliance with Children First: National Guidelines for the Protection and Welfare of Children* (Office for the Minister for Children and Youth Affairs, 2008b).

The original version of the *Children First* guidelines published in September 1999, make little reference to 'race' or racism. In the list of principles for best practice, the guidelines state that 'agencies or individuals taking protective action should consider factors such as the child's gender, age, stage of development, religion, culture and race' (p. 23). This 'catch-all' list, by its inclusion of 'stage of development', raises questions about the report's understanding of the impact of structural factors and stratification in relation to child protection and welfare. Equality legislation (for example, The Equal Status Act 2004) identifies nine grounds for discrimination, including on the basis of 'race' and membership of the Traveller community. The child protection and welfare guidelines make no reference to equality legislation and/or the impact of discrimination on child protection and welfare. It sometimes appears that child care legislation is produced in a vacuum with little or no reference to legislation which does not directly address children and/or their carers. The selective referencing of relevant legislation also occurs in the inclusion and exclusion of various sections of the United Nations *Convention on the Rights of the Child*. For example, while the 1999 *Children's First* guidelines include Article 2 of the Convention, which require States to protect children from discrimination, it omits to mention that Article 2 identifies discrimination on a number of grounds, including 'race', nationality and ethnicity (Christie, 2010).

The three reviews of the *Children First* guidelines largely fail to identify that 'race' and racism might have an impact on child protection and welfare services. The report entitled *Service Users' Perceptions of the Irish Child Protection System* was based on research that analysed the views of 'children, young people, caregivers and extended family members who have been involved with child protection services' (Buckley *et al.*, 2008, p. 1). This research provides insightful information on how service users often view child protection services as 'unsympathetic, powerful and intimidating' (p. 5) and the incongruity that exists between services users' concerns and the concerns of child protection agencies. The findings are based on interviews with 67 services users, of whom 56 were described as 'white Irish', 4 as 'English', 2 as 'Irish Travellers', 3 as 'African' and 2 as 'other European'. While attempts seem to have been made to include Black and ethnic minority services users, the research found that 'discrimination on the grounds of social class, ability or ethnicity was relatively rare' (p. 54). This contrast with research in the UK that demonstrates the significance of 'race' and racism in child protection and welfare services: Black and minority ethnic families are often pathologised/stereotyped, receive more punitive than preventive services, and are often assessed by social workers who use cultural deficit explanations to understand family problems (Williams and Soydan, 2005). Despite the different national context, it seems likely that some of these issues would exist within the child protection and welfare system in Ireland.

The *Analysis of Submissions Made on National Review of Compliance with Children First: National Guidelines for the Protection and Welfare of Children* (Office for the Minister for Children and Youth Affairs, 2008a) provided the opportunity for a wide range of views to be expressed about the child protection and welfare system. Submissions were received from social workers who were particularly concerned about the potential vulnerability of separated children. While the analysis states that there were a number of issues raised in relation to 'non-Irish', these were not discussed in the report. As argued by Nititham (2008, p. 70), the use of the 'non-Irish' suggests that 'Irish' is 'impenetrable and immutable' and that the term 'defines the Other through exclusion of that which is considered "Irish"'. The concerns of Black and minority ethnic children and carers are not given space within the report.

The possibility that 'race' and racism might impact on child protection and welfare system is further elided within the third report, *National Review of Compliance with Children First: National Guidelines for the Protection and Welfare of Children* (Office for the Minister for Children and Youth Affairs, 2008b). This report found that there were no major revisions required in the guidelines and that the only major concerns were inconsistencies in the ways in which the guidelines were applied and the geographical variation in available child protection and welfare resources. There was no mention of the potential vulnerability of separated children, although as stated earlier, one of the senior managers for the Health Service Executive suggests that the child care provision in relation to this group could be potentially defined as racist. This report states that it does not seek to address wider issues that required long-term policy making, so there is no discussion of whether the state's migration polices, including the 'incarceration' of asylum seekers within accommodation centres and the deportation of children and young people, support best practice in child protection and welfare services. It is ironic that staff in the accommodation centres have received training based on the *National Guidelines* which provide no guidance on how the rights of children in such family-unfriendly environments might be protected.

After this review process, it is perhaps not surprising that the revised version of *Children First: National Guidelines for the Protection and Welfare of Children* (Office of the Minister for Children and Youth Affairs, 2010) fails to address whether or how 'race' and racism (institutional and societal) might impact on the child protection and welfare system. The revised version has kept the statement: 'Agencies or individuals taking protective action should consider factors such as the child's gender, age, stage of development, religion, culture and race' (p. 5). Added to the revised guidelines is the statement that: 'Child abuse is not restricted to any socio-economic group, gender or culture. All signs must be considered in the wider social and family context. However, serious deficits in child safety and welfare transcend cultural, social and ethnic norms, and must elicit a response' (p. 12).

This statement addresses the universal nature of child abuse, rather than identifying ways in which racialised differences are recognised and impact on child protection practices. While the vulnerability of separated children was explicitly raised in the review process, they are not identified as a group who are potentially vulnerable and are likely to have particular needs related to their legal status and experiences of migration and 'integration'. By not acknowledging the impact of racism, the revised *Children First* guidelines suggest that some children should be responded to 'first' and others should be treated 'second' and that this group of children's needs are largely invisible when assumptions of white Irishness mark some children's rights as more significant to the state than the rights of other children.

In contrast to the 'absence' of the politics of 'race' within Irish child protection guidelines, the equivalent document produced for use in England and Wales, *Working Together to Safeguard Children. A Guide to Inter-Agency Working to Safeguard and Promote the Welfare of Children* (Department of Children, Schools and Families, 2010) explicitly acknowledges the significance of 'race' and racism in child protection services. This guide acknowledges that, 'children from Black and minority ethnic groups (and their parents) are likely to have experienced harassment, racial discrimination and institutional racism' (p. 202) and that racism impacts on different Black and ethnic minority individuals and communities in a variety of ways. To be able to meet the needs of the Black and minority ethnic children, social workers need to be aware of how wider social factors result in racial discrimination. In particular, social workers are expected to understand how cultural 'difference' may influence their professional assessments. For example, the guidelines state that social workers should guard against racial stereotypes and myths influencing their practice, while at same time suggesting that anxiety about being accused of racism should not deter them from making appropriate decisions to protect and promote the welfare of children.

These guidelines also state that research and abuse inquiries have provided evidence that there can be particular issues for children of mixed parentage and refugee children. However, the guidelines are vague as to what these issues might be. In practical terms, the guidelines recognise that 'the need for neutral, high-quality, gender-appropriate translation or interpretation services should be taken into account when working with children and families whose preferred language is not English' (p. 309). Finally, this section of the guidelines highlights the need for all organisations to address institutional racism (see Macpherson, 1999, p. 202), 'including those operating in areas where black and minority ethnic communities are numerically small'. While the guidelines for England and Wales provide limited acknowledgement of the impact on racism on the lives of Black and minority ethnic children and only give limited guidance on how social workers should start to develop anti-racist practice, they do engage with the politics of 'race' and racism. The 'absence' and 'presence' of the politics of 'race' within Irish and British child protection guidelines both reinforce and potentially destabilise the dominance of whiteness. In the final section of this chapter, I discuss what might be included in the Irish guidelines to underpin the dominant constructions of whiteness that existing child care/protection polices.

Concluding thoughts: destabilising the dominance of white Irishness in child protection polices

As stated earlier, my aim in focusing on whiteness is not to reify white identities, but rather to problematise whiteness as a form of privilege that underpins racism. As both the notions of 'whiteness' and 'Irishness' are 'artificial' and unstable, they cannot exist without being continually reproduced within policies and practices. While in general, policies and practices tend to support hegemonic racial hierarchies,[4] there are always gaps and contradictions where change is possible. These provide potential opportunities for policy makers, including child care/protection policy makers, to develop counter-hegemonic policies that challenge the constantly shifting constructions of 'race' and practices of racism. Therefore there is a need for policies to keep evolving so that they can be used to confront 'the moving target' of 'race' and racism. This suggests that policy makers need to self-reflexively engage in debates on policy making and anti-racism, as a potentially counter-hegemonic process.

Before discussing counter-hegemonic policy making processes, it may be useful to consider some basic potential starting points. One could be the simple acknowledgement that racism exists in Irish society and impacts on child care/protection polices. While Ireland has been promoted internationally as a county of *céad míle fáilte* (a hundred thousand welcomes) and Irishness is used as a form of 'identity currency' to promote 'mass-marketed white homeland fantasies' (Negra, 2006, p. 3), these conceptions of Irish identity tend to reproduce an underlying assumption of whiteness. This was most evident in the debates surrounding the Referendum on Citizenship in June 2004, which denied the automatic right to citizenship for those born in Ireland who did not have at least one Irish parent. The

European Commission's Eurobarometer report on *Discrimination in the EU in 2009*, found that 46 per cent of the Irish population thought that discrimination on the basis of ethnic origin was very or fairly widespread and that 69 per cent of the population thought that the current economic crisis would increase labour market discrimination. Moreover, research suggests that discrimination on the basis of 'race' is on the increase in Ireland, with racist crime increasing and racism becoming significant issue in schools (Crowley, 2010). As described earlier, child protection guidelines in the UK make some explicit statements on the existence of racism and its impact on child care policies. While it is not clear whether these types of statement actually affect child care/protection practices, two basic steps would be to include a statement on combating racism in child care/protection and to make an explicit connection between child care legislation and existing anti-discriminatory legislation.

A second starting point would be to not only acknowledge the impact of 'race' and racism in child care/protection policies and practices, but to recognise whiteness as both a set of social relations and as an analytical framework (Garner, 2006). As the former, whiteness can be understood as a set of norms, a contingent hierarchy and/or a resource, which results in privilege for people who are recognised as white. White Irishness is performed, enacted and claimed in various contexts with differing results; however, white Irishness remains an actual and potential source of privilege for particular individuals and communities and has a direct impact on child care/protection services. Whiteness as an analytic framework involves critiquing dominant discourses and practices and thereby providing the possibility for new insights and possible courses of action in challenging oppression. Critiquing dominant norms is simple because there is evidence of them everywhere, and yet complex because these norms distort the way we see the world and are part of a complex network of interconnecting 'common-sense' norms and values. It is not possible to stand completely outside the influence of dominant understandings of the social world. People who claim to be, and are recognised as, white are implicated in any critique of whiteness. As there are different levels of awareness of Irish whiteness, with whiteness often not visible to those that inhabit it, and/or whiteness only being recognised when it is portrayed in a positive light, this raises the question of who is conscious of white Irishness and how it works to exclude and marginalise. Clearly those who are not recognised as white Irish and/or fully white Irish are likely to have insights into the processes and consequences of racialisation. So another starting point may be to include some of these individuals and groups in developing anti-racist services for all children and their carers/parents. The great danger with adopting this approach is that it can place the burden of developing anti-racist polices and practices unfairly on those who are racially marked as excluded.

In this chapter, I have tried to identify the workings of white Irishness. My emphasis on Irishness is to indicate that 'race' and practices of racism need to be understood within particular historical, social, cultural and economic contexts. While the temptation may be to 'import' anti-discriminatory social work practice from outside Ireland, policies and practices need to be developed within Ireland. This is not to say that 'race' and racism should not be understood as transnational phenomena that are rooted within global capitalism and postcolonial relations. Nor is it to suggest that there is not plenty to be learnt outside Ireland about the development of anti-racist child care polices and practices. The second reason for emphasising white Irishness is to argue that there are different forms of racism and that 'race' does not exist in isolation from other forms of oppression, such as gender, sexual orientation (dis)ability, class and, particularly in the Irish context, oppression against members of Traveller community. While particular structures of oppression are distinguishable, a focus on only one form of oppression can reinforce the unquestioned dominance of other forms of oppression. Individuals who have multiple social privileges, including being recognised in specific contexts as white, may fail to recognise the intersectionality of oppression and privilege. Focusing on only one form of oppression promotes a tunnel vision in which one form of oppression becomes the basis on which other forms of oppression are judged. To reduce the possibility of this false universalisation and potential hierarchy of oppression, child care polices and practices need to address a wide range of forms of oppression. The intersectionality of oppression and privilege is only touched upon in this chapter, but is necessary to all policy analyses.

Having suggested three 'starting points' that could be relatively easily to improve child care policies and practices, I now turn to the more complex issue of how to develop counter policy-making practices. While there are multiple approaches to counter-hegemonic policy making, my focus here is on the processes that have produced the current *Children First* guidelines. The three reports and the revised *Children First* guidelines demonstrate how issues of 'race' are either treated as marginal and/or completely avoided. The report on service users' perceptions of child protection services made some attempt to include the voices of Black and minority ethnic service users, but found that racial discrimination was 'rare'. The report identifies how 'race' is a factor in child protection services in the UK, but states that this appears not to be the case in Ireland. Yet this runs counter to research identified by Crowley (2010), which indicates that racism is a widely recognised feature of Irish society.

It is not clear why the report on service users' perception does not address racial discrimination or the impact of racism. Perhaps an interesting question to have asked all the services users, Black and minority ethnic and white, would be how assumptions of (white) Irish identity influences child care policies and practices. Or perhaps the service users could have been asked to discuss the situation of separated children where there is ample evidence of the impact of being defined as not white. The report which is based on the analysis of submissions from social professionals and NGOs, includes limited discussion of racism, for example, one of the submissions specifically identified the absence of any mention of racism within the *Children First* guidelines. Other submissions highlighted concerns about the treatment of separated children.

While issues of racism and the inadequacy of child protection/care of Black and minority ethnic children were raised in this report, the report on compliance of practice with the *Children First* guidelines and, more importantly, the revised guidelines 'airbrush out' any acknowledgement of the existence of racism. The research processes and the production of reports and revised guidelines provide examples of how a central concern with 'our own' assumed-to-be white Irishness renders Black and minority groups officially 'invisible' and reinforce a particular racialised set of norms, hierarchy of entitlement and access to resources. As stated earlier, focusing on whiteness can result in white identities becoming reified, but a critical study of whiteness can help to identify the processes by which individuals and groups are racially privileged. This privilege exists whether or not individuals who can claim whiteness are aware of it. Using whiteness as an analytic tool focuses attention away from the 'special needs' of Black and minority and refocuses it on the racialisation of dominant groups and possibilities of counter-hegemonic transformation.

Finally, the policy-making process that led to the revised *Children First* guidelines demonstrates that however 'progressive' the review/research methods are, policy making is a political process of inclusion and exclusion. Even the evidence of racism in the reports has had little impact on the revised version of *Children First* guidelines. As policy making is a political process, whether through the influence of political elites and/or through the less direct control of dominant social discourses, those interested in counter-hegemonic policy making need to adopt a critically reflexive approach to the process and engage with a range of stakeholders. Policy making in itself is not enough. Those who want to promote social change though policy making need to make links and alliances outside the 'traditional' boundaries of policy. Without developing these types of spaces, child care/protection will continue to be provided to white children first.

Acknowledgements

Research for this article was funded by an Irish Research Council for Humanities and Social Sciences Development Initiative Grant.

Notes

1 The April 2006 Census identified that there were 419,733 non-Irish nationals living in the Republic Ireland (Central Statistics Office, 2006). They come from 188 different countries and are living in all areas of Ireland.
2 The revised version of *Children First: National Guidelines for the Protection and Welfare of Children* (2010) were downloaded from www.omc.gov.ie on 15 May 2010. At the time of writing, the Department of Health and Children's website states that the revised guidelines are 'not yet operational'. The revised guidelines become operational on the 15th July 2011.
3 '"Separated children" are children under 18 years of age who are outside their country of origin and separated from both parents, or their previous legal/customary primary caregiver' (Separated Children in Europe Programme, 2009, p. 3).
4 See Christie (2010) for examples of how anti-racist polices can reinforce dominant constructions of whiteness.

References

Ahmed, S. (2007) 'A phenomenology of whiteness', *Feminist Theory*, 8(2), pp. 149–168.
Buckley, H., Whelan, S., Carr, N. and Murphy, C. (2008) *Service Users' Perceptions of the Irish Child Protection System*, Dublin, The Stationery Office.
Central Statistics Office (2006) *Principal Demographic Results*, Dublin, CSO.
Christie, A. (2003) 'Unsettling the "social" in social work: Responses to asylum seeking children in Ireland', *Child and Family Social Work*, 8(3), pp. 223–231.
Christie, A. (2010) 'Whiteness and the politics of "race" within child protection guidelines in Ireland', *European Journal of Social Work*, 13(2), pp. 199–215.

Coogan, T. P. (2000) *Wherever Green is Worn: The Story of the Irish Diaspora,* London, Arrow Books.

Crowley, N. (2010) *Hidden Messages Overt Agendas,* Dublin, Migrants Rights Centre Ireland.

Department of Children, Schools and Families (2010) *Working Together to Safeguard Children: A Guide to Inter-Agency Working to Safeguard and Promote the Welfare of Children,* Nottingham, DCFS Publications.

Department of Health and Children (1999) *Children First – National Guidelines for the Protection and Welfare of Children,* Dublin, The Stationery Office.

Department of Justice, Equality and Law Reform (2005) *Planning For Diversity: The National Action Plan Against Racism 2005–2008,* Dublin, Department of Justice, Equality and Law Reform.

Dyer, R. (1997) *White,* London, Routledge.

European Commission (2009) *Discrimination in the EU in 2009,* Brussels, Directorate General for Employment, Social Affairs and Equal Opportunities.

Fanning, B. (2002) *Racism and Social Change in the Republic of Ireland,* Manchester, Manchester University Press.

Garner, S. (2004) *Racism in the Irish Experience,* London, Pluto.

Garner, S. (2006) 'The uses of whiteness: What sociologists working on Europe can draw from US research on whiteness', *Sociology,* 40(2), pp. 257–275.

Gilroy, P. (1987) *There Ain't No Black in the Union Jack: The Cultural Politics of Race and Nation,* London, Hutchinson.

Gray, B. (2004) *Women and the Irish Diaspora,* London, Routledge.

Hartigan, J. (2005) *Old Tribes: Towards a Cultural Analysis of White People,* Durham NC, Duke University Press.

Ignatiev, N. (1995) *How the Irish Became White,* New York, Routledge.

Lentin, R. (2007) 'Ireland: Racial state and crisis racism', *Ethnic & Racial Studies,* 30(4), pp. 610–627.

Lentin, R. and McVeigh, R. (2006) *After Optimism? Ireland, Racism and Globalisation,* Dublin, Metro Éireann.

Lewis, A. (2004) '"What Group?" Studying whites and whiteness in the era of "color-blindness"', *Sociological Theory,* 22(4), pp. 623–646.

Mac an Ghaill, M. (2002) 'Beyond a back-white dualism: Racialisation and racism in the Republic and the Irish diaspora experience', *Irish Journal of Sociology,* 11(2), pp. 99–122.

McIntosh, P. (1988) *White Privilege: Unpacking the Invisible Knapsack,* Wellesley MA, Wellesley College Center for Research on Women.

Macpherson, W. (1999) *The Stephen Lawrence Inquiry,* London, Stationery Office.

McVeigh, R. (1992) 'The specificity of Irish racism', *Race and Class,* 33(4), pp. 31–45.

Miles, R. (1989) *Racism,* London, Routledge.

Murphy, F., Buckley, H. and Joyce, L. (2005) *The Ferns Report*, Dublin, The Stationery Office.

Nayak, A. (2005) 'White lives', in Murji, K. and Solomos, J. (eds) *Racialisation: Studies in Theory and Practice*, Oxford, Oxford University Press.

Negra, D. (2006) 'The Irish in US: Irishness, performativity, and popular culture', in Negra, D. (ed.) *The Irish in US*, Durham, Duke University Press.

Ní Laoire, C. (2008) 'Complicated host-newcomer dualisms: Irish return migrants as home-comers or newcomers?', *Translocations*, 4(1), pp. 35–50.

Ní Shuinéar, S. (2002) 'Othering the Irish (Travellers)', in Lentin, R. and McVeigh, R. (eds) *Racism and Anti-Racism in Ireland*, Belfast, Beyond the Pale.

Nititham, S. (2008) 'Locating the self in diaspora space', *Translocations: The Irish Migration, Race and Social Transformation Review*, 3(1), pp. 69–85.

Office of the Minister for Children (2007) *The Agenda for Children's Services: A Policy Handbook*, Dublin, The Stationery Office.

Office of the Minister for Children and Youth Affairs (2008a) *Analysis of Submissions Made on National Review of Compliance with Children First: National Guidelines for the Protection and Welfare of Children*, Dublin, The Stationery Office.

Office of the Minister for Children and Youth Affairs (2008b) *National Review of Compliance with Children First: National Guidelines for the Protection and Welfare of Children*, Dublin, The Stationery Office.

Office of the Minister for Children and Youth Affairs (2010) *Children First: National Guidelines for the Protection and Welfare of Children*, Dublin, The Stationery Office.

Office of the Minister for Health and Children (2000) *National Children's Strategy. Our Children – Their Lives*, Dublin, Stationery Office.

Reay, D. (2008) 'Psychosocial aspects of white middle-class identities: Desiring and defending against the class and ethnic 'other' in urban multi-ethnic schooling', *Sociology*, 42(6), pp. 1072–1088.

Separated Children in Europe Programme (2009) *Statement of Good Practice*, Copenhagen, Save the Children.

Smyth, J. (2010) 'HSE director criticises care for children seeking asylum', *The Irish Times* (8 February). Available from: www.irishtimes.com/newspaper/frontpage/2010/0208/1224263954887.html (accessed 9 August 2010).

Williams, C. and Soydan, H. (2005) 'When and how does ethnicity matter? A cross-national study of social work responses to ethnicity in child protection cases', *British Journal of Social Work*, 35(6), pp. 901–920.

7

Making 'new connections': The development of a differential response to child protection and welfare

Mark Yalloway, Mary Hargaden and Eilidh MacNab

Introduction

Never before has there been such an intense focus on the delivery of statutory child protection services and commentary on the scope, effectiveness and limitations of the Health Service Executive's legislative mandate to protect children in the Republic of Ireland. The complexities and difficulties present in the operation of the current child protection system have been well documented (Buckley, 1999, 2008, 2009; Shannon, 2010). In 2010, however, the HSE received increased media, political and public attention in the aftermath of the findings of the inquiry reports, reviews and inspections of statutory services (Murphy *et al.*, 2009; Ryan, 2009; Health Information and Quality Authority, 2010; Health Service Executive, 2010b; Ombudsman for Children, 2010). In the context of an increasingly regulatory environment which expects accountability when services fall short of statutory and regulatory requirements (O'Brien, 2010), there is an unprecedented opportunity to radically reform the Irish child protection and welfare system not only in terms of the way it is delivered, but also in relation to how it is perceived and experienced by both staff and members of the public.

This chapter discusses the development of a differential response model (DRM) as an alternative approach to the delivery of child protection and welfare services. It examines some of the international research evidence and benefits of this approach for child protection and welfare practice. We begin by presenting a critique of the current child protection and welfare system in the Republic of Ireland and exploring critical issues and challenges in relation to the implementation of DRM as a national pilot in one local health office within the

Health Service Executive (HSE), namely the Dublin North Local Health Office (LHO). Although implementation only commenced in October 2010, this chapter provides an account of the issues which have emerged in establishing this approach as an alternative response to the current system of service delivery. The Dublin North LHO was selected as the national pilot site owing to its profile as the second largest LHO in the country and 'readiness' to embark on this project, which was a process initiated by the Children Acts Advisory Board (2008, p. 9). Growing awareness of the benefits of DRM has resulted in support for the implementation of this model (see Shannon, 2010). The pilot programme will be evaluated by the Child and Family Research Centre, NUI Galway, with an interim evaluation report scheduled to be ready early in 2012.

Critique of the current child protection and welfare system

North Dublin is the second largest HSE administrative area in the country with some areas of urban disadvantage (Health Service Executive, 2005–9). Its experience of child protection and welfare in recent years has been one of rising referral rates, long waiting lists and cases awaiting allocation. Large numbers of children are being 'screened out' for services because of the need to prioritise available resources to respond to children who are in most need (Health Service Executive, 2005–9). The referral rate to the social work department in this area steadily increased from 517 reports in 2005 to 842 in 2009 (Health Service Executive, 2005–9). The number of referrals confirmed as abuse (156, 21%, in 2008), remains much lower, however, when compared to the overall number of referrals received. This is also reflected in the national statistics: 24,668 reports were received nationally by social work departments across the HSE in 2008, and of these, 2,164 (9%) were confirmed as abuse (Health Service Executive, 2005–9). Although the North Dublin confirmation rates are more than double the national average, this reflects the wide variation in practice across the country concerning referral and assessment of child abuse and service capacity issues in each HSE area. Given these differences when coupled with low confirmation rates, we are arguing that an investigative approach is not the most effective use of available resources when overall outcomes in terms of child well-being and public demands for reform concerning the effectiveness of services are examined (see RTÉ, 2010).

Many community services and professionals in Ireland describe the frustration of not making referrals to the HSE because of their experience of being unable to meet the high threshold for a service, and that when a service is eventually offered, it is frequently too late. Overarching principles of good health service delivery such as equity, accessibility and responsiveness (Department of Health and Children, 2001) become aspirational and difficult to achieve in reality within child protection.

The historic and piecemeal development of child protection and welfare services in Ireland has been recorded comprehensively in recent inquiry reports (see O'Sullivan, 2009), where the evolution of services have been largely influenced by child abuse inquiries both in Ireland and in the United Kingdom (see, for example, McGuinness, 1993; Laming, 2003). In Ireland, service users' perceptions of social work services are generally poor and characterised by feelings of powerlessness and not understanding the process of assessment which users are subjected to (Buckley et al., 2008). As argued by McNulty (2008), commentary in the Irish media concerning child protection can often be critical and unsupportive (see also Chapter 8 by O'Brien for a journalist's view on coverage of child protection in the Irish media). However, it becomes increasingly difficult for practitioners to change such negative perceptions when individual endeavour is often neutralised by constraints in the system within which they operate. In the absence of a capacity to respond in a non-adversarial manner and where the same approach for the investigation of all reported incidents is required, the skills and positive practice approaches which are utilised by practitioners are arguably not as effective as they could be, particularly for cases of lower risk. The challenges of creating a child protection and welfare system that reflects a family support ethos, where interventions by social workers are perceived as being non-threatening and supportive, cannot be under estimated.

Although by no means unique to the Irish experience, traditional child protection systems are hindered by problems of 'over-inclusion' of inappropriate referrals and 'under-inclusion' of families who should be receiving a service. Problems of 'service orientation' also result in an inappropriate emphasis being placed on one approach, for example child rescue (the removal of children at risk of abuse) or family preservation (the provision of supports to enable children to remain at home), when neither approach is suitable for all referred families (Waldfodel, 1998; Dolan et al., 2006). It has been observed that there is no shortage of national family support policies and frame-works to support this shift in practice. However, in the absence of an operational child protection system to support such a family support ethos, it becomes extremely difficult to embed this in practice (Dolan and Curtin, forthcoming).

For many years, the existing statutory child protection system in Ireland has been criticised as being unresponsive to families in need and young people at risk, owing to its incident-driven, investigative focus (Buckley, 1999). Reports into young people who have died in the care of the state have pointed to missed opportunities, and the absence of adequate services and proactive planning for vulnerable young people requiring intervention (Health Service Executive, 2010b). The level of concern surrounding these and other child deaths in HSE care has led to the establishment of an independent review panel to examine the circumstances surrounding the deaths of children in care in Ireland in the last decade (Coulter, 2010; RTÉ, 2010). Social work services in the Republic of Ireland are characterised and experienced as having long waiting lists, which hinder social workers' capacity to respond promptly to concerns of reported child abuse because of other priorities (Clifford, 2010). Although the extent of these difficulties does vary around the country, the presence of varied and inconsistent approaches to practice further compounds existing inequities and inefficiencies in the system. This lack of standardisation has been highlighted in an internal review by the HSE (Health Service Executive, 2005–9) and in successive reviews of *Children First: National Guidelines for the Protection and Welfare of Children,* which were introduced in 1999 (Office of the Minister for Children and Youth Affairs, 2008; Ombudsman for Children, 2010).

Following the publication of the Ryan Report in May 2009, which for the first time revealed the extent of historic abuse suffered by children in institutions run by religious orders on the state's behalf, there have been unprecedented calls from the media and the public for change and reassurance that children currently in the care of the state are adequately protected. A significant investment of resources in terms of additional social work staff and further development of services is contained in the Ryan Report implementation plan (Office of the Minister for Children and Youth Affairs, 2009a), and is reflected in the HSE service plan relating to children and family services (Health Service Executive, 2010a, p. 24). It is in this context that the need to explore and pilot a model which has the potential to address many of these difficulties is receiving increasing support and interest amongt service planners, policy makers and practitioners (see Shannon, 2010).

The inherent danger in the implementation of rapid reforms to a system, which demands increasing standards of performance management and accountability, is that the focus of the service becomes increasingly managerial rather than practice based (Tilbury 2004; Buckley 2008, 2009). The introduction of standardised systems in the United Kingdom has identified considerable concerns in this regard (White *et al.*, 2009). The challenge, therefore, is to ensure that a robust evidence-based practice framework also accompanies, underpins and complements the modern information technology and service planning requirements for measuring activity and performance (Health Service Executive, 2010a). Social work practice needs to influence the design of the required performance measures by focusing on relevant outcomes against which performance can be meaningfully measured so that appropriate indicators that reflect and support changes in practice are used.

The development of a differential response model (DRM), therefore, must identify how the outcomes it seeks to achieve will be different, but also consistent with the goals of national policy. It is anticipated that the successful implementation of DRM in Ireland will mean more rapid assessment of need and a rise in the number of child abuse reports categorised as 'child welfare' rather than 'abuse and neglect'. A core element of DRM is that for medium or low-risk cases, and where the family agree, the focus of the intervention by social workers will be on the assessment of need and not on determining whether the reported incident occurred or not. The outcomes of all initial assessments will be categorised as 'child welfare' unless further concerns emerge in the course of the assessment. This is a significant shift in the approach of the existing child protection system in that only high-risk cases (i.e. non-accidental injury, child sexual abuse, chronic neglect) will receive an investigative response. This will remove the need to categorise reports of abuse as either 'confirmed' or 'unconfirmed' in the vast majority of cases with, over time, only approximately 15 per cent requiring a traditional investigative response (Sawyer and Lohrbach, 2005a).

For North Dublin, using the referral rates outlined earlier in this chapter, it could be predicted that over a period of 5–10 years, as DRM becomes established, in the region of 120 out of a yearly figure of 840 referrals per annum would receive an investigative response. In the Irish context this translates to approximately 3,500 referrals annually. This would ensure that the utilisation of an investigative approach is proportionate to the number of reports which are confirmed each year and would typically require a protective response. Should this be achieved, and with a focus on improving inter-agency working, it will support the realisation of many of the protection, education and welfare goals of the seven national outcomes for children, which include physical and mental health; support for active learning; safety; economic and physical security; positive family and community networks; and inclusion and participation in society (Office of the Minister for Children, 2007, p. 12). This will assist in promoting greater engagement and connection of vulnerable families with services through the introduction of a less adversarial approach from the point of referral, and not after an initial assessment has been completed. DRM will introduce the element of choice and opportunity for greater engagement with families at a much earlier stage in the referral and assessment process.

The experience of many child protection systems around the world is similar to that of Ireland in that they do not achieve the appropriate balance between the provision of a child protection response when needed, and providing necessary supports to families at risk (Department of Health, 1995; Shannon, 2010). The problem of categorising referrals to statutory services as either 'child welfare' or 'child protection' has been noted, particularly in the context of child abuse inquiries (Laming, 2003) and that 'thresholds which act as gateways to restrict services for children, are inconsistent, and are too high' (Laming, 2009, p. 30). By trying to limit responding to only higher-risk referrals, a presumption is also often made that services in the community will be able to meet the needs of all other vulnerable families (Waldfogel, 1998; Waldegrave and Coy, 2005). As a result, child protection systems have the unintended consequence of frequently alienating those who most need assistance (and the services expected to meet their needs), unless effective partnerships are forged with service providers to meet the needs of families who are 'screened out' of statutory services. The following analysis of these issues characteristic of traditional child protection systems, which is equally applicable to the system in Ireland, was made by the *1991 United States National Commission on Children* (cited in Sawyer and Lohrbach's presentation to the Children Acts Advisory Board Seminar, May 2008):

> If the nation had deliberately designed a system that would frustrate the professionals who staff it, anger the public who finance it, and abandon the children who depend on it, it could not have not done a better job than the present child welfare system. (p. 10)

The need for change is self-evident when the present trends in child protection systems here and in other jurisdictions are examined (Buckley, 2007, Buckley et al., 2008). Calls for the introduction of mandatory reporting in Australia, for example, have resulted in the child protection system becoming flooded with referrals. Should such a system be introduced in Ireland, a similar increase in the rate of referrals might be anticipated, the volume of which would seriously hinder the capacity of professionals to respond. Shannon (2010, p. 26) argues that the 'benefits pointed to by the proponents of mandatory reporting are easily refuted'. The focus of already scarce resources would remain dedicated to the investigation of incidents, with low confirmation rates for abuse, rather than on the assessment of need and engagement of families, with support services available to address the reason for a referral being made in the first place. In Minnesota, for example, it has been demonstrated that a shift in focus away from the investigation of incidents, except for those that are considered more serious, does not place children at any more risk (Loman, 2005).

Against a background where Ireland is experiencing the worst recession in almost a century, services designed in the future must be able to cope with the gap between demand and supply, regardless of the availability of additional resources, and have the capacity to provide support services to families who do not meet high thresholds for intervention. In order to achieve this, however, a shift must take place in the way we think about delivering services to children and families in need. It is no longer realistic, nor indeed desirable, that the HSE alone, without close collaboration with others, can succeed in achieving its statutory duty to identify and promote the welfare of children in need of protection, and to provide family support services. This has been highlighted most starkly in media reporting concerning the deaths of children in care (RTÉ, 2010). Although the primary statutory role of the HSE is not at issue, a notable absence in media commentary has been the role of other agencies in meeting the needs of vulnerable children who do not engage with mainstream service provision. Although this shift may be perceived as the HSE seeking to bridge the gap between demand and supply by trying to persuade other services who are already overstretched to take on extra work, we argue that this could not be further from the truth. The issue is one of supporting services that are appropriately placed and who have an ongoing relationship with a family to be more responsive and to intervene earlier.

Greater clarity is required about when the HSE need to be involved through enhanced coordination of services and the use of a common framework to examine child welfare and protection concerns. The establishment of children's services committees, which will be respon-sible for a process of multi-agency planning, funding and delivery of services to children and families in its local area, is a concrete example of government policy in this regard (Office of the Minister for Children and Youth Affairs, 2009b). The implementation of the DRM, therefore, together with common assessment frameworks and practice tools to support practitioners, is regarded as having the potential to provide a single operational framework to achieve these goals. As Buckley (2007) notes, the relationships between voluntary services and the HSE in Ireland has been a difficult one, and this is a significant development in the construction of a new landscape for the delivery of children's services into the future.

A differential response model

Differential response models (DRMs), sometimes referred to as 'alternative response models' or 'multi-track systems' have been developed in a number of sites in the United States, Australia, Canada and New Zealand (Shusterman *et al.*, 2005; Buckley, 2007). Although there may be some variation in approach, the core principles of the model are generally consistent. DRM is a systems approach to dealing with all child protection and welfare reports that is supported by a variety of standardised 'best practice' processes, which guide social workers in how they engage with families in their work, most notably in the utilisation of standardised assessment frameworks and structured decision-making (SDM) tools (Turnell and Edwards, 1999; Johnson, 2004). This facilitates consistency and reduces the tendency for wide variations in practice between areas.

In order to illustrates its operation, DRM can typically be split into three distinct pathways (see figure 7.1):

Path 1: Community response

Families do not meet the threshold for the receipt of statutory services and receive assessment and support from community-based services, where appropriate. Much of the focus of DRM is on developing and supporting the improved coordination of services to families where there may be general child welfare concerns.

Path 2: Family assessment response

A child protection or welfare referral is made to the social work department which indicates 'reasonable grounds for concern' (Office of the Minister for Children and Youth Affairs, 2009b) about a child who requires an initial assessment to be conducted by the HSE. These concerns will relate to the possible abuse or neglect of a child. Family assessments will be conducted for referrals of medium to low risk. Where a family consents to an initial assessment, no determination of abuse will be made and only an assessment of need will be conducted. If concerns emerge during the assessment which indicate a higher level of risk, the assessment will immediately transfer to an investigation pathway. At the end of the assessment, the family decides whether they wish to accept services, unless not to do so would, in the view of the worker conducting the assessment, place the child at risk.

Family assessments may, in certain circumstances, and with family agreement, be conducted by other services in the community under the direction of the HSE. A primary care social worker or a professional working in an agency funded by the HSE are possible alternatives. As part of their Service Level Agreement, The Daughters of Charity Child and Family Service in Dublin North have established an assessment team to undertake some initial assessments on behalf of the HSE for the DRM pilot. The outcome of all assessments conducted are reported back and approved by the HSE social work manager for the area.

An additional *domestic violence response* pathway has been introduced in Olmsted County, Minnesota (Sawyer and Lohrbach, 2005b). The development of this pathway may be of particular interest in the Irish context owing to the recently published policy on domestic, sexual and gender-based violence (Health Service Executive, 2010c) and it has also been estimated that 40 per cent of social work cases include an element of domestic violence (Health Service Executive, 2010c, p. 4). This pathway, which would be included as a possible intervention under the family assessment response (see figure 7.1), would involve the coordination of local services to provide a dedicated response to cases where domestic violence is a factor in partnership with the local HSE social work department. This would enable a much more focused, effective and specialist response to families where there are child protection and welfare concerns of this type. A dedicated response to domestic violence has already been developed in Dublin South West LHO, and is an example of how existing structures and practice approaches can facilitate the introduction of DRM within the HSE in general.

Path 3: Investigative response

A referral is made to the HSE social work department which indicates the possibility that a child may have been abused and neglected and that the nature of this abuse is serious. Examples would include allegations of sexual abuse, non-accidental injury and chronic neglect. A child protection investigation will also be conducted for families where there is An Garda Síochána investigation relating to the referral and /or where the family has a history of child protection involvement, is uncooperative, and/or has made minimal to no improvement in the care of the child(ren).

Under the DRM, the threshold for instigating a child protection investigative response (Path 3) is high, and is restricted only to those reports where serious abuse is suspected/disclosed. Serious abuse relate to referrals of non-accidental injury/serious physical abuse causing bruising, child sexual abuse and chronic neglect *only*. Comprehensive guidance is being developed to assist staff to determine what categories of referral will require an immediate response. For example, where the alleged abuse is a criminal offence; there is reason to believe the parent/guardian will not cooperate and/or there is a history of previous reports which indicate a pattern of concern, these reports will be assigned to Path 3 (see figure 7.1). Where these factors are present, the duty social worker screening the referral and in consultation with his or her manager, is asked whether they pose a serious enough threat to warrant a traditional investigation. Experience of implementing DRM has found that the number of reports which receive a traditional child protection investigative response gradually decreases over time (Sawyer and Lohrbach, 2005, 2008). All other referrals will be brought to a weekly referrals meeting (called the RED team meeting – **R**eview **E**valuate and **D**irect) where the appropriateness of conducting a family assessment will be decided by the multi-agency group.

What is significantly different about the DRM is that where a family assessment response is used, it allows agencies to provide services to more families without a formal determination of abuse or neglect. Studies (Loman, 2005; Shusterman *et al.*, 2005; Siegal and Loman, 2006) and commentary on the operation of DRM systems (American Humane Association, 2005, 2008; National Quality Improvement Center, 2009) have shown that this approach results in no greater risk to the safety of children, and higher levels of service-user satisfaction. Other outcomes associated with this review of the literature provide evidence of greater levels of engagement with families and lower levels

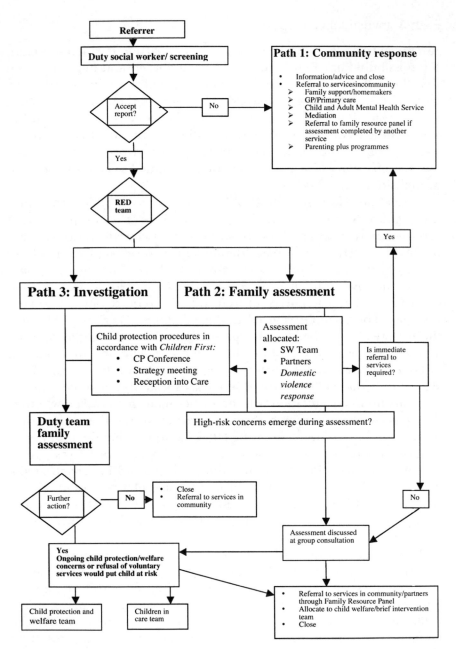

Figure 7.1 Differential response model – referral pathway

of re-reports to social work departments. A reduction in the numbers of children coming into care and lower levels of court applications have also been demonstrated. In addition to evidence which demonstrates that more children and families receive services, greater levels of job satisfaction for staff have also been noted. The outcome measures identified in the research will form part of the evaluation by the Child and Family Research Centre NUIG in evaluating the effectiveness of the DRM pilot in Dublin North.

DRM presents a radical alternative to the traditional way of working for child protection practitioners in Ireland. What is significantly different for us is the involvement of partners, including services funded by the HSE, in the 'core business' of decision making jointly with the child protection social work team at the referral/intake stage, and in the allocation of some initial family assessments. Dublin North is working closely with the Daughters of Charity Child and Family Service (a voluntary, non-governmental organisation) in the restructuring of their service to support the implementation of DRM.

The process of change: initiating the DRM project in Dublin North

Preparing to implement a different system requires a significant change to established ways of working and thinking, not only for staff in the HSE, but also for other agencies and professionals. This process has involved extensive preparation and planning with social work staff, management and community stakeholders. The support of the Child and Family Research and Policy Unit National University of Ireland Galway (NUIG) was secured to provide project planning and evaluation expertise for the pilot project. The evaluation of the pilot will have a key role in informing any future plans to implement DRM more widely across the HSE.

The decision to appoint a dedicated project manager was a critical one in terms of driving the process and putting together a project plan for local implementation. A Dublin North management steering group, chaired by the local health manager/general manager, was established, and met monthly in the initial set-up stages. A comprehensive 'statement of requirements for the implementation of DRM' was prepared and submitted to the local health manager, which identified the resources required to fully implement the model without delay. It is important to note that the identification of additional resources to support the implementation of DRM has been identified as a critical success factor in other jurisdictions (Waldegrave and Coy, 2005; Siegal and Loman, 2006).

The lack of a standardised approach to social work practice has been the subject of much criticism in Ireland (Ombudsman for Children, 2010). It is proposed that *Signs of Safety* (Turnell and Edwards, 1999), which provides a comprehensive and systematic methodology that is easily understood by both clients and professionals, will assist in the process of addressing these concerns and restoring confidence in the operation of the child protection and welfare system. It receives particular attention here, owing to its importance as the practice framework that will underpin the implementation of a pilot system for a differential response in Ireland.

Signs of safety

Signs of Safety (Turnell and Edwards, 1999) seeks to make explicit core practice principles which are embedded and characteristic of good quality, collaborative social work practice with families. In the context of implementing a model for child welfare and protection such as DRM, 'signs of safety' is particularly useful to articulate what client-centred, strengths-based practice means. It focuses on looking for 'exceptions' to incidents of concern about a child and opens the door to examining what is going well for a family (strengths or 'signs of safety'), and balancing this against what the social work department or the statutory agency is concerned about (danger/harm). Most importantly, it clearly articulates in uncomplicated language what the social worker is worried about and develops into a formal 'risk statement' for families and professionals (Sawyer and Lohrbach, 2008). In the Irish context, when used and underpinned by an evidenced-based assessment tool (see, for example, Buckley *et al.*, 2006), the signs of safety approach is invaluable in terms of summarising at a glance the current position pertaining to an open case, the assessment completed to date and what immediate steps/actions are required. The integration of the *Framework for the Assessment of Vulnerable Children and Their Families* (Buckley *et al.*, 2006) with the signs of safety approach and principles has resulted in the production of the HSE North Dublin Practice Framework to guide staff undertaking assessments under DRM.

Wheeler and Hogg (forthcoming) examined the use of 'signs of safety' in Gateshead, England and further underline the usefulness of a solution-focused approach to child protection casework. The examination of how DRM operates in Olmsted County in Minnesota (Sawyer and Lohrbach, 2005, 2008) has informed the development of the pilot project in Dublin North. Wheeler and Hogg (forthcoming) refer to the findings of Turnell *et al.* (2008, pp. 6–7), who describe the impact of utilising the signs of safety approach in the implementation of the DRM by the Olmsted County Child and Family Services (OCCFS):

> In the 12 years to 2007 during a period in which OCCFS has tripled the number of children the agency works with, the agency has halved the proportion of children taken into care and halved the number of families taken before the courts.

Wheeler and Hogg note that these impressive outcomes were accompanied by other structural changes to the department itself. These included implementing changes such as holding more family meetings (for example, a family welfare (group) conference) or safety planning meetings before initiating court proceedings. In order to support staff and create an organisational culture which is committed to sustaining such changes, regular structured times for staff to reflect on their work and to share this with colleagues is necessary. Turnell *et al.* (2008) refers to the process of creating a culture of 'appreciative inquiry' around child protection practice in the implementation of 'signs of safety' as a child protection practice framework. Turnell has also referred to the need to build 'practice based evidence' amongt social workers (Turnell, 2008). As an example of how this can be achieved, Sawyer and Lohrbach (2005) have introduced 'group consultations', which have become integral to the operation of the social work team in Olmsted County.

Group consultation framework

The signs of safety approach is strengthened and made operationally possible by establishing a regular format for group consultations (Sawyer and Lohrbach, 2005). Led by the social work team leaders (supervisors), and using the framework developed by Lohrbach in figure 7.2 (see also Lohrbach, 2008, 2009), key decisions are shared among the wider team and supported by the organisation as a whole, rather than becoming the sole responsibility of an individual social worker/manager. This reduces pressure on staff, enhances peer support, knowledge sharing and expertise. Partnering refers to the key principles and practice of the signs of safety approach where understanding the position of each family member is central. The use of 'scaling' questions to examine the family's willingness, confidence and capacity to bring about change is a key tool in this partnership approach and in facilitating conversations to take place about assessing overall safety. Sawyer and Lohrbach (2005) demonstrate how

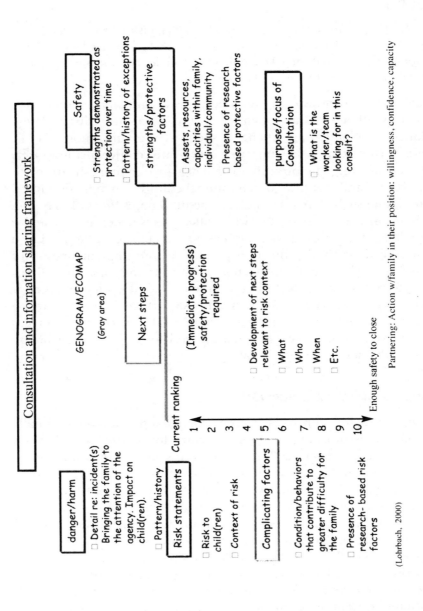

Figure 7.2 Consultation and information sharing framework in child welfare practice

the consultation framework can be used at the point of intake at the Review, Evaluate and Direct (RED) team meeting as a means of examining information contained in referrals received. It is also used throughout the social work department as the model for conducting discussions with colleagues and families and summarising information gathered during initial or further assessment.

Conclusion

Research into the operation of DRM has indicated that this model addresses many of the criticisms and concerns relating to the operation of traditional, incident-driven and investigation-focused child protection systems. It emphasises a family support ethos in the delivery of services and focuses on the identification of family strengths and resources rather than on a deficit model which makes the exploration of 'signs of safety' more difficult. This approach has been shown to be less alienating and threatening for families and, most importantly, is reportedly liked by staff, clients and other professionals.

Challenges in implementing such a new model include the development of enhanced working relationships with other services and professionals. Inherent dangers in this approach are the perception that DRM may be viewed as introducing more stringent threshold criteria relating to the definition of what constitutes a serious child protection concern, rather than on the development of a more responsive system that seeks to intervene earlier. Although it is hoped that improved working relationships and the alignment and coordination of services by the HSE under a common operational and practice framework will result in greater efficiencies in the way services are experienced, an analysis of any remaining core deficits in meeting assessed need must be kept under review.

References

American Humane Association (2005) 'Differential response in child welfare', *Protecting Children: A Professional Publication of American Humane Association*, 20, 2 and 3. Available from: www.americanhumane .org/protecting-children/resources/protecting-children-journal /volumes-and-sample-articles.html (accessed 1 June 2010).

American Humane Association (2008) 'Exploring differential response: One pathway toward reforming child welfare', *Protecting Children: A Professional Publication of American Humane Association*, 23, 1 and 2. Available from:

www.americanhumane.org/protecting-children/resources
/protecting-children-journal/volumes-and-sample-articles.html (accessed
1 June 2010).
Buckley, H. (1999) 'Child protection practice: An ungovernable
    enterprise?', *The Economic and Social Review*, 30(1), pp. 21–40.
Buckley, H. (2007) 'Differential responses to child protection reports',
    Irish Journal of Family Law, 3, pp. 3–7.
Buckley, H. (2008) 'Heading for collision? Managerialism, social science,
    and the Irish child protection system', in Burns, K. and Lynch. D.
    (eds) *Child Protection and Welfare Social Work: Contemporary Themes and Practice
    Perspectives*, Dublin, A. & A. Farmar.
Buckley, H. (2009) 'Reforming the child protection system: Why we need
    to be careful what we wish for', *Irish Journal of Family Law*, 27(2), pp.
    27–31.
Buckley, H., Harworth, J. and Whelan, S. (2006) *Framework for the
    Assessment of Vulnerable Children and their Families*, Trinity College
    Dublin, Children's Research Centre.
Buckley, H., Whelan, S., Carr, N. and Murphy, C. (2008) *Service Users'
    Perceptions of the Irish Child Protection System*, Dublin, Office of the
    Minister for Children and Youth Affairs.
Children Acts Advisory Board (2008) *Evidence to Practice Post Seminar
    Report. A Differential Response Model: Refocusing from Child Protection to
    Family Support, 22 May 2008*, Dublin, Children Acts Advisory Board.
    Available   from: www.srsb.ie/getdoc/eacb0ad0–bccb-4d58–ab65–
    d69ab1a80ff3/DRM-Post-Seminar-Final-Report-web.aspx (accessed 1
    June 2010).
Clifford, M. (2010) 'Cherished equally?', *The Sunday Tribune* (7 March).
Coulter, C. (2010) 'Independent group to examine deaths of children in
    HSE care', *The Irish Times* (3 March 2010).
Department of Health (1995) *Child Protection: Messages From Research*,
    London, HMSO.
Department of Health and Children (2001) *Quality and Fairness: A Health
    System for You*, Dublin, The Stationery Office.
Dolan, P., Curtin, C., Canavan, J. and Brady, B. (2006) *Foyle Trust New
    Beginnings Programme*, NUI Galway, Child and Family Research and
    Policy Unit.
Dolan, P. and Curtin, C. (forthcoming) *Refocusing Social Work Practice
    within a Family Support Framework – New Beginnings a Case for
    Consideration*, Galway, NUI Galway, Child and Family Research and
    Policy Unit.
Health Information and Quality Authority (2010) *Inspection of the HSE
    Fostering Service in HSE Dublin North Area* (online), Cork, HIQA,
    Available from: www.hiqa.ie/publications.asp (accessed 30 July 2010).

Health Information and Quality Authority (2010) *Inspection of the HSE Fostering Service in HSE Dublin North Central Area* (online), Cork, HIQA. Available from: www.hiqa.ie/publications.asp (accessed 30 July 2010).

Health Information and Quality Authority (2010) *Inspection of the HSE Fostering Service in HSE Dublin North West Area* (online), Cork, HIQA. Available from: www.hiqa.ie/publications.asp (accessed 30 July 2010).

Health Service Executive (2005–9) *Dublin North Interim Data Set Returns for the Department of Health and Children*, Dublin, Health Service Executive.

Health Service Executive (2009a) *Social Work and Family Support Survey 1998*, Dublin, Health Service Executive.

Health Service Executive (2009b) *Review of Adequacy Report for Children and Families 2008*, Dublin, Health Service Executive. Available from: www.hse.ie/eng/services/Publications/services/Children/review%2008 .html (accessed 1 June 2010).

Health Service Executive (2010a) *HSE National Service Plan 2010*, Dublin, Health Service Executive.

Health Service Executive (2010b) *Child in Care Death Report: Child Young Person B, April 2010*, Dublin, Health Service Executive. Available from: www.hse.ie/eng/services/Publications/services/Children/reportB .pdf (accessed 1 June 2010).

Health Service Executive (2010c) *HSE Policy on Domestic, Sexual and Gender Based Violence*, Dublin, National Communications Unit.

Johnson, W. (2004) *Effectiveness of California's Child Welfare Structured Decision Making Model: A Prospective Study of the Validity of California Family Risk Assessment*, Sacremento, CA, California Department of Social Services.

Laming, L. (2003) *The Victoria Climbié Inquiry: Report of an Inquiry by Lord Laming*, London, The Stationery Office.

Laming, L. (2009) *The Protection of Children in England: A Progress Report*, Norwich, The Stationery Office.

Lohrbach, S. (2008) 'Group supervision in child protection practice', *Social Work Now: The Practice Journal of Child Youth and Family*, 40 (August), pp. 19–24.

Lohrbach, S. (2009) *Partnership based Collaborative Practice in Work with Children Youth and Families: A Solution and Safety Oriented Approach to Child Protection Casework*. Presentation made to Dublin North Social Work Department, Swords, Co. Dublin (October).

Loman, L .A. (2005) *Differential Response Improves Traditional Investigation: Criminal Arrests for Severe Physical and Sexual Abuse*, A Report of the Institute of Applied Research, St Louis Missouri. Available from: www.iarstl.org/papers.htm (accessed 1 June 2010).

McGuinness, C. (1993) *The Report of the Kilkenny Incest Investigation*, Dublin, The Stationery Office.

McNulty, F. (2008) 'Radical or redundant? Irish social workers, the print media and the Irish Association of Social Workers' in Burns, K. And Lynch, D. (eds) *Child Protection and Welfare Social Work: Contemporary Themes and Practice Perspectives*, Dublin, A. & A. Farmar.

Murphy, Y., Mangan, I. and O'Neill, H. (2009) Commission of Investigation. Reporting to the Catholic Archdiocese of Dublin (online), Dublin, Commission of Investigation, Dublin Archdiocese, Catholic Diocese of Cloyne. Available from: http://www.dacoi.ie/ (accessed 1 December 2009)

National Quality Improvement Center on Differential Response in Child Protective Services (2009) *Differential Response in Child Protective Services: A literature Review*, A project of the Children's Bureau US Department of Health and Human Services. Available at: www .differentialresponseqic.org/assets/docs/qic-dr-lit-review-sept-09.pdf (accessed 1 June 2010).

Office of the Minister for Children (2007) *The Agenda for Children's Services: A Policy Handbook, Office of the Minister for Children*, Dublin, The Stationery Office.

Office of the Minister for Children and Youth Affairs (2008) *National Review of Compliance with Children First: National Guidelines for the Protection and Welfare of Children*, Dublin, The Stationery Office.

Office of the Minister for Children and Youth Affairs (2009a) *Report of the Commission to Inquire into Child Abuse, 2009: Implementation Plan*, Dublin, The Stationery Office.

Office of the Minister for Children and Youth Affairs (2009b) *Children First: National Guidelines for the Protection and Welfare of Children* (2nd edn), Dublin, The Stationery Office.

Office of the Minister for Children and Youth Affairs (2009c) *Children's Services Committees: Toolkit for the Development of a Committee*, Dublin, OMCYA. Available at: http://omc.gov.ie/documents/policy /toolkit_for_development_of_a_commnity.doc (accessed 1 June 2010).

Ombudsman for Children (2010) *A Report Based on an Investigation into the Implementation of Children First: National Guidelines for the Protection and Welfare of Children*, Dublin, Ombudsman for Children's Office.

O'Brien, C. (2010) 'Systemic failures in social services', *The Irish Times* (23 April).

O'Sullivan, E. (2009) 'Residential child welfare in Ireland, 1965–2008: An outline of policy, legislation and practice: A paper presented for the commission to inquire into child abuse', *Commission to Inquire into Child Abuse Report, Volume IV*, Dublin, The Stationery Office.

RTÉ (2010) *Primetime: Ireland's Childcare System* (broadcast on 25 May). www.rte.ie/news/2010/0525/primetime.html (accessed 31 May 2010).

Ryan, S. (2009) *The Commission to Inquire into Child Abuse (Volumes I–V)*, Dublin, The Stationery Office.

Sawyer, R. and Lohrbach, S. (2005a) 'Differential response in child protection: selecting a pathway'. *Differential Response in Child Welfare, Protecting Children: A Professional Publication of American Humane.* American Humane Association, 20 (2 and 3), pp. 44–54.

Sawyer, R. and Lohrbach, S. (2005b) 'Integrating domestic violence intervention into child welfare practice', *Protecting Children*, 20 (2 and 3), pp. 67–77.

Sawyer, R. and Lohrbach, S. (2008) 'Partnership-based Collaborative Practice in Work with Children, Youth and Families'. Presentation made to Children Acts Advisory Board Seminar on Differential Response Model, held at the Gresham Hotel, Dublin (May).

Shannon, G. (2010) *Third Report of the Special Rapporteur on Child Protection: A Report Submitted to the Oireachtas 2009*, Dublin, Office of the Minister for Children and Youth Affairs.

Shusterman, G. R., Hollinshead, D., Fluke, J. D., Yuan, Ying-Ying T. and Walter R. McDonald & Associates (2005) *Alternative Responses to Child Maltreatment: Findings from NCANDS* (online), Office of the Assistant Secretary for Planning and Evaluation (ASPE) US Department of Health and Human Services. Available from: www.aspe.hhs.gov /hsp/05/child-maltreat-resp/ (accessed 14 February 2011).

Siegal, G. L. and Loman, T. (2006) *Extended Follow-up Study of Minnesota's Family Assessment Response – Final Report* (online), A Report of the Institute of Applied Research, St Louis Missouri. Available from: www.iarstl.org/papers/finalMNFARReport.pdf (accessed 14 February 2011).

Tilbury, C. (2004) 'The influence of performance management on child protection welfare policy and practice', *British Journal of Social Work*, 34, pp. 225–241.

Turnell, A. (2008) *Adoption of Signs of Safety as the Department for Child Protection's Child Protection Practice Framework* (online), Western Australia, Department for Child Protection. Available from: www.signsofsafety.net/westernaustralia (accessed 1 June 2010).

Turnell, A. and Edwards, S. (1999) *Signs of Safety: A Solution and Safety Oriented Approach to Child Protection Casework*, New York, W.W. Norton & Company.

Turnell, A., Lohrbach, S. and Curran, S. (2008) 'Working with the "involuntary client" in child protection: Lessons from successful practice', in M. Calder (ed.) *The Carrot or the Stick? Towards Effective Practice with Involuntary Clients*, London, Russell House Publishing.

Waldegrave, S. and Coy, F. (2005) 'A differential response model for child protection in New Zealand: Supporting more timely and effective responses to notifications', *Social Policy Journal of New Zealand*, Issue 25 (July), pp. 32–48.

Waldfogel, J. (1998) 'Rethinking the paradigm for child protection', *The Future of Children: Protecting Children from Abuse and Neglect*, 8(1), pp. 104–119.

Wheeler, J. and Hogg, V. (forthcoming) 'Child Protection', in Franklin, C., Trepper, T., Wallace, J., Gingerich, P. and McCollum, E. (eds), *Solution-Focused Brief Therapy*, Oxford, Oxford University Press.

White, S., Hall, C. and Peckover, S. (2009) 'The descriptive tyranny of the common assessment framework: Technologies of categorisation and professional practice in child welfare', *British Journal of Social Work*, 39, pp. 1197–1217.

8

Social work and the media in Ireland: A journalist's perspective

Carl O'Brien

This chapter explores how social work issues are reported in the Irish media from the perspective of a journalist. It examines why many critically important child protection and welfare issues are often under-reported and, in some cases, distorted by the media. In particular, it focuses on what I consider to be excessive secrecy on the part of the Health Service Executive (HSE) in relation to social care issues, particularly in the area of child protection and welfare, and how this is impacting on media coverage of social work. It goes on to argue for greater openness on the part of the Health Service Executive, a better informed media, as well as a better organised social work profession, and how these could be a powerful force for positive change in ensuring that social work is properly resourced and receives the political priority it deserves. Many of these issues are explored through the story of David Foley, a teenager who died while in the care system.

David's story

David Foley was just 14 when he walked into Pearse Street Garda station on his own. Things were rough at home, he said, and he wanted to be admitted into the care system. He did not look like a child ready for the rough and tumble world of life on the streets. He had a freckled face and big blue eyes. As arrangements were made for his care, he asked An Garda Síochána and social workers whether he had to do his homework that night. 'David wasn't ready for the world he was about to enter', one social worker who dealt with him said (O'Brien, 2008). 'He thought he was streetwise, but he was actually very innocent. He didn't have a clue. Looking back ... [it was] as if he was entering the slaughterhouse' (ibid.).

His needs were simple enough: he needed family support work, a negotiated return home or maybe a care placement in his community. None of it happened fast enough. Instead, as two local health offices (LHOs) disagreed over who was responsible for him, he ended up in an emergency care hostel, known as the 'out of hours' or crisis intervention service.

It is a notoriously dangerous environment. With little to do during the day, most teenagers end up mixing with older, more streetwise young people on the city's streets. With its brutish sub-culture of begging, mugging, drug-dealing and prostitution, it was a toxic environment for a young teenager who had no history of trouble with An Garda Síochána. The speed of David's downward spiral into a world of drugs and crime during his first few months in the out-of-hours service was startling. School was out of the question once other kids on the street told him he could pick up a social welfare cheque if he did not attend. Returning home seemed unlikely as he was adamant that no family member wanted him.

His life became a blur of drinking during the day, getting high, shoplifting or stealing mobile phones. He started failing to keep appointments with social workers, many of whom went to huge efforts to help him. David tried to get to grips with life, but it seemed he was fighting a losing battle. Drugs took over. He overdosed twice. David was found dead in a flat off Blackhall Place in Dublin's north inner city on Saturday, 10 September 2005. It was almost three years to the day after he entered the care system as an innocent 14-year-old.

I wrote about David's story for the first time in *The Irish Times* in October 2008. There had been an internal HSE probe into his death, but nothing was ever put into the public domain about the case. His family were never informed about the report. The public was never alerted to a serious failure in the care system. The only reason I was able to write about David's story was as a result of the bravery and commitment of social workers, care professionals and others who risked their careers to speak to me about the case because they felt it raised profound issues about the child protection and welfare system and crisis intervention service.

David's story is the exception, though. In general, child protection and welfare social work issues are under-reported in the media, despite the vital role the profession plays in day-to-day life. To a large extent, the workings of failures or successes of these services are invisible to the public at large. As a result, I think there is a very poor public understanding about social work and the critical role these professionals play on a daily basis in the lives of children.

Furthermore, this information vacuum feeds a largely negative stereotype about the image of social workers as a kind of over-zealous social police. This view does a huge disservice to social workers: it ignores the positive work being done by very committed professionals on a daily basis in working with families and creating positive outcomes; and it hides the huge strains on a service which urgently needs to be reformed and better resourced.

So why is this the case? I hope to examine what these obstacles are and what we can do to address them. There are three key points I wish to explore. First, there is excessive secrecy surrounding social work services. Second, the fact that it is not a political priority, which means that issues are more likely to be ignored by the media. Third, there is a lack of a well-financed and well-organised professional body to speak out on behalf of social workers and the important work done with vulnerable families.

Excessive secrecy

Trying to access information on child protection and welfare social work can be immensely difficult. Social workers in Ireland are not authorised to talk to media. At HSE level, journalists seeking information are asked to go through press offices, who talk to line managers, who then do not comment on individual cases; or else the HSE issues general, anodyne statements that are of little use to anyone. As a reporter, you then go to the Office of the Minister for Children and Youth Affairs, the policy arm of children's services (see Office of the Minister for Children and Youth Affairs, 2010), which tells you that responsibility for operational issues in health or social services lies with the HSE. Almost everywhere you turn, there is a cul-de-sac.

Even some of the information that is accessible is hardly worth the paper it is written on. For example, the HSE publishes an annual report on child protection and welfare social work services, the *Review of Adequacy of Child and Family Services*, also known as the 'section 8' report (see, for example, Health Service Executive, 2009). It is obliged to do this under the Child Care Act 1991. The raw material for the annual report includes regional dossiers compiled by child care managers in LHOs across the state. Many of these unpublished reports make for disturbing reading, pointing to 'dangerous' numbers of children waiting to be allocated social workers, or 'unsustainable' strains on child protection services. When the actual annual report is eventually published – often years later – these comments are edited or censored out. The published version contains statistics and examples of good practice – but criticism by the HSE's own employees is almost entirely absent.

Far too often, even the most basic information seems to be shrouded in a veil of secrecy. We, as journalists, are forced to use the Freedom of Information (FOI) Act 1997 to find out simple information such as how many children are allocated a social worker; how many reports of abuse or neglect are responded to in a LHO area; how many vacant social work posts are there; what level of family support services exist. (Incidentally, it was through use of the FOI Act that those unpublished LHO reports that contribute to the 'section 8' report entered the public domain through *The Irish Times.*) In tragic cases like the death of David Foley, it has taken years to get answers. After almost two years of questions being raised in the media and Dáil Éireann (Irish Parliament) over his case, the HSE finally published a heavily edited report into the circumstances surrounding his death in April 2010. It highlighted 'tragic systemic failures' and missed opportunities by social workers to provide him with proper support or protection (Health Service Executive, 2010). Many questions were left unanswered. It did not, for example, address key failings, such as the dispute between two LHO areas, which was a central factor in why he never received the kind of support he needed. The delays on the part of the HSE and its reluctance to open itself to scrutiny are highly regrettable. Everyone involved in the lives of these children, including schools, public health nurses, mental health professionals, social workers and the wider community should be learning from these serious failures of the care system.

Yet David Foley's death is just one tragedy. The HSE has since been forced to undertake a major trawl of its files to establish exactly how many children died in care, or while in contact with child protection services. The official number has increased from 21 to a shocking total of 188 (O'Brien, 2010). We can only assume that some of these young people who died in care were quietly forgotten by a system that failed to protect them. The HSE has since adopted guidelines for the reporting of child deaths drawn up by the Health Information and Quality Authority (2010). They stipulate that national reviews be undertaken by a panel of experts whose aim will be to investigate circumstances of deaths and to share these findings with families and the public.

These are positive steps. But secrecy does not end there. It emerged recently that the HSE was refusing to hand over certain files on these deaths to a review group established by the government (Taylor, 2010). It said it was prevented from doing so because of the in camera rules, although this was hotly disputed by many legal experts, and the HSE was forced into an embarrassing climbdown and handed over the files. These obstacles, allied with a culture of secrecy, present a much wider problem. It means social work does not receive the level of informed coverage it merits, despite the crucial role it plays in society. And the public does not get a sense of the real strains and resource problems facing social workers on the ground. Difficulties accessing information – whether it be positive or negative – simply turns most journalists – and their editors – off. Of course, there is a need for sensitivity. We are dealing with families and children who are, in many cases, in crisis. It is only right that, for example, a child's anonymity or a family's identity is protected. But the secrecy surrounding much of the wider work of social services is hugely damaging. Carol Coulter's work in the Family Law Courts could serve as a template for a sensitive but informed public disclosure on child protection matters (Coulter, 2009).

This excessive secrecy can only lead to coverage of social work issues in the media which is either uninformed, simplistic or distorted. In the absence of an informed media, coverage of abuse cases in particular can quickly degenerate into a blame game over who was responsible for failing a vulnerable child or family. In the Roscommon abuse case which made headlines in January 2009 (McDonagh, 2009), the questions being asked by much of the press focused on who the social workers were and why they had abandoned the family. One tabloid newspaper published photos of local social workers on its front page. There was very little, if any, focus on more pressing and relevant issues such as: what kind of resources were available to social work teams in the area?; was there a lack of a developed family support services to allow for earlier intervention?; were these issues common to other social work teams across the state? and; what impact might planned spending cuts have on social work services? This is an issue which is not confined to Ireland by any means. Paul Michael Garrett, Director of Social Work at the National University of Ireland Galway, references similar experiences in the United Kingdom in *Transforming Children's Services: Social Work, Neoliberalism and the Modern World* (2009). The book is dedicated to Lisa Arthurworry, a social worker he believes was unfairly vilified by the media and government in the wake of an inquiry into the horrific death of eight-year-old Victoria Climbié (House of Commons Health Committee, 2003; Lord Laming, 2003).

Greater openness is not something to be feared. It would also lead to more informed coverage. So when the next shocking case of child abuse case makes headlines, the media – and the public – should be not rushing to simply point the finger at social workers. Instead, they should be asking what kind of resources are available to social work teams, whether family support services were available, and why we continue to have services more focused on emergency responses rather than early intervention.

The power of politics

There is another reason why child protection and welfare social work does not get the level of informed coverage it deserves. Much of that is down to the fact that, at government level, it is not a political priority. It is important to remember that journalists are not free spirits wandering the world in search of the truth, but workers expected to produce news to fill newspapers or broadcast time, often on a 24-hour basis. It is no accident that the political arena is where most journalists are found. In fact, media organisations tend to have more reporters covering politics than any other field. *The Irish Times*, for example, has six, sometimes even seven, reporters based in the Irish Parliament, Leinster House.

This is because the political system supplies a never-ending supply of information in an easily transmitted form through briefings and press releases from people with an understanding of deadlines and the media. This also means that, given the investment media organisations make in the political system in terms of staff numbers, many stories only become news when they enter the political sphere. For example, issues such as the mistreatment of patients in nursing homes have become major stories because they became subject to political rows, even though, objectively, it was a major scandal long before TDs (members of Parliament) decided to discuss it.

The problem with social issues is that most politicians and political parties – but not all – see them as being of relevance only to the most marginalised, who are less likely to vote or to be active members of 'civil society'. Because the issues are marginalised politically, they are also marginalised in the media. This is not to exonerate the media. Any news editor, when deciding to run a story, will always ask: 'How many people does this affect?' As a rule of thumb, the more people a story affects – especially those in the middle classes – the more prominence it gets. This is a crucial point: if it affects powerful people like middle classes – the people who vote, the people who buy the material that is advertised in the papers – they are considered even more important. For example, a campaign to reduce stamp duty on the sale of private homes became a major issue in the run-up to the last general election, when, objectively, there were far greater issues affecting society in general. There is a perception on the part of the news media that social work issues affect those who do not read newspapers or listen to the radio, or who are not 'valuable' to advertisers.

There are also more practical obstacles for the media. Lack of access to 'human interest' stories – a key way in which the media tells news stories – is another factor in the under-reporting of social work issues. Everyone can relate to people; telling a person's story is a powerful way of helping people relate to sometimes very complex issues. If you look at broadcast news in particular, almost every story these days begins with a personal angle or story. There are obvious ethical issues about interviewing people in need of support from social workers. In addition, families are often reluctant to talk to the media given the stigma over issues such as mental health, therefore stories of people with mental health problems are under-reported.

There are exceptions. In Ireland newspaper such as *The Irish Times*, *The Irish Examiner* and TV programmes like RTÉ's *Primetime* have helped raise the profile of social work issues from time to time through campaigning journalism. But this is the exception rather than the rule. Ultimately, social work will need to be higher on the political agenda if it is to receive wider coverage. This should not be a counsel of despair, for there are precedents for other, marginalised sectors, becoming more important politically. For example, disability became a much bigger issue in recent years owing to a number of factors, such as representative groupings forming alliances to establish a stronger voice; high-profile court cases being taken by people with disabilities; and campaigns against potentially harmful and restrictive legislation. This resulted in multi-annual funding, a national disability strategy and better legislation. Cancer services, also, have been transformed from a relatively neglected section of the health service to one which even has its own 'Tsar' and dedicated funding stream and national strategy. Similarly, families affected by cancer, lobby groups and even citizens who stood for election on the need for cancer services all helped to push these issues onto the political agenda.

Another very different example is third world aid. It came to the centre-stage of politics through efforts such as the Make Poverty History campaign (Irish Association of Non-Government Development Organisations, 2010), which formed a large coalition of interest groups and led intensive and highly visible rounds of lobbying politicians and governments ahead of the G8 summit.

Mobilising social workers

One of the biggest reasons for the under-reporting of social work issues in Ireland is the fact that social workers themselves are not mobilised or organised in the same way as teachers, nurses, doctors or other vital employees in the public sector. The Irish Association of Social Workers (IASW) is a small and very committed organisation (see IASW, 2009), but its existence owes much to professionals giving whatever spare time they can. But they are almost exclusively involved on a part-time basis. The lack of resources means that the organisation is not in a position to be able to comment publicly as often as it would like. In addition, most social workers, if they are union members, tend to be part of the Impact trade union, a wide-ranging public sector union which represents 65,000 workers. Being in a big union has its advantages at an industrial relations level – but politically, it means the voice of social workers – a relatively small profession – is largely drowned out.

Teachers, for example, are able to use their clout as teacher-only unions – such as the power of withdrawing labour, annual confer-ences, their role in social partnership (a national pay agreement between the government, employers and unions) to dominate the media and get their message across. Every Easter, for example, when the teachers' conferences get underway, the issues affecting teachers dominate the media for at least a week. In an era of 24-hour rolling news schedules and news bulletins, many interest groups are increas-ingly using professional communications advisers to get their message across to pursue their agendas.

In this sense, social workers are increasingly being left behind and are unable to communicate important issues effectively, such as the fact that social work is a community-wide issue and affect all of us; that positive results can be achieved with early intervention; or that the lack of resources and staffing is placing heavy strains on many aspects of child protection and, consequently, that children in need are not in receipt of adequate services, care and protection.

Conclusion

The obstacles to covering social work issues in the media are far from insurmountable; the issues can be pushed up the political agenda, and social workers can become as effective as other representative groups. Of key importance, however, is the issue of excessive secrecy at senior management level, particularly in the HSE. To my mind, the unwillingness to confront failure, to admit that a clearly defective system needs to be changed, or to subject services to proper scrutiny is endemic in Irish public life. This attitude needs to be challenged. It ultimately allows inadequate and under-funded social services to limp along, and it increases the pressure on committed social workers on the ground. Greater openness will only serve to strengthen arguments over, for example, putting more emphasis on resourcing family support and other early intervention services. Perhaps we can take some heart from the reaction to the seminal *Commission to Inquire into Child Abuse Report* (Ryan, 2009), which was commissioned by the government to examine how children were abused in industrial schools over a 70-year period. Subsequent to its publication, the government produced an implementation plan containing 99 recommendations to reform the child protection system (see Office of the Minister for Children and Youth Affairs, 2009).

Taoiseach Brian Cowen described the report at the time as an indictment of the individuals who had perpetrated the abuse – the religious congregations that ran the institutions and the organs of the state that had failed in their duty of care. But it was outpouring of public anger and revulsion which prompted the government into drawing up plans to reform social services. Politicians and policy makers have an important opportunity to change the system and culture and, ultimately, redefine the nature of social work and how it is seen by the public. Let us hope they grasp the opportunity.

References

Coulter, C. (2009) *Family Law in Practice: A Study of Cases in the Circuit Court*, Dublin, Gill & Macmillan.

Garrett, P. M. (2009) *Transforming Children's Services: Social Work, Neoliberalism and the Modern World*, New York, Open University Press.

Health Information and Quality Review (2010) *Guidance for the Health Service Executive for the Review of Serious Incidents Including Deaths of Children in Care* (online), Dublin, Health Information and Quality Authority. Available from: www.hiqa.ie/news_releases/100310 _Guidance_for_Review_of_Serious_Incidents.asp (accessed 9 June 2010).

Health Service Executive (2009) *Review of Adequacy of Child and Family Services 2007* (online), Dublin, Health Service Executive. Available from:www.hse.ie/eng/services/Publications/services/Children /famsupportpub.html (accessed 8 January 2010).

Health Service Executive (2010) *Young Person 'A' Child in Care Death Report* (online), Dublin, Health Service Executive. Available from: www.hse.ie/eng/services/Publications/services/Children/deathsinca re.html (accessed: 9 June 2010).

House of Commons Health Committee (2003) *The Victoria Climbié Inquiry Report. Sixth Report of Session 2002–03*, London, The Stationery Office.

Irish Association of Non-Government Development Organisations (DOCHAS) (2010) *Make Poverty History Irish Campaign* (online). Available from: http://makepovertyhistory.ie (accessed 24 March 2010).

Irish Association of Social Workers (2009) *About Us* (online). Available from: www.iasw.ie/index.php/about-us (accessed 24 March 2010).

Lord Laming (2003) *The Victoria Climbié Inquiry*, London, The Stationery Office.

McDonagh, M. (2009) 'Mother jailed for seven years for incest and abuse', *The Irish Times* (22 January).

O'Brien, C. (2008) 'Life and a death on the street', *The Irish Times* (18 October).

O'Brien, C. (2010) 'Child deaths while in care or contact with services now at 188', *The Irish Times* (5 June).

Office of the Minister for Children and Youth Affairs (2009) *Report of the Commission to Inquire into Child Abuse, 2009. Implementation Plan*, Dublin, Department of Health and Children.

Office of the Minister for Children and Youth Affairs (2010) *Welcome to the Office of the Minister for Children and Youth Affairs* (online). Available from: www.omc.gov.ie (accessed: 24 March 2010). Ryan, S. (2009) *Commission to Inquire into Child Abuse Report (Volumes I–V)*, Dublin, The Stationery Office.

Ryan, S. (2009) *The Commission to Inquire into Child Abuse* (online), Dublin, The Stationery Office. Available from: www.childabusecommission.ie (accessed 1 April 2010).

Taylor, C. (2010) 'HSE admits to data collection flaws', *The Irish Times* (24 May).

9

Two countries, one border: The challenges and opportunities for protecting children on an all island basis – a critical turning point

John Devaney and Colin Reid

There is a strong tradition within social work research of comparative analysis (for example, Duffy and Collins, 2010). And yet, in spite of the shared history and close proximity, very little has been written about how children are protected from abuse and neglect across the whole of the island of Ireland. 'No man [or woman] is an island' perhaps sums up in one metaphor the rationale for looking at child protection within an all-Ireland context while also recognising the challenges to be faced in ensuring that children on both sides of the Irish border are protected. As we move to a new stable era of political cooperation, it is clear that there are, and will remain, pressing grounds for active cooperation on this issue. The safeguarding of children has recently become an agenda item on the working of the North/South Ministerial Council (2006) and its sectoral groups, one of the features of the Belfast Agreement and the Northern Ireland Act 1998. As stated by the Deputy First Minister in September 2009 in his report to the Assembly of the North/South Ministerial meeting of 6 July 2009, 'Co-operation on child protection among agencies and jurisdictions is vital' (Northern Ireland Assembly, 2009).

In both countries the relationship between the State and the family has evolved in separate ways since the Anglo-Irish Treaty of 1921, which resulted in the partition of Ireland. This has been shaped by broader social and economic drivers but has, essentially, seen welfare services which are largely provided by the State in Northern Ireland draw heavily on the broader United Kingdom experience (and, because of direct rule, those of England in particular) (Pinkerton and

Campbell, 2002), while in the Republic of Ireland, a broader European influence can be seen with a more diverse range of providers of services, including a larger role for the non-governmental sector (O'Sullivan, 2001). There is also a belief that the child protection system in the United Kingdom is overly bureaucratised compared to the systems in other European countries, and that this does not necessarily work in children's best interests (Munro, 2004).

However, throughout developed nations, there is a striking similarity in the issues facing modern child welfare systems (Spratt and Devaney, 2009). This relates to the balance to be struck between the provision of support to children and families in times of need compared to the decisions which must be made when it is clear that parents are unable, or unwilling, to provide the standard of care and protection that their child needs (Buckley, 2003). As the tragic deaths in 2007 of the McGovern/McElhill family in Omagh (Toner, 2008) and the Dunne family in Wexford highlight (Brosnan, 2009), there are striking similarities about how professionals need to work together to protect children while also supporting their parents, irrespective of legal jurisdiction.

Any practitioner working in a border county, whether in Ireland or elsewhere, will also know and understand that the border plays an issue in some child care cases in some ways. Families can live on both sides of the border, people work and socialise across it and families move from one jurisdiction to the other. Yet the policy and legislative context for child protection differ substantially between the framework established by The Children (Northern Ireland) Order 1995, and the Child Care Act 1991 and Children Act 2001 in the Irish Republic, and for many years professional practice and social policy have evolved independently in each country.

In this chapter the authors examine, largely from a 'northern' perspective, some of the north–south challenges that exist for the next part of our journey in developing a shared approach to the protection of children from abuse and neglect on the island of Ireland. The authors seek to explore the issues in depth by using the example of sex offenders and public protection, and with particular reference to vetting and barring arrangements, to set out the challenges and the opportunities in addressing the issue of child protection within this transnational paradigm.

Sex offenders and public protection

It is perhaps worthwhile reminding ourselves of why the example of sex offenders is emblematic of the need for political as well as professional action in relation to cross-border cooperation on child protection on the island of Ireland. In February 1990, a young woman revealed to a social worker in Belfast that she had been sexually abused as a child on numerous occasions by a Roman Catholic priest called Father Brendan Smyth (see Moore, 1995). The disclosure marked the beginning of the end of Smyth's offending as a child abuser, while also bringing about the fall of an Irish government and the beginning of a sea change in public perceptions and professional responses in the way sex offenders were dealt with on both sides of the Irish border (McKay, 2009).

The social worker informed the police of the allegations in line with the procedural requirements in place at the time. The police interviewed Smyth in 1991, and he subsequently admitted to the sexual abuse of a number of children. He was charged and released on bail, but promptly returned to his abbey in County Cavan across the border and resumed work as a chaplain. In spite of numerous letters and phone calls requesting his return to Belfast for trial, Smyth, his abbot and others in the Catholic hierarchy failed to respond, and in 1993 the police delivered warrants for his extradition to the offices of the Attorney General in Dublin. There they remained unprocessed for seven months, a matter which, when it emerged, led the Labour Party to withdraw from its coalition with Fianna Fáil and bring about the collapse of the Irish government in November 1994. Smyth eventually returned to Belfast voluntarily, pleaded guilty to 17 specimen charges of abusing boys and girls dating back to the 1960s, and was sent to prison for four years.

The publicity surrounding the arrest and prosecution of Smyth resulted in more of his victims coming forward. It subsequently emerged that he had been abusing children since the 1950s, and that his superiors had been aware back in 1945 that he had what they euphemistically called 'a problem with children' (Kerrigan and Brennan, 1999, p. 267). He had abused children in Ireland, both North and South, Scotland, Wales and the United States. It transpired that the Catholic authorities had received many complaints from distressed parents and victims. The response of the church hierarchy was to move Smyth around, sending him from parish to parish, country to country, never revealing the reason, and often with breathtaking irresponsibility – for example, as noted by McKay (2009),

Smyth was sent to several children's hospitals as a chaplain. As Moore (1995, p. 16) states, 'in blunt terms, instead of caring for the abused, they [the Catholic hierarchy] chose to shelter this criminal'.

On his release from Magilligan in 1997, Smyth was tried in Dublin on 74 charges of child abuse committed between 1958 and 1993. Sentencing him to 12 years in jail, the trial judge said he had 'no doubt but that Smyth was still a risk to children' (McKay, 2009, p. 69). Smyth's lawyers said he had 'made his peace with God'. He died a month later. It later became apparent that the totally inappropriate and irresponsible reaction by the church authorities to allegations and disclosures of child abuse manifest in the Smyth case was widespread, with the Catholic church seeking to avoid bad publicity at all costs by dealing with these matters internally, rather than involving the appropriate police and social services (Ryan, 2009).

Professional practice and the policy framework for working with sex offenders in Northern Ireland have tended to track developments in the rest of the United Kingdom around public protection arrangements. This has focused on multi-agency assessment and management of risk, underpinned by a raft of legislation and policy (McAlinden, 2007; Public Protection Arrangements Northern Ireland, 2009a). This has been driven by the overlapping trinity of media reporting, public opprobrium and professional concern about how to deal with what is often seen as an intractable problem. For example, in 2003, Mrs Attracta Harron was returning to her home in Co. Tyrone from mass in Co. Donegal when she was abducted and murdered by Trevor Hamilton, who had previous convictions for sexual assault and was subject, at the time, to multi-agency public protection monitoring. This case sparked intense media and public scrutiny of the processes in place in Northern Ireland for the monitoring and management of those convicted of serious sexual offences (Criminal Justice Inspection Northern Ireland, 2007). This engendered a sense of a moral panic (Cohen, 2002) that professionals were complacent or impotent in stopping sexual offenders committing further offences. In some ways the recent report from the *Commission to Inquire into Child Abuse* (Ryan, 2009) has similarly heightened public interest in, and reaction to, the systems for assessing and monitoring those who are known to pose a risk of sexual harm to others across the island of Ireland.

Assessing and monitoring adults who pose a risk to others

Notification arrangements for sex offenders (known as sex offender registration) in England, Wales and Northern Ireland were first introduced by the Sex Offenders Act 1997, which brought with it the development of formal multi-agency management arrangements. Following the introduction of the Sexual Offences Act 2003 arrangements were placed on a statutory basis and strengthened by the inclusion of violent offenders in the risk monitoring and management arrangements. New notification timescales and a range of civil orders such as Sex Offender Prevention Orders and Risk of Sexual Harm Orders were introduced, which could be used to restrict and prohibit the activities of individuals who were thought to pose a risk to others. In Northern Ireland, Public Protection Arrangements (PPANI) were relaunched in June 2008 and placed on a statutory footing by the Criminal Justice (NI) Order 2008, allowing the Secretary of State to issue statutory guidance on information sharing and cooperation to a range of named bodies and government departments. Given developments in England and Wales around new provisions for the risk management of violent offenders (Violent Offender Orders) it is likely that the Northern Ireland arrangements will be strengthened further with these provisions and will certainly evolve further, for example, to deal with domestic violence on a multi-agency basis within the structure of PPANI.

The corresponding legislation in the Republic of Ireland, The Sexual Offenders Act 2001, includes a provision that anyone convicted outside of the jurisdiction of a sexual offence is subject to a requirement that they must notify An Garda Síochána of their conviction within seven days of arriving in Ireland. The onus to notify prospective employers about the conviction when applying to do work, that consists mainly of the offender having unsupervised access, or contact, with a child or children, or a mentally impaired person, lies with the offender. If they fail to notify an employer the offender could be fined up to €12,697 or sentenced up to five years in prison, or both. At present, it is unknown what proportion of the individuals with a conviction for sexual offending comply with any of these requirements.

And yet, despite this, as evidenced by cases such as George Finlay, John Murrell and Paul Hunter Redpath, individuals who have been convicted of serious sexual offences against children feel able to cross borders to live in the Republic of Ireland in an attempt to escape the more onerous monitoring requirements in the United Kingdom. This places local communities, families and individuals in an invidious position. It is not the purpose of this chapter to make a detailed comparison between both sets of legal provisions; needless to say there are differences in their workings, for example, regarding notification and risk assessment (see Public Protection Arrangements Northern Ireland, 2009b and Public Service Information, 2007). However, these legal and policy provisions, we would argue, are systemically flawed if the north–south dimension is left unaddressed, although there are some initial signs that progress in this area has begun. The cross-border implications have been recognised by both governments and we have slowly seen the development of more convergent policy in this area. Initiatives have included:

- a memorandum of understanding signed in 2006 between the UK and Irish governments on sex offender information exchange in respect to those travelling from one country to the other (Department of Justice, Equality and Law Reform, 2006);
- the signing of an agreement between the Police Service of Northern Ireland and An Garda Síochána in 2008 on the sharing of personal data in relation to the investigation of sexual offences and the monitoring of sex offenders (Northern Ireland Affairs Committee, 2009);
- arrangements for the sharing of information on sex offenders between respective probation services (Department of Justice, Equality and Law Reform, 2009); and
- planned adoption of the Harris dynamic risk assessment model on an all island basis (Department of Justice, Equality and Law Reform, 2009).

Perhaps one of the most important aspects of harmonisation of the cross-border arrangements relates to the proposed assessment and risk management arrangements for convicted offenders in the Republic of Ireland which, when implemented by the government, should help to bring arrangements more closely into line with those in Northern Ireland.

At present, one of the chief differences is that risk management is largely court directed in the Republic of Ireland, while in Northern Ireland all sex offenders are subject to a static and dynamic risk assessment process and, for offenders with a more serious history of offending, a multi-agency risk management plan (Public Protection Arrangements Northern Ireland, undated). Importantly, this includes those on non-custodial sentences and, on occasions, those who have not been convicted by the courts but who are still deemed to be 'potentially dangerous persons', as a result of their behaviour.

There are, and will remain, differences in cross-border legislation and practice relating to public protection arrangements. But as Northern Ireland policy develops, such as with Violent Offender Orders and in the extension of risk assessment and management to new areas, these differences will be accentuated. One of the challenges, irrespective of underlining legislation, is to ensure that professionals speak a common language, understand collectively what is meant by risk and have largely similar tools to manage those who pose a risk. While it is encouraging to note the Deputy First Minister's recent statement to the Northern Ireland Assembly that:

> Cross-border discussions are continuing on the management of sex offenders. Both jurisdictions now use common assessment standards when dealing with sex offenders, and work is ongoing to bring legislation in both jurisdictions into line as much as possible. (Northern Ireland Assembly, 2009)

– it would be very helpful for the Northern Ireland Department of Justice and the government in the Republic of Ireland to map out current differences in legislation and see, where possible and feasible, that practice and policy can be harmonised. This does not entail identical legislation. While this is potentially helpful, what is needed is operational guidance, clear protocols on information exchange and a common culture of cooperation.

Vetting and barring

We now deal briefly with an associated area. The systems on both sides of the border to vet and bar those unsuitable to work with children are very different and have developed in different ways. In Northern Ireland a voluntary arrangement was developed to check the suitability of those who sought to work with children and to prohibit those who had harmed children previously. This was developed through the voluntary and procedural-led development of the Pre-employment Consultancy Service in the 1990s; a service which was given added impetuous by the inquiry in 1994 into the activities of Martin Huston, who moved between voluntary organisations in an unpaid capacity to gain access to children he subsequently sexually abused (Department of Health and Social Services, 1993). Arrangements were given statutory force by the provisions in the Protection of Children and Vulnerable Adults (Northern Ireland) Order 2003 (referred to as

POCVA) in parallel with arrangements in other parts of the United Kingdom.

The Order, *inter alia*, established statutory requirements for child care organisations to carry out vetting for those seeking either paid or unpaid employment, and reporting of those dismissed for harming children. This allowed the Department of Health, Social Services and Public Safety to establish the Disqualified from Working with Children List. POCVA also enabled the Department of Education to create the Unsuitable Persons List, which was initially intended for teachers and those who worked in ancillary positions in school, but was extended in 2007 to anyone with certain specified criminal convictions which, as a consequence, brought about listing as unsuitable to work with children. Inclusion on either list barred a person from seeking work in regulated activity (in essence, work with children) in the United Kingdom.

The Northern Ireland arrangements were strengthened further with the enablement of Part V of the Police Act 1997 (Northern Ireland was the last part of the United Kingdom to bring in this legislation in 2008) allowing the Northern Ireland Office to establish Access NI, a government agency responsible for providing criminal records information to prospective employers, and bring in enhanced disclosure certificates. This gives the police a statutory power to disclose criminal record information to employers and, importantly and highly significantly, relevant 'non-conviction' data, such as police investigations that did not meet the threshold for a criminal prosecution. This is an area that has been debated in the Republic of Ireland and is currently subject to legislative consideration (Houses of the Oireachtas, 2008), with the incoming coalition government in the Republic indicating in the Programme of Government their intention to legislate for the provision of soft information (Fine Gael, 2011, p. 26).

Probably because of some of the developments in Northern Ireland, and with an ongoing campaign by the Irish Society for the Prevention of Cruelty to Children (ISPCC), pressure has mounted on the Irish Republic's government to do something about criminal record information and its sharing. Up to this point it had been custom and practice only to do checks for the (then) Health Board (now Health Service Executive) posts and funded posts that involved work with children, effectively freezing out non-statutory posts and those undertaking voluntary work with children. The government established a working group and formed a vetting unit within An Garda Síochána leading to a more consistent application of criminal record checks.

However, the Republic of Ireland does not have the equivalences of the barred lists established in the United Kingdom and operating across the border in Northern Ireland, although the Joint Committee on the Constitutional Amendment on Children in the Republic of Ireland has been considering some of the developments across the border (Houses of the Oireachtas, 2008). The new Irish government is subsequently proposing a constitutional amendment on children's rights, which may remove some of the legal difficulties to creating such a structure.

While we could focus on some of the differences of the current schemes, it is with future developments that we may see much more profound differences on a North–South basis. Following the Soham murders and subsequent inquiry (Bichard, 2004), the government in the United Kingdom enacted the Safeguarding Vulnerable Groups Act 2006 and subsequent equivalent Northern Ireland Order.[1] The legislation established the Independent Safeguarding Authority (ISA) to take discretionary barring decisions for England, Wales and Northern Ireland. This has extended regulation into many more posts and spheres of activity with children. The implications for sporting and faith-based groups is particularly important to note, as from 12 October 2009 there has been a new requirement on voluntary and community bodies with posts that involve work with children to refer to the ISA individuals who are suspected of harming or posing a risk to children.

Faith and sporting groups operating across the border in Ireland will need to be aware of this legislation and there will be some complications, in particular for Ulster county activities which straddle the border. Likewise, for faith groups and congregations operating on both sides of the border they will need to be mindful of the requirements of the new arrangements. For example, someone who is a Sunday school teacher in Fermanagh living in Leitrim, will normally have to undergo a vetting check before working in regulated activity with children. In contrast, in the Republic of Ireland they will not have to undergo any criminal record checking at all.

The position of a non-United Kingdom national being subject to vetting and barring arrangements (as amended by the Protection of Freedom Bill announced on 11 February 2011) was raised at an early stage during the passage of the Safeguarding Vulnerable Groups Act 2006 and it is recognised by government that this is a challenge and one of the developmental elements of the arrangements. But it is in Northern Ireland where it has most practical implication with staff working there but domiciled in the Republic of Ireland. In these circumstances it will be necessary to develop protocols for the cross-border sharing of relevant information to facilitate the working of the arrangements, and in particular the continuous updating of enhanced criminal record disclosures and barring referrals. This includes information which would fall short of convictions but would, as in the United Kingdom, be used to make discretionary barring decisions on the grounds of behaviour or risk.

Work has started under the auspices of the North/South Ministerial Council on this issue (Office of the First Minister and Deputy First Minister, 2009). But the vetting and barring arrangements also have implications for the Republic of Ireland in the other direction and that relates to the movement of individuals barred from working with children in the United Kingdom to the Republic of Ireland, where there is no such bar. This is not a theoretical risk and work needs to be done between the Independent Safeguarding Authority in Northern Ireland and the government in the Republic of Ireland on how information might be shared relating to those who are barred in the one jurisdiction but may seek work in the other. Given the many links between the United Kingdom and the Republic of Ireland, the ideal situation is for our vetting and barring systems to be largely similar, and where this is not possible, to ensure that bars are reciprocal, and recognised and clear protocols are in place for information sharing. At the time of writing, it is positive to note that the government in the Republic of Ireland is looking carefully at the possible legislative options. In September 2008 the Joint Committee on the Constitutional Amendment on Children issued an interim report (Houses of the Oireachtas, 2008, p. 4), which recommended the establishment of a statutory scheme:

- for the vetting of all persons involved in working in any capacity with children;
- for the statutory regulation of the manner in which information in relation to records of criminal prosecutions, criminal convictions and 'soft' information may be collated, exchanged and deployed by An Garda Síochána or other Statutory Agencies for the purpose of ensuring the highest standards of child protection within the State; and
- to require that all agencies, organisations, bodies, clubs, educational and childcare establishments and groups working with or involved with children ensure that all of those working under their aegis either in a paid or voluntary capacity with children are subject to vetting.

Whatever the direction of travel on this issue, the government in the Republic will want to consider the cross-border interfaces that undoubtedly exist in the design of any new arrangements.

Conclusion

It was Stanley Cohen who coined the term 'moral panics' in *Folk Devils and Moral Panics* (2002). He defined the concept as a sporadic episode which, as it occurs, subjects society to bouts of worry about the values and principles that society upholds, which may be in jeopardy. He describes its characteristics as a condition, episode, person or group of persons who become defined as a threat to societal values and interests (Cohen, 2002). Cohen goes on to discuss the way in which the mass media fashions these episodes, or stylises them, amplifying the nature of the facts and consequently turning them into a national issue, when the matter could have been contained on a local level.

It could be argued that by introducing the issue of sex offenders and vetting into this discussion about child protection on the island of Ireland we may have contributed to such a reaction. We firmly believe that much good work is done at a local level by practitioners working with families who are vulnerable or in crisis on both sides of the border – our own practice experience and professional contacts confirm this. However, that does not mean that the system itself should be excused scrutiny. As highlighted earlier in this chapter, both challenges and opportunities lie ahead for us all.

In this context there is a place for comparative work that draws on both the common and unique responses to issues that affect our understanding of children's lives, and the interventions that are required. This would allow both jurisdictions to respond to what is distinctive within each country, while also realising that there is much that is similar.

As a professional community we must ensure that the wider system for supporting families and protecting children from harm is as robust as possible. What we have hoped to do is to argue that professional practice must be supported by robust processes and systems and that, in turn, professionals must be open to thinking beyond the limits of their own role, the boundaries of their own organisation and the borders of their own country.

Note

1   Further changes to vetting and barring have been announced by the UK Government and will appear in the Protection of Freedoms Bill which is currently going through the Westminster Parliament.

References

Bichard, M. (2004) *The Bichard Inquiry Report HC653*, London, The Stationery Office.

Brosnan, K. (2009) *Monageer Inquiry*, Dublin, Office of the Minister for Children.

Buckley, H. (2003) *Child Protection Work: Beyond the Rhetoric*, London, Jessica Kingsley Publishers.

Cohen, S. (2002) *Folk Devils and Moral Panics* (3rd edn), Abingdon, Routledge.

Criminal Justice Inspection Northern Ireland (2007) *The Management of Sex Offenders – A Follow-up Inspection* (online), Belfast, Criminal Justice Inspection Northern Ireland. Available from: www.cjini.org/CJNI /files/67/67eca591–a625–4da9–8eb0–280b8dd8c97c.pdf (accessed 5 January 2010).

Department of Health and Social Services (1993) *An Abuse of Trust*, Belfast, Department of Health and Social Services.

Department of Justice, Equality and Law Reform (2006) *New Memorandum of Understanding Signed Regarding Sex Offenders* (online). Available from: www.inis.gov.ie/en/JELR/Pages/PR07000339 (accessed 21 March 2010).

Department of Justice, Equality and Law Reform (2009) *The Management of Sex Offenders – A Discussion Document*, Dublin, Department of Justice, Equality and Law Reform.

Duffy, J. and Collins, M. E. (2010) 'Macro impacts on caseworker decision-making in child welfare: A cross-national comparison', *European Journal of Social Work*, 13(1), pp. 35–54.

Fine Gael (2011) *The Programme for Government between Fine Gael and Labour*. Available at: www.finegael2011.com/viewissues.asp

Houses of the Oireachtas (2008) *Joint Committee on the Constitutional Amendment on Children (First Report) – Interim Report Twenty-Eighth Amendment of the Constitution Bill 2007*, Dublin, The Stationery Office.

Kerrigan, G. and Brennan, P. (1999) *This Great Little Nation: The A–Z of Irish Scandals and Controversies*, Dublin, Gill & Macmillan.

McAlinden, A. (2007) *The Shaming of Sexual Offenders: Risk, Retribution and Reintegration*, Oxford, Hart Publishing.

McKay, S. (2009) 'Dealing with cross border sex offenders: Learning from the North's multi-agency approach', *Journal of Cross Border Studies in*

Ireland, 4, pp. 67–78.

Moore, C. (1995) *Betrayal of Trust: The Father Brendan Smyth Affair and the Catholic Church*, Dublin, Marino Books.

Munro, E. (2004) 'The impact of audit on social work practice', *British Journal of Social Work*, 34, pp. 1075–1095.

Northern Ireland Affairs Committee (2009) *Cross Border Co-operation Between the Governments of the United Kingdom and the Republic of Ireland HC78*, London, House of Commons.

Northern Ireland Assembly (2009) *Record of Proceedings 14th September 2009* (online). Available from: www.niassembly.gov.uk/record/reports2009 /090914.htm#7 (accessed 5 January 2010).

North/South Ministerial Council (2006) *Welcome to the North South Ministerial Council* (online). Available from: www .northsouthministerialcouncil.org/ (accessed 2 March 2010).

Office of the First Minister and Deputy First Minister (2009) *Safeguarding Children – A Cross-Departmental Statement on the Protection of Children and Young People*, Belfast, Office of the First Minister and Deputy First Minister.

O'Sullivan, E. (2001) '"Mercy unto thousands" – constructing the institutional child', in Cleary, A., Nic Ghiolla, M. and Quin, S. (eds), *Understanding Children: Volume 1 – State, Education and Economy*, Cork, Oak Tree Press.

Pinkerton, J. and Campbell, J. (2002) 'Social work and social justice in Northern Ireland: Towards a new occupational space', *British Journal of Social Work*, 32, pp. 723–737.

Public Protection Arrangements Northern Ireland (2009a) *The First Six Months – October 2008 – March 2009* (online), Carrickfergus, Public Protection Arrangements Northern Ireland. Available from: www.publicprotectionni.com/ (accessed 5 January 2010).

Public Protection Arrangements Northern Ireland (2009b) *Managing the Risks Posed by Those Who Have Committed Sexual and/or Violent Offences*, Carrickfergus, Public Protection Arrangements Northern Ireland.

Public Service Information (2007) *Monitoring Sex Offenders in Ireland* (online). Available from: www.citizensinformation.ie/categories /justice/law_enforcement/monitoring-sex-offenders-in-ireland (accessed 21 March 2010).

Ryan, S. (2009) *Commission to Inquire into Child Abuse Report (Volumes I–V)*, Dublin, The Stationery Office.

Spratt, T. and Devaney, J. (2009) 'Identifying families with multiple problems: Perspectives of practitioners and managers in three nations', *British Journal of Social Work*, 39, pp. 418–434.

Toner, H. (2008) *Independent Review Report of Agency Involvement with Mr Arthur McElhill, Ms Lorraine McGovern and their Children*, Belfast, Department of Health, Social Services and Public Safety.

10

Why child protection is so difficult

Harry Ferguson

The critical issue in child protection and welfare that I want to address in this chapter is: why is child protection so difficult? Why is it that professionals struggle and sometimes fail to keep children who are known to be at risk safe? What might make the work easier, or at least more effective, so that abused children can be well protected? These are of course very big questions and I want to try and answer them by exploring three themes: how child protection is never (and can never be), simple, and the fallacy of media representations and policy statements which suggest that it is not difficult; the complex relationships that so often exist between professionals and families in high-risk cases and what we are learning about how parental resistance and deception makes child protection so difficult; and the nature of welfare organisations and the extent to which they provide the support and conditions for workers to practice confidently and safely.

Child protection is never simple

To say that child protection is difficult is not as obvious as it first sounds. Certainly, the impression given by the much of the media is that it is not hard, that the key problem is with bungling social workers and other professionals who failed to see the obvious. This can be seen in the media response to the death of 'Baby Peter' when the case hit the headlines in England in late 2008. He died aged 17 months, with over 50 injuries on his body. He had been placed on the child protection register 7 months before he died, when he was 9 months old, because of confirmed physical abuse and neglect. One of his older siblings was on the register for neglect. Serious consideration had been given to taking the children into care, and frequent announced and unannounced visits were made by the social worker. The police had some involvement and a health visitor and family support service were also involved, visiting the family at home. The family had some

60 contacts with social work, health staff, and police during Peter's short life (Haringey, 2009). On one of the many front pages that it devoted to the case and extreme criticism of social workers, the *Sun* newspaper wrote (21 September 2009): 'Maria Ward became Baby P's social worker six months before he died, when he was already being tortured. She repeatedly failed to spot the abuse and lies told by the child's mum.'

While a series of media outlets were scathing in their criticism of social workers, The *Sun* was the most vicious, to the extent of organising a petition to have the social work staff who worked with, and managed the case, sacked. It gained an astonishing 1.4 million signatures and the social work staff were eventually sacked. The Director of Children's Services for Haringey, Sharon Shoesmith, was sacked by the Labour government minister responsible, Ed Balls, who referred righteously to the *Sun* campaign when announcing publicly that he had ordered her sacking. The impact of this vilification on Sharon Shoesmith's life has been extreme in that she became a public hate figure, received death threats and her career and livelihood appear to be ruined.

While the *Sun*'s tactics are indefensible, in some respects the incredulity of this kind of commentary is understandable. For how do we as professionals satisfactorily explain to one another, never mind the public, how children can be missed like this when so much contact is being made with them? A striking example of how professionals can oversimplify the nature of child protection is seen in the highly influential inquiry report into the death of Victoria Climbié. Victoria died with 128 separate injuries to her body after suffering months of torture and abuse by her great-aunt Marie Therese Kouao and Kouao's lover, Carl Manning, who are serving life sentences for her murder. She was brought to London by Kouao from the Ivory Coast less than a year before she died. Her parents hoped this would give her the opportunity of a better education and life, yet Kouao never enrolled Victoria in a school. Victoria was starved, beaten and left in a freezing bathroom, trussed up in a bin bag, lying in a bath with her own urine and faeces. A public inquiry into the circumstances which lead to Victoria's death, chaired by Lord Herbert Laming and published in January 2003, argues that a massive system failure occurred, and that there were an estimated 12 bungled occasions when Victoria could have been protected (Laming, 2003).

The Laming report undoubtedly explains a lot as the source of the failures to protect Victoria are put down to a combination of events and woefully incompetent practices. Evidence of profound organisational malaise and an absence of leadership was exemplified by senior managers' apparent indifference to children's services, which were underfunded and neglected. Local child protection procedures were long out of date and this was compounded by major staffing problems and low morale among staff who were invariably overworked and 'burning out'. Front-line workers got little support or quality supervision and were uncertain about their role in child protection. Extremely poor administrative systems existed for tracking referrals and case information. Inter-agency communication was poor or non-existent and there was a consistent failure to engage with the child in any meaningful way as a service user or to assess the child's needs. The focus throughout was on Kouao, Victoria's carer, as the client in the case (Laming, 2003).

Much of this is already familiar from the many other high-profile inquiry cases and child death reviews (Reder *et al.*, 1993; Brandon *et al.*, 2008). What is distinctive about Victoria's case is that she was not a child who was hidden away. She was actually admitted to hospital on two separate occasions with suspicious injuries, on one of which she was diagnosed by a consultant paediatrician as having scabies. While the inquiry adjudged this to have been an accurate diagnosis, the opinions of other doctors who suspected non-accidental injury were not given the same prominence as the scabies, especially by social services. Injuries were also misinterpreted as marks from where Victoria scratched the infected area. Some staff wrongly attributed these marks to being 'normal' for a child brought up in African culture, an assumption that was racist.

Despite casting its net wide in terms of examining key issues and events, the Laming report ultimately exemplifies the limitations of such texts in how the primary emphasis, in seeking to improve child protection, is in need of better management and accountability. The underlying premise on which the recommendations for change are based is naive in the extreme, as one of the central messages of the report is that the way forward is in 'doing the simple things properly' (Laming, 2003, p. 105), and 'Doing the basic things well saves lives' (p. 69). What the report is alluding to are so-called 'simple' tasks, such as speaking to other professionals about concerns, writing up case notes, reading faxes, files, or even reading the child protection guidelines, never mind following them, engaging with the child and challenging her suspected abusers, and doing home visits – none of which were done.

But why is it that the so-called simple things are, so often, not simple? Why are the basic things not done well? A consistent finding of all such child death inquiry reports is that seemingly straightforward tasks, just did not get done. Nothing is simple. This requires us to in many ways explain the unexplainable and to focus on the neglected psychological and emotional features of child protection work, as well as the kinds of organisations professionals work in. Time and time again, we see in such cases well-intentioned, often very experienced professionals from all disciplines who simply cannot explain their inaction in the face of evidence of marks and injuries. In Victoria's case there were grounds for clear suspicions of non-accidental injury, and on one occasion, sexual abuse. Things do not appear to be much simpler than writing up an observation in case notes. Yet during one of Victoria's stays in hospital in July 1999, for instance, Laming (2003, p. 272) writes that:

> Numerous witnesses from the hospital came before me and gave disturbing accounts of the injuries they saw on Victoria's body. I heard a variety of nurses say that they thought Victoria had been bitten, branded and beaten with a belt buckle.

On one occasion, as many as five nurses observed Victoria's injuries while she was taking a bath. On another, a Nurse Pereira who was bathing Victoria was so disturbed by what she saw that she called in Nurse Quinn to observe the marks, 'which she thought may have been caused by a buckle belt. She also noticed that Victoria's arm was bruised and swollen' (p. 266). Laming concludes from this:

> I have found it very difficult to understand why important observations of this nature were not recorded in the notes. Both Nurse Pereira and Nurse Quinn were aware that Victoria was a child about whom there were child protection concerns, and Nurse Pereira had seen fit the previous evening to make a note in the critical incident log concerning the master–servant relationship between Kouao and Victoria. Nurse Pereira was frank enough to accept that she should have made a note of her observation that night. Nurse Quinn simply told me that she could not account for why she chose not to do so. (Laming, 2003, p. 266)

Similar examples could be given for social workers, the police and housing officials. So why is it so difficult to identify and act on apparently clear signs of child abuse?

Resistance to child protection and manipulation of professionals

Child protection work is difficult because it is surrounded so much by secrecy and deception, because those who abuse children have a vested interest in keeping it hidden. Parents and other abusive carers resist detection, sometimes in a violent and intimidating manner (Littlechild, 2005). Practitioners face huge challenges in gaining access to children whose parents and other carers resist professionals getting to know about them. In one study I found that 34 per cent of all cases reported and worked with by social workers were defined by them as involving families who did not want a service – 'involuntary clients' (Ferguson and O'Reilly, 2001). Only a proportion of those were actually intimidating or violent, but ambivalence towards child protection professionals was rife. Such resistance is also evident in high proportions of cases of child death and significant harm (Brandon *et al.*, 2008).

The difficulties involved here apply wherever the children and family are seen, whether it is in the school, family centre, mental health service, social work office, or hospital. However, dealing with resistance, hostility and deception is especially difficult on home visits (Ferguson, 2009). The serious case review into the Baby Peter case provides a vivid example of this.

> On 30 July 2007 all the children were seen on a planned home visit by the social worker on their own and with Ms A. Peter was in the buggy, alert and smiling but overtired. His ear was sore and slightly inflamed. He had white cream on the top of his head and Ms A. thought the infection had improved. Peter's face was smeared with chocolate and the social worker asked that it be cleaned off. The family friend took him away to do so and he did not reappear before the social worker left. Ms A. said she had a GP appointment and mentioned grab marks on Peter. She was worried about being accused of harming him. (Haringey, 2009, p. 13)

In some respects, the practice here came close to being acceptable. The social worker saw the two older children on their own, which was good. However, the fact that she saw them in the home while their mother, the suspected abuser, was in the vicinity was not good, because of what we know about how difficult it is for children to feel safe enough to speak the truth about their lives in such circumstances (Jones, 2003). The social worker saw Peter too – from a distance at least – and was presumably concerned enough to want to see more of him, so asked for his face to be cleaned. She did not however follow it through when the family friend did not bring Peter back. The poignancy of this scene is all the greater given that three days later Peter was dead. This was the last time the social worker saw him alive. At the time of his death he had over 50 injuries on his body, including a broken back; and a tooth was found in his stomach, which is assumed to have been knocked out by a blow.

In the last two days of his life, that is, after the social worker's home visit, a paediatrician saw Peter but did not examine him for injuries. His GP also saw him a day or so before he died and described him as being in 'a sorry state', but he did not examine him either. Peter had an infected scalp which is why he had the white cream on his head when the social worker visited. His childminder who had been given a key role in the child protection plan, had refused to look after him any longer owing to the infection. It is now also known that the chocolate was deliberately plastered on to Peter's face to conceal some of his most visible injuries. Unless professionals touch children, either in the case of medical and health practitioners to examine them for injuries, or to ensure that substances like chocolate and dirt are removed from areas of the body that are visible, hidden injuries will not be discovered. A vitally important – but too often ignored reason why child protection is difficult – is because professionals are afraid to touch children, either because they fear allegations of inappropriate behaviour (Piper and Stronach, 2008) or because they fear contamination by diseased children.

It is now known that Peter's mother Tracey Connelly had a cohabitee whose brother was also resident in the home, and these men were abusing and torturing Peter, but Tracey Connelly hid their presence in the home from professionals. She also told social workers that Peter's biological father had hit Peter in the past and social workers did not assess him as a potential carer for Peter, when, by all accounts, he may have had something positive to offer. Research has shown that this tendency for professionals to take the mother's account of the father as the truth of the matter without directly engaging with the father himself is a common reason why men are not worked with (Ferguson and Hogan, 2004). Other than in cases of known danger to workers, fathers should always be directly assessed.

It would have taken real skill, knowledge, insight and courage for a social worker to have seen through all this deception and acted to protect Peter. To have insisted on the child being brought back, and his face being seen clean, required authority and a capacity to negotiate with the mother to achieve this; and ultimately, if necessary, to insist on having him removed. For social workers and other professionals to inquire more deeply into the presence of men in the home requires them to check if there are signs of men in the bedrooms and bathroom. We know little of a systematic nature in terms of evidence from research about whether social workers make such checks and inspect homes, and this shows how much face-to-face practice has been neglected in research studies (Forrester *et al.*, 2008; Hall and Slembrouch, 2009). What can be said is that requesting to look around the home like this, and enter people's most intimate spaces is very difficult, partly because a deeply ingrained respect for people's privacy is in us all.

Yet cases such as this reveal the pressing need for agencies to find ways for such actions to be performed, irrespective of how difficult they are. Little attention has been given in the literature of social work or child protection to the ethical dilemmas involved in performing these practices and no direction on how it can be done, and this needs to change (Ferguson, 2010). The ethical imperative of social work continues to be defined in terms of the importance of respecting service user's rights and working in partnership with them. Thus Peter's mother Tracey Connelly was clearly shown a lot of compassion. She had suffered abuse in her own childhood, but those effects were not adequately taken into account in the attachment and relationship problems she had with her children, and with social workers in the way she mistrusted, manipulated and deceived them. Showing compassion and adopting an ethic of care based on partnership is all very well when the circumstances allow, but the lack of a knowledge base and access to professional wisdom about the nitty-gritty of how authoritative work can be done undoubtedly makes child protection more difficult than it needs to be.

The same can be said about the need to reach better understandings of the kinds of relationships that go on between service users and social workers and which can do justice to their complexity. From a psychoanalytic perspective (Bower, 2005), something seems to happen in these difficult high-risk cases where service users project their neglect and disregard for the child's welfare onto the workers, who then act it out by not asking difficult questions about seeing the children, who lives with them, not looking around the house, and so on. Or, as shown in the above extracts from the Victoria Climbié case, nurses do not ask about or act on visible injuries. As the above quote shows, one nurse had made a note in the critical incident log 'concerning the master–servant relationship between Kouao and Victoria' (Laming, 2003, p. 266). Within the complex psychological dynamics which characterise the impact of projection in helping relationships, not only children but workers become 'slaves' to 'masterful' abusive carers. Becoming aware of when and how this is happening is incredibly difficult and requires the kind of reflective organisational culture, support and supervision which can bring these dynamics and their emotional and practical effects to light and enable workers to counteract them by refocusing on the child (see Chapter 15 for more on supervision in child protection work).

Organisational, cultural and systemic factors

It is crucial not to regard the difficulties social workers experience in taking action in such cases as in any simple way an individual failure of character, or personal or professional inadequacy. Character and the worker's own life history, experience and capabilities do matter. But fundamentally there are also systemic issues and processes at work here and crucial solutions lie in social, political and organisational changes. A considerable literature now exists on the ways in which organisational changes have resulted in an the increase in paperwork to ensure accountability for decisions and the rise of managerialism, where workers' practice is scrutinised much more for possible mistakes and in order to avert risks. The amount of time practitioners now spend at their computers limits the time they can spend providing quality work with children and families (Garrett, 2004, 2009; Munro, 2004; Parton, 2006; Webb, 2006). Broadhurst *et al.* (2009) showed that in some English local authority teams social workers spend the majority of their time at their desks, which leads to speedier assessments, shortcuts being taken, and more superficial work than is in the best interests of children. This is compounded by high caseloads, and staffing problems, arising from recruitment and retention problems (HM Government, 2010).[1] If social workers are to be better able to deal with the difficulties they routinely face they need more resources, and especially time and permission to do quality work with children and families.

Conclusion

Yet, as I have been arguing in this chapter, while having more time is crucial it is not enough. If practitioners had all the time in the world, to be effective at child protection they would need to know how best to use it. And, no matter how much time you have, there will always be families you won't want to spend time with, because you know they don't like you, and it's mutual. What is needed is a deep understanding of just how difficult child protection is and the complex and often deeply conflict-ridden relationships in which professionals and families are embroiled. To achieve this practitioners need supervision that gives time and space to think, and which addresses the emotional impact of the work

(Cooper, 2005). This has to include acknowledgement of very difficult feelings such as fear and disgust, with supervisors and peer supporters engaging in what I have elsewhere called 'embodied listening' (Ferguson, 2009). A clear vision of what child protection has to involve needs to be available and implemented, including the importance of seeing around homes and inquiring about, and seeing, fathers. Finally, it is crucial to let the media and public know just how difficult child protection is, how doing even the so-called 'simple things' well is enormously difficult because of the psychological, emotional and organisational pressures that this chapter has drawn attention to (see Chapter 8). Yet, very often, child protection work *does* succeed as practitioners manage to overcome the difficulties and keep children safe. It is vitally importance that we learn from how child protection is done in the countless instances when it is done well.

Note

1   Recent research by Burns (2011) has questioned the common view in child protection and welfare that turnover is high. Burns's review of turnover rates for children's and families social workers in the United Kingdom using data from the Social Care Workforce reports, demonstrates that turnover rates are actually reducing and does not support the perception that turnover rates are high.

References

Bower, M. (ed.) (2005) *Psychoanalytic Theory for Social Work Practice*, London, Routledge.

Brandon, M., Belderson, P., Warren, C., Howe, D., Gardener, R., Dodsworht, J. and Black, J. (2008) *Analysing Child Deaths and Serious Injury Through Abuse and Neglect: What Can We Learn?* Nottingham, Department of Children, Schools and Families Publications.

Broadhurst, K., Wastell, D., White, S., Hall, C., Peckover, S., Thompson, K., Pithouse, A. and Davey, D. (2009) 'Performing "Initial Assessment": Identifying the latent conditions for error at the front-door of local authority children's services', *British Journal of Social Work*, pp. 1–19, Advance Access, doi:10.1093/bjsw/bcn162.

Burns, K. (2011) *Retaining Social Workers in Child Protection: The Influence of Career Pathways, Social Exchanges and 'Myths'*, Research Seminar Series, University of Sussex.

Cooper, A. (2005) 'Surface and depth in the Victoria Climbié inquiry report', *Child & Family Social Work*, 10(1), pp. 1–9.

Ferguson, H. (2009) 'Performing child protection: Home visiting, movement and the struggle to reach the abused child', *Child & Family Social Work*, 14(4), pp. 471–480.

Ferguson, H. (2010) 'Walks, home visits and atmospheres: Risk and the everyday practices and mobilities of social work and child protection', *British Journal of Social Work*, 40, pp. 1100–1117.

Ferguson, H. and Hogan, F. (2004) *Strengthening Families Through Fathers*, Dublin, Department of Family and Community Affairs.

Ferguson, H. and O'Reilly, M. (2001) *Keeping Children Safe: Child Abuse, Child Protection And The Promotion Of Welfare*, Dublin, A. & A. Farmar.

Forrester, D., Kershaw, S., Moss, H., and Hughes, L. (2008) 'Communication skills in child protection: How do social workers talk to parents', *Child & Family Social Work*, 13, pp. 41–51.

Garrett, P. M. (2004) 'Social work's "electronic turn": notes on the deployment of information and communication technologies in social work with children and families', *Critical Social Policy*, 24(4), pp. 529–553.

Garrett, P. M. (2009) *'Transforming' Children's Services? Social Work, Neoliberalism and the 'Modern' World*, Maidenhead, Open University/ McGraw-Hill.

Hall, C. and Slembrouch, S. (2009) 'Communication with parents in child welfare: skills, language and interaction', *Child & Family Social Work*, 14(4), pp. 461–470.

Haringey (2009) *Serious Case Review, Baby Peter, Executive Summary* (online), Haringey Local Safeguarding Board. Available from: www.haringeylscb.org/executive_summary_peter_final.pdf (accessed on 1 October 2010).

HM Government (2010) *Building a Safe and Confident Future: Implementing The Recommendations of The Social Work Task Force*, Department for Children, Schools and Families, the Department of Health and the Department for Business, Innovation and Skills in partnership with the Social Work Reform Board, London.

Jones, D. P. H. (2003) *Communicating with Vulnerable Children: A Guide for Practitioners*, London, Gaskell.

Laming, H. (2003) *The Victoria Climbié Inquiry*, London, Stationery Office.

Littlechild, B. (2005) 'The nature and effects of violence against child protection social workers: Providing effective support', *British Journal of Social Work*, 35, pp. 387–401.

Munro, E. (2004) 'The impact of audit on social work practice, *British Journal of Social Work*, 34, pp. 1075–1095.

Parton, N. (2006) *Safeguarding Childhood: Early Intervention and Surveillance in a Late Modern Society*, New York, Palgrave Macmillan.

Piper, H. and Stronach, I. (2008) *Don't Touch! The Educational Story of a Panic*, New York, Routledge.

Reder, P., Duncan, P. and Gray, M. (1993) *Beyond Blame*, London, Routledge.

Webb, S. (2006) *Social Work in a Risk Society*, Basingstoke, Palgrave.

11

'Walking a tightrope': Exploring uncertainties in the initial assessment of suspected non-accidental head injury to an infant in statutory child protection and welfare

Pat Kelleher and Deborah Lynch

Introduction

A serious head injury to an infant is a traumatic and potentially catastrophic event. Where there are concerns that the injury may have been caused non-accidentally, social workers working within statutory child protection and welfare face significant responsibilities to ensure the welfare and safety of the child, in collaboration with other key agencies and professionals. Social workers are not removed from the tragedy of such events. They become part of them in the unfolding story, in an attempt to fulfil a role in protecting the child if the injury sustained is considered to be a consequence of abuse. This role also extends to ensuring that any siblings in the home, or other children born into that family in the future, are protected from harm.

This chapter draws on the author's experience as a social work practitioner working within a statutory child protection and welfare team for over 10 years in Ireland. This work has underlined the uncertainties inherent in the initial assessment of cases of serious suspected non-accidental head injury (NAHI) to an infant. Involvement in these complex cases as a social work practitioner has exposed the 'fine line' between potentially missing abuse and making an incorrect judgement that the injury was caused non-accidentally. In their empirical exploration of child protection assessment following serious injuries to infants (including head injuries), Dale *et al.* (2005, p. 1) refer to 'fine judgements' as those assessments and judgements made by child protection professionals and courts in relation to whether the child's injuries are the consequence of abuse, and decisions taken regarding interventions in such cases. These authors highlight the consequences of professionals 'making a mistake', such as missing evidence of child abuse or incorrectly attributing abuse to parents, with devastating consequences (see Dale *et al.*, 2005, pp. 7–25).

In an Irish case reported in the media of suspected NAHI where a five-month-old infant Rebecca Whyte died, initial medical opinion by three senior clinicians appeared conclusive that the head injuries the child sustained were a consequence of abuse. However, following the final report of the state pathologist it was concluded that the injuries were due to an underlying medical condition and abuse was not a factor (Cody, 2009). This illustrates the complexity of such cases where there may be conflicting opinion and different conclusions reached in relation to the cause of the injury. In this particular case, there were serious implications for the family who were under suspicion for a period of months and the father was prevented from seeing his child from another relationship during this time (Cody, 2009).

As in any child protection matter, analytical, critical and reflective thinking are essential processes for social workers and other professionals working together to achieve the best possible outcomes for children (Turney, 2009). According to MacDonald (2001, p. 265), child protection assessment is a multi-professional or inter-agency approach that must be 'tailored to address the needs of a particular set of circumstances and is a sequential, iterative process which requires knowledge, skill and the exercise of professional judgment'. In cases of serious suspected non-accidental head injury, the initial assessment is undertaken at a crisis point where an infant may be gravely ill in a hospital intensive care unit. The medical risks associated with this type of injury to very young children have been well documented (Karandiker *et al.*, 2004; Minns and Brown, 2005; Cobley and Sanders, 2007; Stipanicic *et al.*, 2008). These studies demonstrate high mortality rates (20–25%) and devastating neurological damage resulting in permanent disabilities, cognitive impairment, developmental delays and other associated health issues.

Initial interviews with the child's parents or caregivers in these uncertain, grief-laden and emotionally fraught circumstances are very challenging, even for the most experienced social work practitioner. Our social work values of respect and client self-determination can make intruding into this private family space at such a critical time feel very uncomfortable. The experience of seeing a child with severe injuries as a result of possible abuse is uncommon, and at the human level practitioners may need to regulate their own emotional response given the gravity of the assessment tasks ahead. Parents and caregivers may be in a state of shock and confusion given the serious nature of the child's injury and need for emergency medical treatment. For the practitioner, there may be uncertainty as to whether the injuries were caused by abuse, or whether the injuries were accidental or due to a medical condition. Social work interventions therefore take place in an uncertain and emotionally tense environment where the main focus tends to be investigative rather than therapeutic. Therefore, from the outset, for the child protection social worker, it can feel like 'walking a tightrope'. We explore this analogy in more detail later.

This sets the context for our chapter which focuses on some of the uncertainties and dilemmas inherent in statutory child protection and welfare social work in relation to the initial assessment of cases of suspected NAHI within an inter-agency and multi-disciplinary practice framework. Differentiating between abuse and an alternative accidental or medical explanation is a critical issue and we discuss some of the complexities inherent in these situations at this early stage where the emphasis is on the safety of the child (Office of the Minister for Children and Youth Affairs, 2010). We draw on international literature in our broader discussion and then focus on qualitative research studies that provide rigorous analysis and insights into key issues relating to the investigation and assessment of cases of suspected NAHI to infants. We hope that our chapter will assist social work practitioners to navigate their way through some of the complexities, expectations, uncertainties and challenges presented by such cases.

Our review of the literature is practice led and case informed, and we draw on Irish legislation as well as policy and practice guidance. By using relevant research to develop our practice themes, we hope to stimulate ideas and generate insights into this complex area of social work practice (Research in Practice, 2006). We undertook a literature search on NAHI in children using web and electronic databases to identify empirical studies, articles and reviews that addressed our practice themes of uncertainty, complexity and dilemmas in the assessment process from a social work perspective. We were particularly interested in any Irish research in this area.

Our chapter highlights limitations within our Irish child protection guidelines and practice frameworks in relation to NAHI and the limited nature of Irish statistics and research in this area. We begin with a brief overview of this form of child abuse and then shift our focus to the child protection process and Irish legislative and policy frameworks.

Non-accidental head injury to an infant: an overview

We use the generic term 'non-accidental head injury' (NAHI) to encompass a range of brain injuries to an infant or very young child sustained as a consequence of abuse. This term is widely used in the literature and considered acceptable in contemporary medical, legal and social frameworks (Cobley and Sanders, 2007). Other terms used interchangeably are 'inflicted head injury', 'abusive head trauma' and 'shaken baby syndrome' (Wheeler, 2003; Evans, 2004; see National Society for the Prevention of Cruelty to Children (NSPCC), 2008; Koe et al., 2010). Serious injuries to the brain are the leading cause of death among children who have been abused (Reece and Sege, 2000; NSPCC, 2008). The early years in a child's life is the period when they are most likely to suffer physical harm. In a Welsh study, severe physical abuse was found to be six times more common in babies under 1 year (54 children per 100,000 population) than in children 1 to 4 years of age (9.2 children per 100,000 population) and 120 times more common than in 5 to 13-year-olds (0.47 children per 100,000 population) (Silbert et al., 2002, p. 267). Specifically, babies under the age of 1 year are more vulnerable to serious forms of abuse such as brain injury – including subdural haemorrhage (more commonly referred to as 'shaken baby syndrome') and fractures – than older children (Silbert et al., 2002). Suspected non-accidental injury to infants or very young children is the focus of our discussion in this chapter.

In the international literature, non-accidental head injury to an infant is considered an uncommon event. Kelly et al. (2009) conducted an exploratory study on outcomes of NAHI in New Zealand statutory social work services and highlight a notably consistent incidence of NAHI in international epidemiological studies with rates of 20–30 per 100,000 infants under 1 year of age (see Kelly et al., 2009). However, a review of incidence studies of NAHI in infants (<1 year) in the UK suggests a much lower incidence of approximately 10–14 per 100,000 infants per year (Minns et al., 2008, p. 132). A prospective population study in the Southeast of Scotland from a national database conducted by Minns et al. (2008) shows a mean incidence of 33.8 per 100,000 infants per year. While these authors note that their incidence figure is much higher than those suggested in their UK review, they emphasise the rigour of their methodological approach and consider this to be an accurate reflection of incidence for the region. They raise the issue of under-reporting which is also a concern highlighted in the literature on NAHI in infants (see Sanders and Cobley, 2007). We return to this issue later in the chapter.

We do not have annual incidence figures for NAHI in infants in the Republic of Ireland. We found only one Irish study on NAHI in infants, which reflects the limited nature of Irish research in this area. The study offers a retrospective analysis, over a 10-year period, of admissions and transfers to one large children's hospital in Dublin of children with suspected non-accidental head injury. They identified 22 confirmed cases of NAHI in children with an age range from 1 to 54 months, with a median of 4 months and a mean of 7 months (Koe et al., 2010).

The incidence of serious physical abuse towards infants and young children in the Republic of Ireland is difficult to quantify, owing to the limitations of official statistics and information (see Buckley, 2008). The implementation of a National Child Care Information System (NCCIS), which is an information management system utilising information communication technology designed to support standardised child care practices and services, should address this issue in the future (Health Service Executive, 2009a). Currently available statistics show that in 2008 there were 24,668 individual reports of possible abuse or welfare concerns to the statutory social work services. Specifically, 2,399 or just less than 10 per cent of these referrals related to concerns of physical abuse. Furthermore, 476 of these cases were found to be confirmed cases of physical abuse (Health Service Executive, 2009b). These basic statistics cover the wide spectrum of physical abuse and do not differentiate between NAHI and other forms of physical abuse. The figures relate to all children up to the age of 18 and we have no official reference point to determine the extent of NAHI or serious physical abuse in Ireland. Given that NAHI has been recognised internationally as the main cause of fatal child abuse in children under 2 years of age, this is a serious shortcoming. However, a prospective study on NAHI in Ireland is currently being established by the Paediatric Surveillance Unit (Koe et al., 2010). This will be the first time that information of this nature will be available in the Irish public domain and it is anticipated that this will provide data into what is one of the most serious forms of child physical abuse.

We could not complete our overview of NAHI in infants without commenting on the finding in several studies that male children are over-represented. In the Irish review of cases of NAHI presenting to one hospital, the authors note a male to female ratio of 3:1. In Dale et *al.*'s case review of 45 children with serious/fatal injuries in the UK, 31 (69%) children were male and 14 (31%) were female (2002, p. 300). Other UK researchers, Cobley and Sanders (2007), who specifically investigated NAHI in children, noted that of the 54 children referred to the police and social services, 38 (70%) were male and 16 (30%) female. Furthermore, in a more recent retrospective review of NAHI cases admitted to a hospital in Auckland, New Zealand by Kelly *et al.* (2009) there were 23 (59%) boys and 16 (41%) girls. The literature suggests it is an international phenomenon that 'baby boys are consistently more likely to be seriously/fatally abused than baby girls although there is no generally agreed understanding of why this is so' (Dale *et al.*, 2005, p. 30). This is an interesting issue that warrants further research and analysis. We now move the discussion on to child protection processes and Irish legislative, policy and practice frameworks.

Critical processes: referral, initial child protection assessment and An Garda Síochána (police) investigation

Where an infant presents to an Accident and Emergency Department with a serious and potentially life-threatening head injury, hospital staff are 'in a pivotal position to identify cases where reasonable grounds for concern exist regarding the welfare and protection of children' (Office of the Minister for Children and Youth Affairs, 2010, p. 28). Under the Irish national child protection guidelines, *Children First: National Guidelines for the Protection and Welfare of Children* (hereafter, *Children First*) 'all front-line staff, particularly in emergency departments, must be alert to indicators of actual or potential child abuse' and coordinated working arrangements between hospitals and statutory child protection and welfare services should be in place (Office of the Minister for Children and Youth Affairs, 2010, p. 29). Child protection procedures are also outlined in the context of a multi-disciplinary approach. In the Irish study, 14 cases of suspected NAHI out of 22 were referred to social work services within four days of admission to the emergency department of the Children's University Hospital (Koe *et al.*, 2010). These findings show that there was early social work involvement in most of these cases. However, this study was limited to one children's hospital and, clearly, further research is needed.

Once a child has been identified as having sustained a serious head injury and there is a medical concern that this is a possible non-accidental injury, two processes are initiated: a child protection assessment/investigation by the statutory social work services, and a An Garda Síochána (Police) investigation in relation to potential criminal justice issues. The legislative basis for statutory social work intervention centres on Section 3 of the Child Care Act 1991. Section 3 (1) states that:

> It shall be a function of every health board to promote the welfare of children in its area who are not receiving adequate care and protection, and

> (2) 'in the performance of this function, a health board shall (a) take such steps as it considers requisite to identify children who are not receiving adequate care and protection and co-ordinate information from all relevant sources relating to children in its area.

In addition, Section 3 (3) states that 'a health board shall, in addition to any other function assigned to it under this Act or any other enactment, provide child care and family support services ...' This legislation clearly reflects the dual aspect of the statutory social work role, namely: assessing and responding to risk, and meeting needs by providing supports for children and their families. In cases where there is a concern that children have been injured by their parents or carers, the initial approach is investigative with the primary aim being to establish whether the injury is a consequence of abuse, and if protective action is required. This process is underpinned by the key principle that the welfare of the child is of paramount importance (Office of the Minister for Children and Youth Affairs, 2010). This statutory role poses significant challenges for social workers as it is at odds with principles that traditionally underpin helping relationships in social work practice, such as client self-determination (Barber, 1991; Healy and Meagher, 2007).

The An Garda Síochána mandate for their intervention where a child survives, relates to potential criminal justice issues, specifically, the Non-Fatal Offences Against the Person Act 1997. Both the child protection assessment and An Garda Síochána investigation will be dependent on medical expertise, opinion and the outcome of any diagnostic investigations by the assigned medical team and allied health professionals. The most critical factors in cases of NAHI which may arouse suspicion as to how the injuries were caused include:

- the plausibility of any explanation provided by parents or carers;
- analysis of the child's medical, social and family history; and
- the developmental stage of the child. (Dale *et al.*, 2002; NSPCC, 2008).

In addition, a suspicion can arise when no explanation is provided for injuries in cases where medical personnel expect there to be a significant traumatic incident. This issue is explored in some detail later.

Following a referral regarding suspected child abuse/NAHI, the statutory social work role within the multi-disciplinary team is to establish if abuse or neglect has been a factor leading to the presenting injuries and to consider the safety needs of any siblings arising from this. In the Irish context, NAHI is recognised in *Children First* which defines physical abuse as:

> Any form of non-accidental injury or injury that results from wilful or neglectful failure to protect a child. Examples of behaviours that cause physical injury include: Shaking, Use of excessive force in handling; Deliberate poisoning; Suffocation; Fabricated/induced illness; Allowing or creating a substantial risk of significant harm to a child. (Office of the Minister for Children and Youth Affairs, 2010, pp. 8–9)

Under the signs and symptoms of physical child abuse, it is noted that 'shaking is a frequent cause of brain damage in very young children' (p. 87). However, in this document there is an emphasis on procedural duties with limited guidance and information for practitioners in relation to identifying signs and symptoms of this type of abuse. Furthermore, this current policy framework has not been mandated for use by the statutory social work services in child protection and welfare in Ireland, which has drawn criticism (see, for example, Shannon, 2010; Ombudsman for Children, 2010). However, under the implementation plan of the *Report of Commission to Inquire into Child Abuse* (Office of the Minister for Children and Youth Affairs, 2009), it is recommended that these guidelines are underpinned by legislation and implemented nationally.

The social work tasks in the initial assessment phase will take the form of preliminary consultations with medical personnel, various network checks relating to any previous contact with social services, general practitioners, public health nurses and other professionals and services in contact with the family. In addition, preliminary inquiries with the child's parents/carers and wider network are critical. These inquiries focus on the full circumstances of the situation which has led to the child being admitted to hospital. In addition, a detailed analysis and exploration of the child's family context, medical, social history and development (including care arrangements; activities, routines, developmental milestones and presentation leading up to the admission) is undertaken. All care-givers and others who had contact with the child leading up to hospitalisation should also be identified in the overall assessment. There will also be early consultation and checks with the An Garda Síochána in view of the possibility that a crime has occurred.

As a basis for joint protocols between social work personnel and An Garda Síochána, *Children First* (Office of the Minister for Children and Youth Affairs, 2010) identifies a strategy meeting as an important resource in the initial period of assessment which is instigated, organised and chaired by the social work department and attended by all relevant professionals. Specifically, the guidelines identify the objectives of a strategy meeting as: (i) to share available information; (ii) to consider whether immediate action should be taken to protect the child and other children in the same situation; (iii) to decide if Section 16(1)(b) of the *Criminal Evidence Act, 1992* interviews should take place (this refers to joint An Garda Síochána and social work interviews of children – in cases of NAHI in infants this legislation could be applied if there are child witnesses or older siblings in the family); (iv) to consider available legal options; (v) to plan early intervention; (vi) to identify possible sources of protection and support for the child; (vii) to identify sources of further information; to allocate responsibility; and (ix) to agree with An Garda Síochána, how the remainder of the enquiry will be conducted (2010, p. 64).

However, within these objectives there appears to be a bias towards confirmation that abuse has occurred when this is likely to be one of the most complex and important issues to resolve in cases of NAHI in infants and needs to be a key area for discussion at this stage. These meetings provide an opportunity for clarifying information between the key agencies (medical services, An Garda Síochána and the statutory social work services). As noted by Macdonald (2001, p. 254), 'unless there is a strategic approach to making sense of a range of information from different professionals it is highly likely that erroneous conclusions will be drawn, or important patterns missed'. Exploring hypotheses around the injury are very important at this point in time. A repeat cycle of hypothesising and revising the hypotheses is implicit in this process and can be a 'demanding and potentially uncomfortable activity', which 'requires an agency culture that will accept not knowing and encourage respectful uncertainty' (Turney, 2009, p. 7).

At the initial stages of these cases, there are key similarities in the information required by both child protection social workers and An Garda Síochána authorities. However, the complexity of these cases is such that there is a danger that there could be a 'blurring' of roles. This issue was highlighted in a UK study relating to the police and social workers working together with one finding that the police tend to see themselves as the 'lead agency' (Garrett, 2004). This could compromise a key aspect of multi-disciplinary approach in these cases, which is meaningful collaboration to achieve the best possible outcome for each stakeholder. It is within this context that a strategy meeting is important in that it affords the opportunity for the respective agencies to work together under a wider child protection and welfare remit while maintaining and identifying the operational boundaries and objectives of each agency.

Furthermore, the strategy meeting offers a forum for collective analyses, planning and decision making. Engaging in a transparent process through 'making explicit the assumptions upon which decisions and judgement are made, and making judgements on the best available evidence, or the most sound interpretation of data', are critical processes from the outset (Macdonald, 2001, p. 254). 'Evidence' is integrated with the expertise of the practitioner (van de Luitgaarden, 2009; see Buckley, Chapter 12 for a discussion of evidence-informed practice). This process can be summed up as 'a combination of evidence-based practice grounded in knowledge with finely balanced professional judgement' (Department of Health *et al.*, 2000, p. 16). There has been an emphasis on developing and implementing assessment frameworks for practice which are evidence-based and we now look at their use in relation to assessing cases of NAHI in infants.

Assessment frameworks and the assessment of risk

Social work policy and practice in Ireland have been influenced by many developments in the UK. A significant feature of this is the UK developed *Framework for Assessment of Children in Need and their Families* (Department of Health *et al.*, 2000) with its distinctive triad of domains namely: child's developmental needs, parenting capacity and family/environmental factors. The use of this framework by statutory child protection and welfare social services in England and Wales is mandated (Dale *et al.*, 2005), and this assessment framework has been adopted or used in Scotland and Northern Ireland as well as a number of other countries including Australia, Canada, Sweden, Romania, United States of America and the Russian Federation (Horwath, 2010).

In Ireland, the UK assessment framework has been used in conjunction with, or integrated with, *Children First* in recent years resulting in procedural and practice models being established. However, the use of this assessment framework is not mandated, and as a consequence, we do not have an assessment framework that is universally applied. A national standardisation project is currently underway (Health Service Executive, 2009a) with a view to integrating and standardising child welfare and protection processes from first contact with the Health Service Executive (HSE) social work department through to case closure. While the UK assessment domains are integrated into the National Child Care Information System (NCCIS) assessment record, the accompanying guidance emphasises flexibility in relation to the adoption of appropriate assessment frameworks and tools in the assessment process (Health Service Executive, 2009a).

The strengths of the UK assessment model in relation to the assessment of cases of suspected NAHI are noted by Ennis and Henry (2004, p. 211):

> It is grounded in reliable research findings on child development, parenting capacity and the impact on environmental factors on families' functioning. It is attractive to practitioners for a number of reasons; it clearly locates the child as the focus of professional activity, extensive guidance is provided, it is easily accessible on the internet and assessment tools are freely available.

In this regard it is a valuable resource for front-line practitioners in the assessment and delivery of social work services to children and their families. However, a general criticism of the UK framework has been the lack of an applied conceptual framework of 'risk' (Ennis and Henry, 2004, p. 211). As noted by Macdonald (2001, p. 257), 'the assessment of risk should be seen as a thread running throughout child protection case management'. At its most salient, the initial social work task in cases of suspected NAHI in infants is to decide if protective action is warranted for the injured infant and their siblings. However, as Macdonald states, 'a reliance on risk assessment checklists is unlikely to be much use, and may well mislead' (Macdonald, 2001, p. 258). The ecological approach (that underpins the UK assessment framework) emphasises 'the interactional nature of risks, instead of a "summative" approach i.e. the more risk factors the more risk' (Macdonald, 2001, p. 258). Thus the emphasis becomes 'the *meaning* of events and circumstances for adults caring for a child and how they – and the child(dren) are perceived' (p. 258). In this context, she stresses the value and importance of constructing a genogram and completing a social history. A chronology can provide a basis for a sequential analysis of key events in the life of the child and the family.

Dale *et al.* (2005) strongly criticise the assessment framework in the context of its benefit in social work assessment where a child has sustained a suspected non-accidental injury: 'There is no domain relating to exploring and understanding the circumstances of serious events, the injury incident' (p. 142). This is particularly relevant to any assessment of suspected NAHI in infants or very young children, owing to the complexities which are often inherent in these cases. Despite this shortcoming, the framework contributes to an overall in-depth assessment to obtain the fullest understanding of the child and family. Munro (2002, p. 67) advocates for a comprehensive assessment in such cases when she expresses that:

> The narrow risk assessment has an essential role in front line work but, even with cases of immediate danger, it is not generally adequate on its own. The broader family assessment is needed for the basis of planning and intervention.

In this regard, other authors support the idea that the integration of specialist knowledge within the context of the broader UK assessment framework in these cases would be of value in assessing and investigating cases of suspected NAHI in infants (see Ennis and Henry, 2004).

The child protection social work role in cases of suspected NAHI to an infant can be demanding and arduous, and the initial assessment and analysis, professional judgement, decision making and intervention can take place in an uncertain environment, as described earlier. Therefore, establishing working relationships with families and other professionals in completing the assessment and intervention process is integral to achieving the best possible outcome. Brandon *et al.* (2008) also highlight the critical role of effective and accessible supervision in these highly demanding and emotive practice contexts in order 'to help staff put in practice the critical thinking required to understand cases holistically, complete analytical assessments and weigh up interacting risk and protective factors' (p. 326).

We now turn to the complex issue of differentiating between abuse and an alternative accidental or medical explanation of the head injury in an infant or young child at the initial assessment stage.

Differentiating between abuse and alternative explanations: a complex medical-legal issue

The UK study conducted by Cobley and Sanders (2007) analysed 68 cases of children under 2 years old who had been diagnosed with serious internal head injuries. In 54 of these cases, referrals had been made to the social services and police authorities. It was found that, of the 68 cases of children presenting to hospital, 14 had not subsequently been referred to the police or child protective social services. Of this number, 9 were identified as having another cause in which abuse was not suspected (pp. 69–70). In a retrospective examination of available records, 5 were considered suggestive of non-accidental injury, and they express their concern about this finding, owing to the serious implications inherent in not examining these situations within the wider child protection framework. In effect, they are proposing some degree of misdiagnosis or under-reporting. A level of under-reporting by hospital staff is acknowledged in the broader literature on non-accidental injury in children (see Sanders and Cobley, 2005; Ince *et al.*, 2010).

There is no clear basis to suggest that there is a level of misdiagnosis and underreporting in Ireland and until similar research is carried out in the Irish context, the level of any under-reporting will remain unknown. However, there is anecdotal acknowledgement of 'under-recognition' in the Koe *et al.* study (2010, p. 104):

> as data collection occurred during a time period (1998–2009) when the recognition and diagnosis of Abusive Head Trauma (AHT) was evolving, it is possible that in the early period some cases of AHT may not have been recognised.

Differentiating between suspected abuse and an alternative accidental or medical explanation is a complex medical-legal issue in its own right. Cobley and Sanders (2007, p. 61) capture the essence of this perplexing issue, which needs to be considered by social workers and An Garda Síochána:

> Although clinical investigations can offer a likely pattern of injuries and offer clues as to whether they indicate a possible non-accidental cause, they cannot conclusively show on their own that the injuries were non-accidental.

On a range of key issues, our dependence on the medical professionals to assist us in making accurate assessments is not in question. The advancement of medical knowledge and technologies has been significant in relation to the identification of physical child abuse and particularly NAHI in young children (Wheeler, 2003; Evans, 2004; Togioka *et al.*, 2009). However, our expectations in relation to the degree of accuracy which can be offered by these services can be unrealistic. Therefore, a comprehensive multi-disciplinary approach remains the core principle underpinning the assessment and investigation of suspected NAHI in infants (Sanders and Cobley, 2005; Office of the Minister of Children and Youth Affairs, 2010). Cobley and Sanders (2003, p. 114) describe the process of 'evidence-building', as cases of non-accidental head injury move through the child protection system along a 'spectrum' ranging from suspicion of non-accidental injury (when the child protection referral is made), to possible non-accidental injury, to probable non-accidental injury, to proven non-accidental injury (court finding). This reflects the processes of assessment/investigation that may be involved in such cases.

The plausibility of the explanation (or lack of one) for the head injury in line with medical opinion may be a significant factor in any decision to refer the matter to An Garda Síochána and/or social work department (see Sanders and Cobley, 2005).

NAHI: exploring uncertainties

We now focus on the uncertainties inherent in these situations and our discussion begins with the issue of parental explanations relating to the cause of the presenting injury(s). We highlight the findings of the two UK studies which explored qualitative and quantitative issues where a child had suffered serious significant physical harm of a non-accidental nature. We have referred earlier to the study by Cobley and Sanders (2007) which specifically related to NAHI in young children. The other study by Dale *et al.* (2002) reviewed 21 cases within a 14-year period where children had sustained a range of very serious injuries, including NAHI. In addition, they examined a further 17 cases where a serious case review had taken place, primarily where there had been the death of a child. This study involved a total of 45 children aged between 0 and 2 years from 38 families. Both these authors specifically analysed parental explanations relating to the cause of the presenting injury(s). What is striking is the similarity of findings between the two studies, highlighting the complexity involved in such matters from both a social work and criminal justice perspective. This is where the parents can offer no explanation (or else a questionable explanation) for the injuries to the infant.

In the Dale *et al.* study of 21 cases where children suffered serious injuries, it was noted that at the initial stages of the medical investigations, there were no explanations offered by parents or carers in 14 cases as to the cause of any diagnosed injuries. In the larger study by Cobley and Sanders this was also the case where 'The most common response offered by parents when asked how the injury could have occurred was to provide no explanation' (p. 171). An additional pattern was also noted in both studies where, as child protection and police inquiries progressed, at times, differing and changing explanations for the injury were given by parents/carers. The Irish study by Koe *et al.* (2010) identified that no explanation was provided in the majority of cases examined and in 3 cases a 'low fall' was given as a possible explanation. In only 4 of the cases out of 22, an admission was made by the parent or carer that they had shaken the child. It was not clear at what stage of the assessment this admission had occurred.

A common theme emerges which can be summed up by Dale *et al.* (2002) who commented that: 'There are few incentives for parents to acknowledge responsibility when they have caused an abuse-related serious injury, and many reasons (psychological, social and legal) to adopt and reinforce a stance of denial' (p. 25). This is an important matter to consider in any assessment and needs to be balanced with the fact that there could well be an accidental or medical basis to any diagnosed injuries.

In situations where there is a significant suspicion that a child's injury has been caused in a non-accidental way, one would expect that there would be challenges for professionals in establishing a working relationship with parents. In this situation, parents/carers are likely to experience added stressors related to their being 'under suspicion' and communication with professionals can often be difficult (Ince *et al.*, 2010). Both studies indicate that, for the most part, practitioners' perceptions of parental cooperation were rated as high. However, Cobley and Sanders (2007) do note that a decision to apply for a care order subsequently had a detrimental effect on the social work relationship with parents. This finding of perceived cooperation is an interesting one and while this may be considered somewhat positive in the context of an overall assessment, it is also an issue for assessment where a practitioner may 'overweigh' this fact when deciding whether the injury was a result of abuse. Ennis and Henry (2004, p. 213) raise two critical issues in this regard:

> how and whether genuine co-operation can be distinguished from plausibility; and resistance, lack of co-operation and collusion between protagonists – which may be exacerbated if criminal justice processes are not pursued and the absence of charging with an offence is used to undermine professionals concerns about a child.

They argue that these factors, among others, in such complex cases, highlight the need for professional support systems such as supervision and inter-agency dialogue and the application of decision-making theory in combination with the assessment framework (p. 213).

However, of critical importance throughout the assessment process, is keeping the child in focus (Horwath, 2010).

Finally, the issue of coexisting injuries is another factor of critical relevance in the assessment and investigation of suspected NAHI in infants. Both UK studies found that in the majority of cases where a serious non-accidental injury was suspected, the child had other coexisting injuries of varying severity. For example, in the Cobley and Sanders study, 25 out of the 54 children also had fractures. In the Koe *et al.* (2010) study, 4 children out of 22 were found to have suspicious bruising (3 had bruising to the face and one infant had extensive bruising to the face and body). This issue of coexisting injuries is very important for an initial child protection assessment where every identified injury must be investigated in isolation as well as collectively. Any coexisting injuries can also alert medical personnel to increase their suspicion that a non-accidental cause is more plausible and make it more likely that a conclusion of NAHI can be agreed upon.

Identity of perpetrator(s) and criminal justice outcomes

Of note in the Dale *et al.* (2005) study was that the identity of the perpetrator was unlikely to be identified in child protection inquiries and more likely to be established in the course of the police investigation. A key focus of the assessment for social work practitioners is establishing that the injury(s) have been conclusively caused in a non-accidental manner. The Gardaí are best placed to establish who is directly responsible for these although in the Dale *et al.* study, there were some instances where the identity of the person responsible became known in the course of child protection inquiries. Clearly, it is important in any initial social work inquiries with parents/carers that comprehensive and detailed attention is given to the events preceding the intervention of the medical services. In this context, social workers are becoming key witnesses in potential criminal investigations.

The nature and outcome of any criminal investigation into a situation where a child has sustained a serious injury has a very significant bearing on the child protection and welfare process and consequently for any siblings, or future children born into that family. The best case scenario from a criminal justice point of view in situations where a child has sustained non-accidental injury(s) is where the person or persons responsible have been clearly identified, charged (assuming it is an adult) with the offence, appear in court and receive the appropriate sanction. This in effect represents a 'gold standard' that any social work assessment and intervention can benefit from, particularly if the identity of the perpetrator becomes known at the initial stages of the process. However, this represents an optimal situation, which is not the likely scenario as in the Koe *et al.* study, out of the 22 cases of NAHI, 'just one criminal prosecution is being pursued at present' (p. 104) and in Cobley and Sanders' study (2007), out of the 54 cases of confirmed abuse, there was a low rate of only 8 convictions.

These figures are quite disturbing and they underline the serious complexities for the criminal justice authorities in investigating such matters. Gaining a full understanding from the family how injury was sustained is a critical issue for the social work department in identifying sources of risk. Central to this is identifying the person(s) responsible and, as we have seen, this may be very difficult. On this matter, Cobley and Sanders (2007) articulate what can be a key dilemma in the UK for the child protection and welfare social services, the police and courts: 'The research findings indicate that the question of who caused the injuries (as opposed to how they were caused) is frequently the most difficult issue to prove in cases of NAHI' (p. 95). This in itself represents a particularly challenging issue for social workers in their relationship with a child and their family and highlights major implications for any assessment of risk if the situation remains unchanged. Social workers often have to work with children and their families for long periods in this context, where the management of risk can become a central feature of ongoing intervention with a family.

However, in the New Zealand retrospective study of 39 cases of NAHI referred to statutory child protection services, the conviction rate was much higher (14 convictions). Despite this, the long-term child protection outcomes are extremely concerning. This study is noteworthy for the extensive time-frame. Some 9 (27%) out of 33 children had been placed permanently outside the home and 2 (6%) with unrelated care-givers. It was found that 14 children (44%) were re-notified for abuse or neglect to statutory child protection services (the median time from referral to review was 11.7 years). Interventions were variable in the Irish study, where 6 children returned home to parents, 7 went to relatives of the parents, 6 went to foster parents (5 voluntarily), 1 child left the country and 1 child died (Koe *et al.*, 2010). However, there is a lack of qualitative information on the assessment and decision making in these cases, and the question of long-term child protection outcomes in NAHI to infants remains to be addressed.

Conclusion

Child protection and welfare social workers can and do play an important part in the lives of families where a child has sustained a serious head injury and it is suspected that this has been caused non-accidentally. The necessity for social workers, medical staff and An Gardai Síochána to 'get it right' in terms of the assessment at the initial stages in what can be uncertain and emotionally fraught circumstances cannot be overstated. The balance in the assessment between potentially missing actual abuse and making an inaccurate determination that abuse has occurred can be precarious, and for the social work practitioner (owing to all the complexities discussed in this chapter) it can feel like 'walking a tightrope'.

In simple terms, an inaccurate determination can result in an injustice. Alternatively, abuse can be missed with the result that no action is taken to protect the child. It is not just our knowledge base, skills and systems of working we rely on, the medical services and An Garda Síochána occupy key roles and we very much depend on their expertise as well. Working relationships based on trust, as well as confidence to challenge each other's decisions, is crucial for effective practice in a high-risk environment (Gardner and Brandon, 2009). The studies reviewed advocate for each discipline to work together effectively to achieve the best possible outcome for the child. They emphasise that while each discipline has their particular area of expertise, no one agency has a monopoly, given the magnitude of the child protection issues involved. In this context, there is a clear need for continuing professional development and interdisciplinary training that is targeted, useful, evaluated and ultimately beneficial to the children and their families with whom we engage, as highlighted in the *Implementation Plan of the Report of the Commission into Child Abuse* (Office of the Minister for Children and Youth Affairs, 2009). In assessments of this nature, social workers have to be very clear about their role within the multi-disciplinary practice framework. This requires confidence and the capacity to form professional judgements based on expertise, experience and sound knowledge. We need to continue to build new forms of knowledge and theory for child protection practice, and develop our skills base (Healy and Meagher, 2007).

Our chapter highlights limitations within our Irish child protection guidelines and practice framework and the limited nature of Irish statistics and research in the area of suspected NAHI in infants. Prevention of this form of abuse through raising both public and

professional awareness (Russell, 2010) and undertaking early interventions in the context of a broad child and family welfare response
to children at increased risk (Macdonald, 2001; Gilbert *et al.*, 2009)
are critical strands. However, we are encouraged by current developments such as the prospective study being conducted by the Paediatric
Surveillance Unit, and urge the Irish government to implement fully
the recommendations of the *Report of the Commission into Child Abuse*
(Office of the Minister for Children and Youth Affairs, 2009), which
we believe will impact significantly on the protection, welfare and
rights of children in Ireland.

Acknowledgement

The authors would like to acknowledge Caroline Shore for her
comments on this chapter.

References

Barber, J. (1991) *Beyond Casework*, London, Macmillan.
Brandon, M., Belderson, P., Warren, C., Gardner, R., Howe, D.,
    Dodsworth, J. and Black, J. (2008) 'The preoccupation with thresholds
    in cases of child death or serious injury through abuse and neglect',
    Child Abuse Review, 17, pp. 313–330.
Buckley, H. (2008) 'Heading for collision? Managerialism, social science,
    and the Irish child protection system', in Burns, K. and Lynch, D. (eds)
    *Child Protection and Welfare Social Work: Contemporary Themes and Practice
    Perspectives*, Dublin, A. & A. Farmar.
Cobley, C. and Sanders, T. (2003) 'Shaken baby syndrome: Child
    protection issues where children sustain a subdural haemorrhage',
    Journal of Social Welfare and Family Law, 25, pp. 101–119.
Cobley, C. and Sanders, T. (2007) *Non-Accidental Head Injury in Young
    Children: Medical, Legal and Social Responses*, London, Jessica Kingsley
    Publishers.
Cody, C. (2009) 'Father tells of ordeal after baby-death probe', *The
    Independent* (17 July).
Dale, P., Green, R. and Fellows, R. (2002) 'Serious and fatal injuries to
    infants with discrepant parental explanations: Some assessment and
    case management issues', *Child Abuse Review*, 11, pp. 296 – 312.
Dale, P., Green, R. and Fellows, R. (2005) *Child Protection Assessment
    Following Serious Injuries to Infants: Fine Judgements*, Chichester, John
    Wiley and Sons.
Department of Health, Department for Education and Employment and
    Home Office (2000) *Framework for the Assessment of Children in Need and*

their Families, London, The Stationery Office.

Ennis, E. and Henry, M. (2004) 'A review of social factors in the investigation and assessment of non-accidental head injury to children', *Pediatric Rehabilitation,* 7(3), pp. 205–214.

Evans, H. (2004) 'The medical discovery of shaken baby syndrome and child physical abuse', *Pediatric Rehabilitation,* 7(3), pp. 161–163.

Gardner, R. and Brandon, M. (2009) 'Child protection: Crisis management or learning curve', *Public Policy Research* (December 2008–February 2009), pp. 177–186.

Garrett, P. M. (2004) 'Talking child protection: The police and social workers 'working together', *Journal of Social Work,* 4(1), pp. 77–97.

Gilbert, R., Kemp, A., Thoburn, J., Sidebotham, P., Glaser, D. and MacMillan, H. (2009) 'Recognising and responding to child maltreatment', *The Lancet,* 373, pp. 167–180.

Health Service Executive (2009a) *Report of the National Child Care Information System (NCCIS) Business Process Standardisation Project,* Health Service Executive. Dublin.

Health Service Executive (2009b) *Review of Adequacy of Services for Children and Families 2008* (online), Dublin, Health Service Executive. Available from: www.hse.ie (accessed 19 October 2010).

Healy, K, and Meagher, G. (2007) 'Social workers' preparation for child protection: Revisiting the question of specialisation', *Australian Social Work,* 60(3), pp. 321–335.

Horwath, J. (2010) *The Child's World. The Comprehensive Guide to Assessing Children in Need* (2nd edn), London, Jessica Kingsley Publishers.

Ince, E., Rubin, D. and Christian, C. (2010) 'Parental perceptions of hospital care in children with accidental or alleged non-accidental trauma', *Child Abuse and Neglect,* 34, pp. 403–406.

Karandikar, S., Coles, L., Jayawant, S. and Kemp, A. (2004) 'The neurodevelopmental outcomes in infants who have sustained a subdural haemorrhage from non-accidental head injury', *Child Abuse Review,* 13, pp. 178–187.

Kelly, P., MacCormick, J. and Strange, R. (2009) 'Non-accidental head injury in New Zealand: The outcome of referral to statutory authorities, *Child Abuse and Neglect,* 33, pp. 393–401.

Koe, S., Price, B., May, S., Kyne, L., Keenan, P., McKay, M. and Nicolson, A. (2010) 'Medical, social and societal issues in infants with abusive head trauma', *Irish Medical Journal,* 103(4), pp. 102–105.

Macdonald, G. (2001) *Effective Interventions for Child Abuse and Neglect: An Evidence-based Approach to Planning and Evaluating Interventions,* Chichester, Wiley.

Minns, R. and Brown, J. (2005) 'Neurological perspectives of non-accidental head injury and whiplash/shaken baby syndrome: An overview', in Minns, R. and Brown, J. (eds) *Shaking and Other Non-accidental Head Injuries in Children*, London, Mac Keith Press.

Minns, R., Jones, P. and Mok, J. (2008) 'Incidence and demography of non-accidental head injury in Southeast Scotland from a national database', *American Journal of Preventive Medicine*, 34, pp. 126–133.

Munro, E. (2002) *Effective Child Protection*, London, Sage Publications.

National Society for the Prevention of Cruelty to Children (2008) *Core Information from the Welsh Child Protection Systemic Review Group* (online), London, NSPCC Publication. Available from: www.core-info .cardiff.ac.uk (accessed 21 October 2009).

Office of the Minister for Children and Youth Affairs (2009) *Report of the Commission to Inquire into Child Abuse Implementation Plan*, Dublin, The Stationery Office. Available from: www.omc.gov.ie (accessed 26 February 2010).

Office of the Minister for Children and Youth Affairs (2010) *Children First: National Guidelines for the Protection and Welfare of Children* (revised 2nd edn), Dublin, The Stationery Office. Available from: www.omc.gov.ie (accessed 22 August 2010).

Ombudsman for Children (2010) *A Report Based on an Investigation into the Implementation of Children First: National Guidelines for the Protection and Welfare of Children*, Dublin, Ombudsman for Children's Office.

Reece, R. and Sege, R. (2000) 'Childhood head injuries: Accidental or inflicted?', *Archives of Pediatric and Adolescent Medicine*, 154, pp. 1–5.

Research in Practice (2006) *Firm Foundations: A Practical Guide to Organisational Support for the use of Research Evidence*, Dartington, Research in Practice.

Russell, B. (2010) 'Revisiting the measurement of shaken baby syndrome awareness', *Child Abuse and Neglect*, doi: 10.1016/j.chiabu.2010.02.008.

Sanders, T and Cobley, C. (2005) 'Identifying non-accidental injury in children presenting to A&E departments: An overview of the literature', *Accident and Emergency Nursing*, 13, pp. 130–136.

Shannon, G. (2010) *Third Report of the Special Rapporteur on Child Protection. A Report Submitted to the Oireachtas 2009*, Dublin, Office of the Minister for Children and Youth Affairs.

Silbert, J., Payne, E., Kemp, A., Barber, M., Rolfe, K., Morgan, R., Lyons, R. and Butler, I. (2002) 'The incidence of severe physical child abuse in Wales', *Child Abuse and Neglect*, 20, pp. 267–276.

Stipanicic, A., Nolin, P., Fortin, G. and Gobeil, M. (2008) 'Comparative study of the cognitive sequelae of school-aged victims of shaken baby syndrome', *Child Abuse and Neglect*, 32, pp. 415–428.

Togioka, B., Arnold, M., Bathurst, M., Ziegfeld, S., Nabaweesi, R., Colombani, P., Change, D. and Abdullah, F. (2009) Retinal hemorrhages and shaken baby syndrome: An evidence-based review, *The Journal of Emergency Medicine*, 37(1), pp. 98–106.

Turney, D. (2009) *Analysis and Critical Thinking in Assessment* (online), Dartington and University of Sheffield, Research in Practice Series. Available from: www.rip.org.uk/publications (accessed 21 October 2009).

Van de Luitgaarden, G. (2009) Evidence-based practice in social work: Lessons from judgement and decision-making theory, *British Journal of Social Work*, 39, pp. 243–260.

Wheeler, P. (2003) 'Shaken Baby Syndrome: An introduction to the literature', *Child Abuse Review*, 12, pp. 401–415.

12

Putting research evidence to work in child and family social work

Helen Buckley and Sadhbh Whelan

The majority of inquiries and reviews of child protection practices in Ireland have tended to focus on professional and systemic failures (see, for example, Western Health Board, 1996; North Eastern Health Board, 1998), with minimum attention paid to the considerable successful work being carried out with children and families (see Ferguson, 2001). This skewed emphasis on the deficits of the services has done little to engender confidence in social work and has contributed to the turbulence currently being experienced in the profession. Although the most common response to perceived weaknesses in child protection is a tightening of guidelines and policies, this is an area of work that is both complex and unpredictable, and regulation alone will not be sufficient to improve its outcomes. In fact, increased proceduralisation and standardisation often fail to address the core issues needing attention. The achievement of competent and reflective practice is dependent on a number of influential factors; some are organisational and some professional, and significant among them are a sound evidence base and the willingness and motivation of staff to keep abreast of the evolving state of knowledge and research. This chapter examines a number of key issues surrounding the application of research to practice in the child welfare sector. It draws on a review of international literature together with the findings of a study highlighting the barriers and facilitators that are perceived by staff to determine the extent of research utilisation (Buckley and Whelan, 2009).

The aspiration towards evidence based and informed practice is part of a global trend, and is supported in Ireland by central government. For example, in December 2007 the Office of the Minister for Children and Youth Affairs launched the *Agenda for Children's Services* (Office of the Minister for Children, 2007), described as a 'broad policy framework document' the aim of which is to assist policy makers, managers and front-line practitioners to engage in reflective practice and effective delivery, to be informed by best Irish and international evidence and to identify their own role within the agenda. Thus, it underlined the importance of accessing and applying research to the policy development and delivery of practice interventions to children and families.

Research evidence

What do we mean by research? Among the many definitions offered in the literature is a useful one by Marsh and Fisher (2005, p. 16), who describe it as 'a form of structured enquiry capable of producing generalisable knowledge', the capacity of which to deliver messages depends on its relevance and applicability. Nutley *et al.* (2007, p. 20) describe the type of research that is likely to be accessed by key public service professionals in health care, education, social care and criminal justice as that which is 'aimed at understanding the social world, as well as the interactions between this world and public policy/public service'. Debates about the quality of research evidence in the social sciences generally include questions about robustness, validity, generalisabilty and reliability. There are comparisons of the merits of experimental design (randomised control tests), statistical analyses and studies based on experiences and attitudes, with the former tending to be more esteemed in the research hierarchy, often known as the 'gold standard' because cognitive bias is effectively eliminated (Macdonald, 2001; Lewig *et al.*, 2006). Overviews of subject-related literature are also categorised into two different types comprising 'mainstream' and 'systematic' reviews, which synthesise results from several different studies on the same topic, the latter incorporating predefined inclusion criteria and a particular set of quality standards with regard to methodology, accountability and replicability (Hannes *et al.*, 2007). Case control studies, cohort studies and research-based protocols provide other examples of research evidence.

Evidence-based and evidence-informed practice

The current drive towards evidence-based practice (EBP) in social work is part of an international trend, based on the belief that assessment and interventions that are informed by research evidence about the nature of social problems and the best means of addressing them will ultimately achieve better outcomes for service users. Typically, EBP involves the steps of formulating problems or questions, sourcing the best evidence to answer the question, critically appraising the evidence for validity, integrating the evidence with practice experience and specific contextual factors, taking action and then evaluating effectiveness (adapted from Mullen *et al.*, 2008).

One of the principal proponents of evidence-based social work in the United States, Eileen Gambrill, has identified EBP as a philosophy and process designed to forward effective use of professional judgement, systematic approaches to improving services and transparency in policy making (Gambrill, 1999). Gambrill is extremely critical of a tendency in social work literature in particular to continued use of unrigorous research reviews of practice and inflated claims to effectiveness and the practice of simply relabelling models of practice as evidence-based with no mention of critical reviews arguing otherwise. She argues that EBP helps to avoid bias, 'authority based' decision-making and 'jumping to conclusions' (Gambrill, 2006).

Although many policy documents, including the *Agenda for Children's Services* (Office of the Minister for Children, 2007), refer to 'evidence-based practice', the term 'evidence-informed practice' is now commonly used in the literature to take account of the myriad influences on policy and practice operating within an organisational and wider environmental context, including values and ideologies, organisational culture, resources and politics (Lewig *et al.*, 2006; Research in Practice, 2006; Nutley *et al.*, 2007). It has been argued that there is, in fact, very little evidence to suggest that policy and practice in social care fields draw extensively from research, certainly in comparison to medicine, where its implementation is more frequently referred to and worked through in terms of implications for practice (Barnardo's, 2000). Indeed, the concept of 'evidence' is itself open to different interpretations and needs to be seen in relation to other factors that influence and shape the nature of child protection and welfare work. As Barratt and Cooke (2001, p. 2) have observed, practice should be 'informed by the best available evidence of what is effective, the practice expertise of professionals and the experience and views of service users'. Nutley *et al.* (2007) also point out that the term 'evidence-informed' practice is intended to denote the role played by evidence, while acknowledging that other factors continue to exert some influence.

A similar claim that the impact of research on decision making in social care is 'subtle' and 'indirect' is made by a UK-based organisation, Research in Practice (RIP), who point out that the nature of research in social care is that it is often more about increasing background understanding, giving insights into the nature of problems, changing attitudes and beliefs and generating ideas rather than prescribing action (Research in Practice, 2006). In fact, RIP are quite firm in their assertion that:

> The practitioner goes through a considered and thoughtful process where a range of factors (including research) influence the judgement or proposal made. It is this process that we call evidence-informed practice. (Research in Practice, 2006, p. 14)

For the purpose of this chapter, however, the terms 'evidence-based' and 'evidence-informed' will both be used, given the still widespread use of the former term in both policy and research literature.

Critiques of evidence-based/informed practice

The concept of evidence-based/informed practice is not without its critics, some of whom claim that it can undermine 'traditional professional practice' and legitimate the managerialism that is creeping into social work, whose ambiguous, complex and uncertain nature does not easily lend itself to technical rationality (Parton, 2000; Webb, 2001). Furthermore, the assumption that research can be readily 'translated' into practice has been challenged, for example by Brady and Dolan (2007) who consider that the vulnerability of research to a range of methodological flaws means that it should not be totally relied upon, to the exclusion of other demonstrations of good practice such as 'show-casing'. It has been argued by Trinder (2000) that the principles applying to evidence application in a science such as medicine, where an element of cause and effect may be anticipated (for example, medication is likely to have a predictable effect), cannot be replicated in areas such as social work and probation. She argues that clients come with their own histories and understanding and are far from being passive recipients of an intervention so are not ideal subjects for study of a technical rational nature. Nonetheless, evidence-based practice has become firmly embedded in the health care and education sectors, and social work has some catching up to do.

The remainder of this chapter reports from a recently completed research study, identifying some of the reasons for the slow take-up of this process in children's services. It also outlines the factors that appear to promote research use in practice.

The current study

The current study was commissioned in the Republic of Ireland by the Children Acts Advisory Board (CAAB) and published in late 2009 (Buckley and Whelan, 2009). The overall aim of the study was to ascertain the level of research use in practice in children's services along with the factors that facilitated and impeded it.

The study was conducted in two different phases, consisting of an international review of literature on research utilisation and evidence-informed practice, followed by consultation with staff from the four sectors of health, welfare, justice and community-based organisations who were involved in the delivery of child and youth welfare services. Thirty-one per cent of the participants were from the health and welfare sector, which included social workers in the Health Service Executive (HSE), 28 per cent worked in community-based non-governmental or voluntary organisations, 20 per cent were from the justice sector including Gardai and probation officers, and the remaining 20 per cent came from the education sector. Seventy-five percent of the participants were either front-line managers or practitioners, while 25 per cent were senior managers.

Data was collected by means of a survey and focus groups. Questionnaires were completed by 155 staff members at four separate seminars organised by the CAAB, and a slightly smaller number participated in a total of thirteen focus groups at the same events. A summary of the findings are presented here under the following headings:

- The factors perceived to influence day-to-day decision-making in practice in children's services;
- The relevance of research to practice and the benefits of accessing and applying it;
- The extent to which staff members applied research evidence in their work;
- The barriers to research utilisation;
- Factors that facilitate research use, and
- How best to promote research utilisation.

The factors perceived to influence day-to-day decision-making in practice in children's services

In order to explore the attitudes of staff to research utilisation, participants were initially asked to identify the factors that most influenced their day-to-day decision-making. The 'legal context', particularly in respect of participants from statutory services, application of standards, vigilance about child protection issues, procedures, guidelines and the requirement to develop care plans were all identified. 'Risk assessment tools', other methods of assessment and specific models of practice were also cited, as was the view that 'client needs' often determined the type of action to be taken. Many cited the importance of experience, in the form of 'proven programmes and proven techniques that worked in the past' combined with knowledge about what families preferred. Some said that they would be particularly influenced by their specific training and background. In keeping with previous research findings (Macdonald, 2001; Munro, 2007), some participants claimed that their decision-making was, to a degree, intuitive and based more on the family's capacity to engage, their circumstances at the time, and pragmatic factors such as access to resources. A senior manager pointed out that decision-making was also influenced by financial issues. While some commented that many of their guidelines and policies were research based, there was little overt identification by participants of the way that research influenced day-to-day practice.

The relevance of research to practice and the perceived benefits of accessing and applying it

Though the findings in general supported the use of research, when asked about the relevance of research to their everyday work, most participants had reservations about the research available to them in terms of its usefulness. Some were critical about its lack of applicability, claiming that it overlooked some of the sensitivities and complexities of work in children's services, such as the importance of relationships between workers and service users. There was criticism of statistics, with claims about how easily they might be manipulated, as one person argued: 'it's a bit about ... tell me what you want me to prove and I'll prove it for you'. Despite the publication of a substantial amount of Irish research on child protection and welfare issues and children's services since the mid-1990s, a number of participants perceived a lack of 'real', 'local' and 'up-to-date' Irish research, the lack of a database of Irish research[1] and an over-reliance on studies from other countries. Some also expressed caution about the limits to which research is relevant in social care, as the environment is dynamic and constantly changing. It was also suggested by staff from different community-based organisations that research cannot be generalisable to the differing needs and circumstances of service users; as one pointed out: 'What may be a good outcome for one client may not necessarily be for another' and another participant added: 'Each client is different so success may not be quantifiable.'

However, despite the qualms expressed about the relevance of research to practice, when focus group participants were asked why the use of research might be considered beneficial, they identified a number of positive reasons. The way in which it facilitated them to 'promote a culture of change' and 'question' their practice was highlighted by several who pointed out that 'people think in certain ways and they need to think differently'. Another participant suggested that using research might 'shake up the system ... it could be thought provoking', and a third suggested that it might overcome 'practitioner resistance' to new ideas or ways of working. At a practice level, the use of research was considered necessary to inform practitioners about the impact of social problems, such as the effects on children of parental mental illness or domestic violence. It was also considered important to use research-based tools to measure the degree to which desired outcomes had been attained.

An application of research in practice considered particularly useful was the evaluation of current interventions and programmes, particularly if the provider organisation was required to make a case for the continuation of funding. It was also suggested that evaluation which is carried out prospectively would have the capacity to indicate, at the end of a funding cycle, which aspects of the project were most effective and would ultimately positively inform choice.

The extent to which staff members applied research evidence in their work

The survey findings indicated that the majority of participants were regular, though perhaps not frequent, research users; one quarter 'looked up' or consulted research evidence at least weekly, with around half accessing it either monthly or every two months. The remainder accessed it sometime between once or twice yearly. The most commonly reported method of accessing research evidence cited by almost 80 per cent of the respondents was via Internet sites. These were mainly government sites, with very low usage of websites dedicated to disseminating knowledge about child welfare such as Research in Practice.[2] The next most frequently identified method of accessing research cited by two-thirds was through reading reports. Smaller numbers of respondents reported using seminars books or journal articles as a way of familiarising themselves with current research.

While the survey was unable to pick up the quality or depth of engagement exercised by the participants with research, the focus group discussions indicated that it varied considerably with only half of participants indicating that the work of their organisations was informed by research. It may be that the rolling out of continuing professional development, spurred by the Health and Social Care Professionals Act may provide a stimulus for practitioners to consult research more frequently (see CORU, 2010). However, the findings from this study indicate that access to, and application of, research may be subject to a number of exigencies, which are detailed below.

The barriers to research utilisation

While it was generally agreed that using research was beneficial to inform and challenge practice and to evaluate projects and programmes, it became clear that a number of obstacles need to be addressed if the rate of research utilisation in the child welfare sector is to improve. These could be categorised into three different types: barriers to research use by individuals, barriers identified in respect of research material, and organisational barriers to research utilisation.

Barriers to research use by individuals
The most frequently cited individual barrier was lack of time. Participants identified a combination of a busy workload, 'getting caught up in practical day-to-day matters' and a lack of dedicated time for consulting research. There was a general view that prioritising the study of research over other duties in busy organisations was not considered to be acceptable and even finding the time to attend conferences and seminars was considered difficult for some. Several spoke of 'feeling guilty' if they spent time looking up information about their practice on the Internet, with 'colleagues thinking you are doing nothing' and as one participant suggested: 'If I were to sit at my desk reading ... you would feel like you were not doing your job.'

However, some identified barriers that were personal to the staff themselves. It was suggested, for example, that some staff slightly exaggerated their 'busyness' to avoid having to engage with research, denoting 'lack of real motivation'. 'Resistance to change' was cited as another barrier; it was observed that staff often preferred to rely on traditional methods of practice rather than sourcing other options. Some participants acknowledged that research evidence may be avoided if it compelled an individual to move outside their 'comfort zones'.

Part of the negativity about using research was reflected in participants' attitudes to taking part in research conducted in respect of their own organisations. The belief was expressed by some that there was little real connection between the data they provided for research purposes and the outcomes for their own work. As one person expressed: 'When you have people coming in ... basically and looking for all types of information and making all kinds of work you feel – where is it going?'

Other individual barriers included limited access to research materials in some cases, although the Internet was available to most participants and many belonged to organisations that had libraries, although books and articles were difficult to access for staff particularly in small organisations. In a slightly contrary vein, 'overload' of available research evidence was seen as off-putting to several participants who felt they could 'get lost' in the wealth of available information. Overall, however, there was a strong sense of conflict between workplace pressures; 'the need for immediate solutions' and taking the time to source and consider research evidence on everyday practice.

Barriers identified in respect of research material
Barriers identified in respect of the nature of research material included the fact that reports and articles are often written in 'inaccessible' and 'problematic' language, as well as complicated statistical presentations, which caused people to 'tune off'. One participant used the analogy of 'looking into a field of thistles' to describe his struggle with 'turgid' research on which he was reluctant to expend 'the time, energy or the mental capacity'.

The view was also expressed that research is often out of date by the time it is published, that it was 'very subject to fashion' replete with 'buzz terms' and that samples are often very small and unrepresentative, particularly where studies are carried out by students. While it was generally felt that research from a 'reputable' source such as a university or a journal was trustworthy, many expressed scepticism about the Internet as a source of evidence, for example, the need to 'wade through a lot of rubbish to get to the quality'.[3]

Organisational barriers to research utilisation
The 'lack of a research culture' in the workplace was cited by several of the participants as an organisational barrier. By this they meant lack

of encouragement and support for staff and a low regard for the value of research. One participant expressed her fear of being considered an 'upstart' if she mentioned research, indicating a negative organisational attitude. The fact that some organisations had commissioned studies, including evaluations, and failed to engage with the results was cited as a discouraging factor. Some participants complained that they had been expected to take part in studies or provide statistical data for purposes that were never made clear to them, which engendered a certain amount of mistrust and resentment towards research. Inadequate means of disseminating research within organisations were also seen as barriers. The habit of some organisations to 'randomly' email research references and material to staff was highlighted as 'pointless', given that most of it would not be used.

Factors that facilitated research use

Despite the barriers and difficulties highlighted above, participants in this study were able to identify a number of factors that actively promoted their use of research. As above, these are categorised into factors that facilitate individual research use, facilitators related to the nature of research and organisational factors.

Factors that facilitate individual research use
Along with access to research, personal interest and involvement in further study were cited as two individual facilitators. Personal motivation was identified as stemming sometimes from intellectual curiosity, professional codes of practice, or from simply wanting to find out the best way to respond to a critical situation. Having 'exposure' to outside organisations or working with a colleague that was involved in studying and having the opportunity to share new knowledge with, for example, a student on placement, were identified as providing incentives to further investigate new evidence. Participants whose work obliged them to prepare annual reports or presentations found that these activities motivated them to use research.

Facilitators related to the nature of research
Given the criticisms voiced about complicated and unfriendly research publications, it was not surprising to find participants suggesting that material presented in a simple format, which had practical relevance, would be attractive to them. Evidence in 'bite-sized pieces' was considered useful. Provision of up-to-date and

'timely' summaries with key messages with minimal inclusion of statistics and methodologies, briefing papers and bullet pointed lists were also suggested. Although the Internet had been identified as the main medium for research use, a significant number of participants indicated a strong attachment to hard copies of books and articles. There was also support for interactive fora such as seminars and conferences, but some also suggested that the use of diverse media such as CDs, DVDs, and podcasts would enhance the likelihood of research being accessed and applied.

Organisational factors

Focus group members identified a number of organisational factors that facilitate research use, such as maintaining a library and journal subscriptions, 'generating' interest and giving 'permission' to practitioners to become more research focused. Funding staff to undertake further study was also seen as a signal that research is valued.

Similarly, overcoming staff resistance by fostering a 'culture of reflective questioning' was proposed. The appointment of a research officer within the organisation was cited as another facilitator. There were several examples of where such appointments had been recently made, enabling the relevant organisations to integrate statistical data and evaluations to their strategic plans, as well as providing a person who can 'mediate' research use. In addition, several organisations had dedicated teams or units, such as training and development units that took responsibility for disseminating research to staff. In some smaller organisations there were deliberate efforts at knowledge sharing, for example, using team meetings for feedback and discussion of a new report or article, or identifying blocks of time for reading. It was also considered that the creation or strengthening of links between service-provider organisations and research units in universities would have a positive effect.

The use of incentives was suggested, such as making the funding of staff for further study conditional on the ultimate production of a piece of research that will benefit the staff member's own organisation. It was also suggested that job descriptions and staff appraisals should encompass research utilisation.

How best to promote research utilisation

The findings of this study identified a good deal of support for research use in child welfare practice and identified many reasons why it should be promoted. However, the data also indicate a number of obstacles to its application, both practical and attitudinal, from individual and organisational perspectives. Reservations were also expressed about the adequacy of Irish research on child welfare, in terms of its currency, relevance and the way it is presented. Overall, therefore, it can be assumed from the study that availability of research material is no guarantee that staff will apply it. Some element of mediation is clearly required in order to both facilitate and persuade staff towards increased use of evidence to inform practice. The outcomes from the current study indicate that a holistic approach will need to be taken if this aspiration is to be taken seriously and achieved.

In taking a systematic approach, the challenges need to be met by all the stakeholders involved. These include the organisations that commission research, service provider organisations, and organisations that produce research. Research is normally commissioned by either service providers who require specific pieces of work, or dedicated research funders whose main goal is to enhance research capacity. The findings from this study indicate that research which is commissioned should be relevant to service provision and should fill an identified gap. The required outputs should include, in addition to a research report, strategies for disseminating the research in a variety of formats.

The study findings have identified a number of implications for service provider organisations if research utilisation by staff members is to be enhanced. A very basic requirement is the promotion of an organisational culture that is supported by senior management and signifies the importance of research while continuing to value professional experience and expertise. Where it is currently insufficient, access to research material should be provided within organisations by means of the Internet or print materials. While it may not always be affordable or practicable, the appointment of dedicated research staff is likely to have a positive impact on the attitude of staff towards using and participating in research. Likewise, the involvement of staff in research that is commissioned, and the encouragement and utilisation of individuals who have a special interest in research, is likely to generally add to its perceived value. Strong incentives would be provided by the planned and purposeful dissemination of research within organisations. Many organisations already facilitate staff attendance at seminars and support further study that includes a research component. It is important that the value of these activities is recognised in the current economic climate. An excellent example of organisational promotion of research use is to be found in the Department of Community Services (DoCS), New South Wales, Australia, which delivers a programme called 'Research to Practice' to staff. It includes regular seminars, dedicated time to access research and a regular newsletter providing updates and summaries of recent research.[4]

The organisations that produce research need to ensure that their materials meet the needs of practitioners by providing clearly written, jargon-free reports that clearly demonstrate implications for practice. Outputs should be presented in a number of formats such as reports, briefing papers and summaries, and different media such as interactive seminars, CDs, podcasts and webcasts should be employed to suit individual tastes and contexts.[5]

In addition to the implications for the aforementioned groups, the findings suggest a role for central government, in developing a national research strategy which identifies and addresses gaps in Irish research. A recent audit of child protection literature, which highlighted specific deficits such as a shortage of robust research on child protection practice in the statutory sector, should help to inform such a strategy (Buckley *et al.*, 2010). Additionally, the establishment of a national knowledge brokering organisation[6] specifically to meet the research needs of child welfare professionals would similarly provide a mechanism for the dissemination of research data. The North South Child Protection Hub (www.nscph.com), established in 2010, is a useful all-Ireland development. However, the hub is limited by the fact that it only provides links to existing research, unlike other sites which also provide briefings, issues papers and research summaries, for example the Australian Child Protection Clearinghouse (www.aifs.gov.au/nch).

Finally, however, while organisational and professional support is important to promote research utilisation it is ultimately up to individual social workers to avail themselves of the learning opportunities presented, and to appraise their own practices in the light of evidence about their likely effectiveness. Social work practitioners can increase their research utilisation by consulting subject-specific resources in print or on the Internet, such as some of the sites listed at the end of this chapter, which provide overviews and summaries of research (for example, the National Clearinghouse on Child Protection). Following the example of clinical colleagues, the establishment of journal clubs could provide a useful forum for discussion and exchange of knowledge. These activities could enhance their practice in two respects. First, by basing their assessments on known evidence of the impact of particular types of harm on specific aspects of child development, practitioners will be making more informed and accurate judgements. Second, by planning interventions on the basis of what is known to be successful in that particular circumstance, they will increase the potential for effective change. Using evidence this way will also add credibility to the professional judgements of social workers. The ability to evaluate current and planned activities in a transparent and auditable fashion will help them to withstand some of the current pressures to which their profession is currently subjected.

Notes

1   See new research databases published recently by the Children Acts Advisory Board (CAAB) on their website which goes some way towards addressing this issue:www.caab.ie/Research/publications-database.aspx.
2   See end of chapter for a list of useful websites. Research in Practice can be located at www.rip.org.uk.
3   See end of chapter for a list of useful research websites.
4   See www.community.nsw.gov.au/research_centre/research_to_practice_program .html.
5   For examples of relevant webcasts on child abuse and neglect see www.evertechnology.com/apccan/.
6   Knowledge brokering organisations promote research use in policy and practice by means of a number of activities including providing research summaries, helpdesks, consultancy and training. Examples are Research in Practice based in the UK, the Child Welfare Information Gateway in the US and the National Child Protection Clearinghouse in Australia. A list of the websites are provided at the end of this chapter.

Useful websites

California Evidence Based Clearinghouse for Child Welfare
    www.cebc4cw.org/
The Campbell Collaboration
    www.campbellcollaboration.org/(Norway/International)
Centre of Excellence for Child Welfare www.cecw-cepb.ca/ (Canada)
Chapin Hall www.chaplnhall.org/ (USA)
Child Welfare League of America www.cwla.org/default.htm
Childlink www.childlink.ie/(Ireland)
Children Acts Advisory Board

www.caab.ie/Research/publications-database.aspx(Ireland)
Children's Database www.childrensdatabase.ie (Ireland)
International Society for Prevention of Child Abuse and Neglect
    (ISPCAN) www.ispcan.org/ (USA/International)
Ministry of Development Practice Centre
    www.practicecentre.cyf.govt.nz/(New Zealand)
Multi-Agency Resource Service www.mars.stir.ac.uk/ (Scotland)
National Child Protection Clearinghouse
    www.aifs.gov.au/nch/ (Australia)
New Zealand Family Violence Clearinghouse www.nzfvc.org.nz/
North South Child Protection Hub nscph.com (Ireland)
Promising Practices Network on Children, Families and
    Communities www.promisingpractices.net/ (USA)
Research in Practice www.rip.org.uk/ (UK)
Scottish Child Care and Protection Network
    www.sccpn.stir.ac.uk/index.php
Social Care Institute for Excellence www.scie.org.uk/ (UK)

Bibliography

Barnardo's (2000) 'What Works? Making Connections: Linking Research and Practice'. A review by Bardardos Research and Development Team supported by the Joseph Rowntree Foundation, Essex, Barnardo's.
Barratt, P. M. and Cooke, J. C. (2001) REAL Evidence Based Practice in Teams: Action Pack, Research in Practice, Sheffield, Sheffield University.
Brady, B. and Dolan, P. (2007) 'Exploring good practice in Irish child and family services: Reflections and considerations', Practice, 19, pp. 5–18.
Buckley, H. and Whelan, S.. in association with the Children Acts Advisory Board (2009) Putting Research Evidence to Work: Key Issues for Research Utilisation in Irish Children's Services, Dublin, Children Acts Advisory Board.
Buckley, H., Corrigan, C. and Kerrins, L. (2010) Report of an Audit of Child Protection Research in Ireland 1990–2009, Dublin, Children Acts Advisory Board.
CORU (2010) Education-Continuing Professional Development (online), Health and Social Care Professional Council. Available from: www.coru.ie/education-section/cpd/(accessed 20 May 2010).
Ferguson, H. (2001) 'Promoting child protection, welfare and healing: The case for developing best practice', Child & Family Social Work, 6, pp. 1–12.
Gambrill, E. (1999) 'Evidence-based practice: An alternative to authority based practice', Families in Society: The Journal of Contemporary Human Services, 80, pp. 341–349.

Gambrill, E. (2006) 'Evidence-based practice and policy: Choices ahead', *Research on Social Work Practice*, 16, pp. 338–357.

Hannes, K., Claes, L. and the Belgian Campbell Group (2007) 'Learn to read and write systematic reviews: The Belgian Campbell Group', *Journal of Social Work Practice*, 17, pp. 748–753.

Lewig, K., Arney, F. and Scott, D. (2006) 'Closing the research-policy and research-practice gaps: Ideas for Child and Family Services', *Family Matters*, 74, pp. 12–19.

Macdonald, G. (2001) *Effective Interventions for Child Abuse and Neglect*, Chichester, Wiley.

Marsh, P. and Fisher, M. (2005) *Developing the Evidence Base for Social Work and Social Care Practice*, Bristol, Policy Press and London, Social Care Institute for Excellence.

Mullen, E., Bledsoe, S. and Bellamy, J. (2008) 'Implementing evidence-based social work practice', *Research on Social Work Practice*, 18, pp. 325–338.

Munro, E. (2007) 'Research governance, ethics and access: A case study illustrating the new challenges facing social researchers' *International Journal of Research Methodology*, 1, pp. 1–11.

North Western Health Board (1998) *The West of Ireland Farmer Case: Report of Review Group*, Manorhamilton, North Western Health Board.

Nutley, S., Walter, I., and Davies H. (2007) *Using Evidence: How Research Can Inform Public Services*, Bristol, Policy Press.

Office of the Minister for Children (2007) *Agenda for Children's Services: A Policy Handbook*, Dublin, Office of the Minister for Children and Youth Affairs.

Parton, N. (2000) 'Some thoughts on the relationship between theory and practice in and for social work', *British Journal of Social Work*, 30, pp. 449–463.

Research in Practice (2006) *Firm Foundations: A Practical Guide to Organisational Support for the Use of Research Evidence*, Dartington, Research in Practice.

Trinder, L. (2000) 'Evidence-based practice in social work and probation' in L. Trinder and S. Reynolds (eds) *Evidence-Based Practice: A Critical Appraisal*, Oxford, Blackwell.

Webb, S. (2001) 'Some considerations of the validity of evidence-based practice in social work', *British Journal of Social Work*, 31, pp. 57–79.

Western Health Board (1996) *Kelly – A Child is Dead*, Dublin, The Stationery Office.

13

Young people exiting homelessness: The role of family support

Paula Mayock, Mary Louise Corr, Eoin O'Sullivan

Introduction

Uncovering what facilitates or hinders young people's transition from homelessness to stable housing is significant for several reasons. Homelessness is a demeaning experience for all individuals but is particularly damaging for the young. Living on the streets or without stable housing increases vulnerability to criminal activity, arrest and committal to prison (Hagan and McCarthy, 1997; Baron, 2007) and in these same contexts young people are also vulnerable to victimisation, including verbal and physical abuse, robbery, sexual harassment and violence (Baron, 2003; Gaetz, 2004). Exposure to homelessness is also associated with a broad spectrum of health problems, ranging from malnutrition to drug addiction (McCarthy and Hagan, 1992; Greene and Ringwalt, 1996; Clatts *et al.*, 1998; Clatts and Davies, 1999; Dachner and Tarasuk, 2002). It is now reasonably well established that a longer duration of homelessness increases susceptibility to these negative outcomes (Chamberlain and MacKenzie, 1994; Johnson and Chamberlain, 2008). Thus, identifying those processes and factors that enable successful exits from homelessness is critical if services and interventions are to be responsive to the needs of those children and young people who leave home prematurely.

A key objective of these services must be to ensure that young people return to stable housing at the earliest possible juncture. However, it is only in recent years that research has moved beyond a focus on the reasons why young people become homeless. Driven in large part by a recognition that homelessness need not result in a progressive downward spiral towards long-term homeless states (Anderson and Tulloch, 2000; May, 2000; Clapham, 2002), research in the United Kingdom, North America and Australia has begun to investigate those factors, mechanisms and experiences that enable young people to exit homelessness (Fitzpatrick, 2000; Kurtz *et al.*, 2000; Milburn *et al.*, 2009; Mallet *et al.*, 2010).

This chapter examines young people's exit routes from homelessness in the Irish context based on selected findings from an ongoing biographical longitudinal study of youth homelessness in Dublin. Drawing on the biographical accounts of young people, we highlight the enabling role of family support as a facilitator to exiting homelessness. It is argued that existing services and interventions need to focus to a greater extent on building and fostering reconnections between young people and family members as a worthwhile and cost-effective strategy to ensure that adolescents exit homelessness as rapidly as possible, and thus avoid the deleterious effects of prolonged homelessness.

The homeless pathways of young people

Critical of the static nature of much homelessness research, Fitzpatrick's (2000) Glasgow-based study was one of the first to attempt to track homeless young people over time. A major finding arising from this research was that young people took different pathways through homelessness, with some moving to stable housing. Three factors – remaining in the home community near established networks, receiving competent help from formal agencies, and being female – were identified as facilitating young people's progress out of a homeless situation. Those who had made the best progress had better employ-ment and housing circumstances as well as the closest contact with their families. More recently in Los Angeles, Milburn *et al.* (2009) tested the likelihood of adolescents exiting homelessness, based on a longitudinal study of 183 newly homeless adolescents followed over a two-year period. Focusing on how socialisation experiences across four levels of organisation – family, peers, social services and formal institutions – affect the chances that adolescents will exit homelessness, this study found that engagement with pro-social peers and continued school attendance significantly increased the likelihood of a stable exit. Maternal social support, described as a 'striking' predictor of exiting, was consistently associated with the transition out of homelessness (Milburn *et al.*, 2009, p. 779).

In Australia, based on a subgroup of 40 newly homeless young people selected from a larger sample of 165 who had been living away from a parent or guardian for less than six months, Mallet *et al.* (2010) examined the pathways followed by these young people into and through homelessness over a period of two years. In identifying factors that aided the achievement of stability of housing, this study also highlighted the benefit to young people of their ongoing relationships with various family members and/or a partner, as well as social service intervention, particularly from an individual service worker, as providing support that was enabling in terms of moving out of homelessness. In a similar vein, in the United States, but through a focus on the perspectives of young people on what enabled them to resolve their homelessness, Kurtz *et al.* (2000) found that help from others – particularly from family, friends and professional helpers – was a critical enabler to their transition to stable housing. Although most of the study's young people had histories of volatile relationships with their families, their parents and other family members were, nonetheless, identified as important sources of caring and support.

Thus, a reasonably consistent finding arising from recent research on homeless young people across a number of jurisdictions relates to the positive impact of supportive family relationships in bolstering young people's ability to exit homelessness. What is perhaps less clear is how precisely this kind of support materialises and is negotiated, either with or without the direct intervention of professional agencies. It does appear, however, that services and interventions have an important role to play, with most studies highlighting the importance of both family and professional supports as facilitators to the process of exiting homelessness (Kurtz *et al.*, 2000; Milburn *et al.*, 2009; Mallet *et al.*, 2010).

The importance of understanding exit routes from homelessness

There are many barriers to exiting homelessness, particularly for those young people who have been homeless for longer. Separating from street or hostel environments and from street peers can be daunting (Karabanow, 2008) and drug or alcohol problems exacerbate the challenges associated with exiting (Piliavin *et al.*, 1996). Available research suggests that, irrespective of age, the homeless pathways and housing transitions of people who experience homelessness are influenced by a range of social, structural, personal and situational factors (Piliavin *et al.*, 1993, 1996; Wong and Piliavin, 1997; Stojanovic *et al.*, 1999; Fitzpatrick, 2000). Homeless experiences and pathways are also influenced by individuals' access to and interaction with services and service providers (Gerstel *et al.*, 1996). In the Irish context, while a considerable amount is known about why young people become homeless (Kelleher *et al.*, 2000; Mayock and O'Sullivan, 2007; Mayock and Carr, 2008), little is known about the routes they subsequently take through and out of homelessness.

This chapter specifically explores the role of family support as a facilitator to young people exiting homelessness. The data presented highlight the positive impact of family contact on young people who leave home prematurely as well as ways in which this contact and support facilitate positive housing and non-housing transitions, including participation in education/training and engagement with drug treatment. Thus, while much of the existing research highlights fractured family relationships as contributing to young people's premature home-leaving, we argue that the role of families is not uni-dimensional; rather, a more complex dynamic is evident whereby families are also significant in enabling young people to exit homelessness.

Methodology

The study, which is qualitative and longitudinal, was designed to examine the experiences of homeless young people over time. To date, two waves of data collection have been completed: the first between September 2004 and January 2005 and the second between September 2005 and August 2006.[1] During the first wave of data collection (Phase I) life history interviews were conducted with 40 homeless young people aged between 14 and 22 years, living in the greater Dublin area. Contact was re-established with 32 of these respondents during Phase II of the study and details regarding living situations were collected for an additional 5 young people. Information was therefore available to the research team on 37 of the 40 young people interviewed during Phase I and, of these, a total of 30 were re-interviewed. One young person was deceased by Phase II of the study.

Young people were initially recruited through hostels, residential settings, night shelters and drop-in centres as well as a number of strategically chosen street-based settings (see Mayock and O'Sullivan, 2007 for a detailed account of access and recruitment issues). At the time of follow-up, many had moved at least once since the time of initial contact with them and, for a considerable number, their place of residence was still of a temporary nature (for example, living in a homeless hostel, bed and breakfast accommodation or sleeping rough). Others had moved to more stable living situations, housing transitions which were categorised as homeless exits. There were numerous challenges associated with re-establishing contact with the study's young people (see Mayock *et al.*, 2008), including their transience and/or rapid movement through accommodation of various kinds. Nonetheless, the study's retention rate is satisfactory, particularly in light of the problems associated with retaining homeless people in longitudinal studies (Conover *et al.*, 1997).

The study's core method of data collection is the life history interview. With a central place given to the narration of personal biography, life history interviewing allows participants to actively remember and reconstruct their lives through the telling of their stories (Denzin, 1982). The study's baseline interviews commenced with an invitation to young people to tell their 'life story' and several topics and issues were then targeted for questioning. These included family life and family relationships, peer groups and networks, drug and alcohol use, criminal behaviour, physical and mental health, and experiences of victimisation, among other topics. A strong emphasis was placed on eliciting narratives about becoming homeless and also on the establishment of a chronology of housing/living situations since homelessness was first experienced. During the follow-up interviews, conducted between 12 and 18 months after the point of initial contact with research respondents, young people were encouraged to update their life stories, including descriptions of changes in their social networks and family relationships, housing situations, homelessness, health and service utilisation practices. They were also encouraged to reflect on events, past and present, and to identify experiences which they felt had specific positive or negative consequences. This focus on personal experience allowed young people to articulate their views and to discuss transition and change in the telling of their stories over time.

Young people's exit routes from homelessness

The analysis of young people's pathways through and out of homelessness was based on a detailed examination of the narratives of the 30 young people re-interviewed at Phase II.[2] At the time of follow-up, young people reported a range of housing transitions, with 17 having achieved greater stability of housing and 13 remaining homeless, that is, living in emergency hostels, on the street, or in other unstable places of residence. Thus, a larger number of follow-up study participants had achieved greater stability of housing by Phase II of the study compared to those who remained homeless. This finding is significant since it signals success stories and demonstrates that young people who experience residential dislocation can make successful transitions out of homelessness.

The living situations of those who transitioned out of homelessness differed and were categorised as either *independent* or *dependent* exits. Those who exited independently were categorised in this way to reflect their relative independence from state-subsidised housing or other non-statutory interventions at the time of follow-up (although private rented sector occupants may have been receiving rent allowance). This distinguishes them from those who made dependent exits to state-subsidised transitional/supported housing or to state care. Table 13.1 presents a breakdown of the number of young people assigned to the two exit routes identified.

Table 13.1 Young people's exit routes from homelessness

Exit routes	Young men	Young women	All
Independent exits from homelessness Family home (6); private rented sector accommodation (1)	2	5	7
Dependent exits from homelessness Transitional/supported housing (7); state care (3)	3	7	10
Totals	5	12	17

Immediately obvious from the figures above, and similar to research findings elsewhere (Fitzpatrick, 2000), is that females were more likely than males to have exited homelessness. Only one young person had entered the private rented sector, signalling possible challenges to young people in accessing and negotiating accommodation of this kind. Three young people had moved from emergency hostel accommodation to state care, a transition which might be queried as an exit route, particularly since the study previously identified a history of state care as a pathway *into* homeless (Mayock and O'Sullivan, 2007). Nonetheless, these young people had moved on from out of hours service (OHS)[3] emergency (hostel) accommodation and, in general, they regarded their living situations as more stable than at the time of their baseline interview.

The process of exiting homelessness

For the majority of young people, the process of exiting homelessness was one with a number of transitions and negotiations attached. Like becoming homeless, exiting was not a single event. While the circumstances and developments associated with the transition differed for each individual, it was possible to identify factors, events and experiences that facilitated the move out of homelessness. Among these, access to appropriate and affordable housing was a key issue. Those who exited – whether by moving home, to private rented sector accommodation, transitional housing or state care – had clearly entered into more stable living situations. Low levels of movement between short-term, emergency or other unstable living situations was a second important facilitator, with several who had exited reporting no or few changes in accommodation since the time of their Phase I interview. For example, five of the seven who accessed supported or transitional housing by the time of follow-up had moved directly to these settings from their places of residence at Phase I. This situation contrasts sharply with those young people who remained homeless and who almost always reported rapid transitions between multiple living situations.

Other facilitators to exiting homelessness included access to, and engagement with, drug treatment and participation in education/training, with six of the seven respondents who moved to transitional housing, five of the six who had moved home, and all who moved to state care, having re-engaged in education or training. Alongside these facilitators, family support featured as a strong positive influence on young people and their ability to exit homelessness. The following sections explore the process of exiting with particular attention to the role of family support as a facilitator to moving home and to transitional housing, the two exit routes where the positive impact of family contact was particularly evident.

The concept of family support in much of the literature stresses the types of support that should be made available to families to enable them to support transitions to adulthood for troubled or 'troublesome' young people (see Pinkerton and Dolan, 2007 for an accessible overview). Such supports include emotional support, advice support and esteem support. In this chapter, we add to this fertile area of debate by suggesting that such support ought not to be viewed solely in terms of external agencies supporting families through professional interventions, but rather focus on ways in which families support and cajole young people through a variety of strategic decisions and actions that encompass exclusionary as well as inclusionary negotiated relationships. As the data reveal, resolving the difficulties that contributed to premature home-leaving involved, in some cases, young people desisting from certain activities and relinquishing certain peer networks while, in others, it was the parent(s) who made significant lifestyle changes. Some young people moved home while others accessed transitional housing. Both groups benefited from the support of their families, albeit to varying degrees and, in some cases, in conjunction with the help of professionals.

Moving home

Six respondents had exited homelessness by moving home. The home-leaving of three of these young people (two females and one male) was associated with their 'problem behaviour', including drinking and drug use, staying out late, and so on. During the period prior to becoming homeless all three described themselves as associating with the 'wrong crowd', and both of the young women were emotionally involved with a person of whom their parent(s) disapproved. Two others (both young women) left home for the first time following a period of profound instability or trauma, including sexual abuse in one case. One of these experienced housing disruption and parental alcohol abuse during childhood. With tensions running high, she left and stayed with a cousin initially, later with a family friend, and subsequently entered the statutory out of hours service emergency (hostel) accommodation. A second had an extremely fraught relationship with her mother and was the victim of physical and sexual abuse within her home. The final participant in this group was born outside Ireland and moved to Dublin at the age of 11. She had lived in an emergency residential setting for several years and, at the time of follow-up, was about to move to a suburban locality to live with a family member.

As might be expected, given the differences in the circumstances surrounding their home-leaving, the process associated with returning home differed for each individual. Nonetheless, there were a number of identifiable themes. For young people whose 'problem' behaviour was a factor in their homelessness, specific conditions were invariably attached to their return to the family home. All three had become heavily involved in drug use during their teenage years and two had criminal records. Sarah* had a lengthy history of drug use and criminal activity and had served two prison sentences. Since the age of 15 when she first left home she had slept rough, lived in England for a period, and had made use of adult hostels on many occasions. At the time of her Phase I interview she was living in a step-down unit from prison and was enrolled in a drug treatment programme. However, she subsequently relapsed, moving between unstable living situations, and was incarcerated for a second time. This second period in prison appeared to constitute a turning point experience, providing her with respite from street life and an opportunity to address her drug use. Prison 'didn't feel like a punishment', she explained, and helped her to 'get clean' (drug free). On release Sarah moved home, a development she attributed in large part to the intervention of her father. She went on to depict her father as having played a critical supportive role during her time in prison and felt that her situation would be very different had he not intervened at this juncture: 'I would be back in the hostels. I know I wouldn't have stayed clean on me own, you know.' Remaining drug free was a clear condition attached to her return to the family home:

> I had put them [parents] through an awful lot and they still came back like and I am so lucky to have them like but they don't tolerate it when I am active [using drugs], which is fair enough. They won't have me near the house or they won't let me live at home when I am like that, you know. So there was tight restrictions around even me parents taking me home like. (Sarah, age 23)

Sarah, like others who had moved home, described troubled relationships with her parents during her Phase I interview. The home-based difficulties and tensions reported by young people ranged from conflict between parents and young people over their behaviour (for example, mixing with 'troublemakers', drug use, staying out late) to resentments on the part of young people towards their parents linked to feelings of abandonment and neglect. As stated earlier, a number had left home under extremely difficult circumstances having suffered trauma in their homes as children. But improved family relationships were important enablers to moving home and a number openly acknowledged that their return home was facilitated by the support they received from their parents. Anna is another participant who highlighted the crucial role of parental support:

> I'd be lost without them [parents] because they're huge support for me and they'd do anything for me. So I can't complain about them too much [laugh] ... She's [Mum] learned to trust me and that's the biggest thing, there's a bit more trust in the family. (Anna, age 19)

Exiting homelessness was therefore strongly associated with a process of resolving issues that had previously served to undermine their ability to access and maintain a secure living situation. Those who moved home had made significant lifestyle changes and there was also a sense in which they had embraced new responsibilities and routines. Disassociating from former 'street' peers was another dimension of the lifestyle changes they described:

> We [referring to network of homeless peers] were bad influences on each other, do you know that kind of way ... Like I totally disconnected from all the old people I used to hang around with. (Anna, age 19)

These young people often talked about the importance of demonstrating to a parent(s) that they had made clear and tangible efforts to change. Julian (age 24) explained:

> I'm going to see counsellors and doctors, you know, they take urines and the urines are clean and all that. Once me Da sees that, it's a big improvement to him like, 'me son's trying to clean himself up'.

For others, however, resolving home-based difficulties relied to a far greater extent on change in the behaviour of their parents. Amy's home-leaving was strongly related to her mother's heavy drinking. During childhood, she and her family had lived in hostels and bed and breakfast accommodation for periods and Amy and her siblings were subsequently placed in care. Amy's care placement broke down, at which point she accessed emergency accommodation through the out of hours service and was placed in emergency hostel accommodation. By Phase II, her mother's situation had improved dramatically and she was in a position to care for some of her children, having stopped drinking and moved to local authority housing. Amy had maintained regular contact with her mother between Phases I and II of the study and, at the time of follow-up, was living five nights a week with her mother and two nights in a residential care setting. Professional supports had played an important role in her return home:

> Well she (key worker), anything I say to her like she'll get it done for me and all, do you know what I mean, me saying I wanted more access and she'll get back on to the social worker and say to her about me and what days I stay with me Ma, do you know what I mean. (Amy, age 17)

For the majority, moving home was a process that largely hinged on the ability of young people and their parents to resolve past tensions and conflicts. In general, strengthening family relationships through communication, behaviour change and trust were all important to the process of exiting. Conditions imposed by parents, such as commit-ments to remaining drug free and to breaking connections with street 'scenes', were almost always attached to a young person's move home. In this sense parents, while providing care and support, also held their children accountable.

Moving to transitional housing

All seven of the young people who had moved to transitional or supported housing reported some level of contact with their families and five felt that their relationship with family members had improved since the time of their previous interview. However, they told a somewhat different 'story' about family contact and relationships. These young people reported less frequent contact with their families compared to those who moved home and did not rely as heavily on family members for practical or emotional support. For example, practically all had negotiated their entry to a transitional living situation independent of family members, mostly with the help of professionals. Nonetheless, typical accounts suggest that family support played a positive and enabling role in their move to transi-tional housing. One young man, for example, had succeeded in building a stronger relationship with his mother and visited home on a regular basis. He depicted his mother's role as pivotal in his return to education and the affirmation he received at home appeared to be an important motivator: 'You get pride in paying things like that, paying the ESB (electricity bill), because like I'm showing to me Ma I can survive' (Sean, age 22). Another young woman described a vastly improved relationship with her mother as well as increased levels of support from home. These developments were closely associated with her pregnancy:

> I need me Ma. I'm having a baby and I need her help, do you know that way ... she's trying her best to be involved in this and she wants to be. She's putting a lot of effort into that ... so I want her to feel involved in it as well and let her know that I need her there. (Caroline, age 17)

Caroline further noted that she was not 'isolated in any way' and felt she was in a very different position to 'a young girl going through the out of hours' because of the support she had from her mother and friends. Others, however, who reported improved family contact did not have this level of support. One young woman explained that while her family relationships had improved she still felt uneasy and awkward when she spent time at home:

> I'm talking to me Ma all the time now and I'm talking to all me brothers
> which is better but I don't know, it's just weird being around me ma 'cos
> I don't know what to talk about. (Roisín, age 17)

For a number, then, the process of resolving past conflicts with parents
was clearly an incremental one. Neil's account highlights the tensions
and challenges surrounding his efforts to rebuild relationships with
his mother. Nonetheless, for this young man, contact with family
members was important even if the process of conflict resolution was
sometimes fraught:

> It [relationship with mother] was great up until the point where she says
> she didn't want me in the house anymore. That kind of makes you feel
> rejected ... it was getting really bad because I was like a lodger instead
> of a son in the house. I'm happy go lucky, I will go back if she wants. I'd
> rather not be away from my family and, like it or not, my mother is part
> of my family. (Neil, age 22)

Although all of the young people who moved to transitional housing
had some level of contact with home, not all reported a high level of
support from their families. However, those who had contact with
their families did feel supported by them to some extent and
appeared to benefit from their communication with their mothers, in
particular, and from the positive endorsements they received for their
efforts and achievements. Others had resolved some issues and home-
based difficulties and, although not completely at ease with their
parent(s), wanted to maintain these connections. Reports of not
wanting contact with parents or siblings were rare, with most express-
ing a willingness and desire to renew or improve contact with their
family and to rebuild these relationships.

Discussion

Moving out of homelessness was a challenging and sometimes lengthy
path for those young people who exited. Young people had to address
a range of issues in order to make the transition to stable housing,
including their drug use and drug problems, in some cases, and/or
their friendships – steps which required them to relinquish their
connections with former street, and drug-using, peers. They also
needed to significantly restructure their daily routines and a majority
had succeeded in returning to school or to a training programme.
Irrespective of the route taken by young people, family support
featured centrally in their stories of exiting homelessness, which

typically emphasised the importance of improved contact and communication with their parent(s). Overall, the data strongly suggest that continued contact with family members throughout a young person's homeless experience can facilitate a smoother transition to stable housing. This level of contact with family contrasts sharply with those young people in the study who remained homeless and who typically had weaker family ties, leaving them more reliant on other homeless youth for help and support (Mayock *et al.*, 2008).

Irrespective of whether young people moved home or to transitional housing, the process of rebuilding relationships with family members served important functions. In many cases, young people and their parents negotiated and redefined their relationships independently, that is, without the support of specific services, while others clearly availed of the supports available through formal programmes and interventions (for example, key workers, social workers, drug treatment programmes). Young people often identified 'critical moments' or turning point experiences that appeared to motivate them to seek alternative and more stable living situations. Parental support at this juncture acted in some cases as the catalyst for change and, in others, as a motivator or source of encouragement. Thus, exiting homelessness emerged as a process that differed according to the circumstances surrounding young people's home-leaving, their experiences of living out of home, and the level of social support available to them from family, professional agencies and others.

Clearly, a return to the family home is not always possible; and may be neither desirable nor appropriate for some young people who leave home prematurely (Fitzpatrick, 2000; Milburn *et al.*, 2009). Yet, the accounts of those young people who moved to transitional housing indicate that they valued their contact and relationships with family members. This support was a source of positive identification, even in situations where continued tensions served to undermine the quality of their family relationships. While the intensity and quality of support available to young people from their families differed, with lower levels typically available to those who transitioned to supported housing, compared to those who moved home, young people for whom moving home was not an option nonetheless valued their connections with family members.

That a considerable number of the study's young people had exited homelessness at the time of follow-up is significant, particularly in light of the challenges and difficulties they experienced both prior to and during their homelessness, and is a promising finding from the viewpoint of interventions. The findings presented signal variation in the routes taken by young people out of homelessness and indicate that they will rely to a greater or lesser extent on the support of professional agencies in attempting to resolve their homelessness. The positive impact of family support was striking, particularly for those young people who returned home but also for those who exited by transitioning to supported housing.

Concluding comments

In 2001, the *Youth Homelessness Strategy*, published by the Department of Health and Children, outlined its core objective, which was: 'To reduce and if possible eliminate youth homelessness through preventative strategies and where a child becomes homeless to ensure that s/he benefits from a comprehensive range of services aimed at reintegrating him/her into his/her community' (Department of Health and Children, 2001, p. 19). The first of twelve objectives set out by the *Youth Homelessness Strategy* states that, 'Family support and other preventive services will be developed on a multi-agency basis for children at risk of becoming homeless' (Department of Health and Children, 2001, p. 20). More broadly, family support is accepted as integral to the 'whole child/whole system' approach expressed clearly in the *National Children's Strategy: Our Children, Our Lives* (Government of Ireland, 2000). It is in this policy context that this chapter has attempted to explore the role of family in supporting young people to exit homelessness.

Social support is significant for all individuals but is particularly important during adolescence because of the number of transitions and potential challenges that young people typically face during this period. People generally access support from the informal sources of the nuclear family and, to a lesser extent, from friends (Cutrona, 2000; Canavan and Dolan, 2003). According to Pinkerton and Dolan (2007, p. 221), 'the ultimate goal of social support is to achieve the rights of young people through meeting their needs within the family'. However, the development of family support services in Ireland is not as strategically integrated as the systems operating in other jurisdictions and has a lower profile than child protection work (Buckley, 2002). Furthermore, despite the strategic emphasis placed on 'joined up thinking', 'there continues to be a tendency to think in practice of the child welfare system as being made up of three very distinct systems – child protection, out-of-home care (residential and foster care) and family support' (Pinkerton, 2006, p. 182).

The findings presented in this chapter strongly suggest that family-based interventions that work with homeless young people and their families may be viable and underdeveloped alternatives to address problem behaviour and issues of family conflict and communication. However, as noted in previous publications arising from this research (Mayock and O'Sullivan, 2007; Mayock *et al.*, 2008), current services targeting homeless youth in the Dublin region are predominantly *crisis orientated*. Many in our study who entered the out of hours service spent months and, in some cases, years moving between emergency hostels for the under-18s. These young people were far less likely to exit homelessness than their counterparts who moved relatively quickly to stable housing, and their ties with family members were weaker and more tenuous, particularly as time progressed (Mayock *et al.*, 2008). The timing of support intervention is clearly critical (Dolan and Holt, 2002). As Milburn *et al.* (2009, p. 782) point out, 'When adolescents first leave home, they are not yet committed to a pathway of chronic homelessness.' Early supportive intervention with homeless young people and their families could provide a positive starting point to securing a speedy resolution to young people's home-based difficulties. Noteworthy in this regard is that a Cork-based study of out-of-home young people (Mayock and Carr, 2008) found the Liberty Street Adolescent 'Out of Home' Service, which places a strong emphasis on working with young people and their families, to be effective in securing a return home for a considerable number of young people.

Much of the debate on the relationship between family circumstances and homelessness has focused on the role of family difficulties in propelling young people into homelessness. This chapter has attempted to explore another dimension of family dynamics, that of the role of families in enabling young people to exit homelessness. The findings documented have implications for social work practice and highlight the importance of a strengths perspective, which views the family both as a resource and target of intervention, when seeking to intervene in the lives of young people who leave home prematurely. Families, often viewed as the primary contributors to youth homelessness, may also provide the solutions required to ensure positive outcomes for homeless young people.

Notes

1   A third wave of data collection commenced in August 2009.
2   Although information was available on the whereabouts and living situations of an additional seven young people, this analysis draws solely on the narrative data available from the study's Phase I and Phase II interviews.

3 The Out of Hours Service (OHS) was established in 1992 by the Eastern
   Health Board to provide children and young people (under the age of 18) in
   crisis with the necessary services when all other options were closed
   (O'Sullivan and Mayock, 2008). The OHS is a social work, rather than a
   specific accommodation, service but much of its remit relates to 'out of home'
   young people. In order to access this service, a young person must report to a
   Garda station and declare him/herself as homeless, at which point the Gardaí
   contact the out-of-hours social work service. A social worker then attends and
   determines whether it is possible for the young person to return home. In
   cases where this is not possible, the young person is placed in OHS emergency
   (hostel) accommodation.
   * Pseudonyms are used for all of the young people quoted.

References

Anderson, I. and Tulloch, D. (2000) *Pathways through Homelessness: A Review of the Research Evidence*, Edinburgh, Scottish Homes.

Baron, S. W. (2003) 'Street youth, violence, and victimisation', *Trauma, Violence, & Abuse*, 4(1), pp. 22–44.

Baron, S. W. (2007) 'Street youth, gender, financial strain, and crime: Exploring Broidy and Agnew's extension to general strain theory', *Deviant Behavior*, 28(3), pp. 273–302.

Buckley, H. (2002) *Child Protection and Welfare: Innovations and Interventions*, Dublin, Institute of Public Administration.

Canavan, J. and Dolan, P. (2003) 'Policy roots and practice growth: Evaluating family support on the west coast of Ireland', in Katz, I. and Pinkerton, J. (eds), *Evaluating Family Support: Thinking Internationally, Thinking Critically*, Chichester, Wiley.

Chamberlain, C. and MacKenzie, D. (1994) 'Temporal dimensions of youth homelessness', *Australian Journal of Social Issues*, 29(1), pp. 1–254.

Clapham, D. (2002) 'Housing pathways: A post modern analytical framework', *Housing, Theory and Society*, 19(2), pp. 57–68.

Clatts, M. C. and Davis, W. R. (1999) 'A demographic and behavioral profile of homeless youth in New York City: Implications for AIDS outreach and prevention', *Medical Anthropology Quarterly*, 13(3), pp. 365–374.

Clatts, M. C., Davis, W. R. Sotheran, J. L. and Atillasoy, A. (1998) 'Correlates and distribution of HIV risk behaviors among homeless youths in New York City: Implications for prevention and policy', *Child Welfare*, 77(2), pp. 195–207.

Conover, S., Berkman, A., Gheith, A., Jahiel, R., Stanley, D., Geller, P., Valencia, J. and Susser, E. (1997) 'Methods of successful follow-up of elusive urban populations: An ethnographic approach with homeless men', *Bulletin of the New York Academy of Medicine*, 74(1), pp. 90–108.

Cutrona, E. E. (2000) 'Social support principles for strengthening families: Messages from America', in Canavan, J., Dolan, P. and Pinkerton, J. (eds) *Family Support: Direction from Diversity*, London, Jessica Kingsley.

Dachner, N. and Tarasuk, V. (2002) 'Homeless "squeegee kids": Food insecurity and daily survival', *Social Science & Medicine* (54)7, pp. 1039–1049.

Denzin, N. K. (1982) 'Contributions of anthropology and sociology to qualitative research methods', *New Directions for Institutional Research: Qualitative Methods for Institutional Research*, 34(2), pp. 17–26.

Department of Health and Children (2001) *Youth Homelessness Strategy*, Dublin, The Stationery Office.

Dolan, P. and Holt, S. (2002) 'What families want in family support: An Irish case study', *Child Care in Practice*, 8(4), pp. 239–250.

Fitzpatrick, S. (2000) *Young Homeless People*, Basingstoke, Macmillan.

Gaetz, S. (2004) 'Safe streets for whom? Homeless youth, social exclusion and criminal victimisation', *Journal of Criminology and Criminal Justice*, 46(4), pp. 423–455.

Gerstel, N., Bogard, C. J., McConnell, J. J. and Schwartz, M. (1996) 'The therapeutic incarceration of homeless families', *Social Service Review*, 70(4), pp. 543–572.

Government of Ireland (2000) *The National Children's Strategy: Our Children, Their Lives*, Dublin, The Stationery Office.

Greene, J. M. and Ringwalt, C. L. (1996) 'Youth and familial substance use's association with suicide attempts among runaway and homeless youth', *Substance Use & Misuse*, 31(8), pp. 1041–1058.

Hagan, J. and McCarthy, B. (1997) *Mean Streets: Youth Crime and Homelessness*, Cambridge, Cambridge University Press.

Johnson, G. and Chamberlain, C. (2008) 'From youth to adult homelessness', *Australian Journal of Social Issues*, 43(4), pp. 563–582.

Karabanow, J. (2008) 'Getting off the street: Exploring the process of young people's street exits', *American Behavioral Scientist*, 51(6), pp. 772–788.

Kelleher, P., Kelleher, C. and Corbett, M. (2000) *Left Out on Their Own: Young People Leaving Care in Ireland*, Dublin, Focus Ireland and Oak Tree Press.

Kurtz, D. P., Lindsey, E. W., Jarvis, S. and Nackerud, L. (2000) 'How runaway and homeless youth navigate troubled waters: The role of formal and informal helpers', *Child and Adolescent Social Work Journal*, 17(5), pp. 381–402.

Mallett, S., Rosenthal, D., Keys, D. and Averill, R. (2010) *Moving Out, Moving On: Young People's Pathways In and Through Homelessness*, East Sussex, Routledge.

May, J. (2000) 'Housing histories and homeless careers: A biographical approach', *Housing Studies*, 15(4), pp. 613–638.

Mayock, P. and Carr, N. (2008) *Not Just Homelessness ... A Study of 'Out of Home' Young People in Cork City*, Cork, Health Service Executive South.

Mayock, P. and O'Sullivan, E. (2007) *Lives in Crisis: Homeless Young People in Dublin City*, Dublin, The Liffey Press.

Mayock, P., Corr, M. L. and O'Sullivan, E. (2008) *Young People's Homeless Pathways*, Dublin, Homeless Agency.

McCarthy, B. and Hagan, J. (1992) 'Surviving on the street: The experiences of homeless youth', *Journal of Adolescent Health*, 7(4), pp. 412–430.

Milburn, N. G., Rice, E., Rotheram-Borus, M. J., Mallett, S., Rosenthal, D., Batterham, P., May, S. J., Witkin, A. and Duan, N. (2009) 'Adolescents exiting homelessness over two years: The risk amplification and abatement model', *Journal of Research on Adolescence*, 19(4), pp. 762–785.

Piliavin, I., Entner-Wright, B., Mare, R. and Westerfeld, A. H. (1996) 'Exits from and returns to homelessness', *Social Service Review*, 70(1), pp. 33–57.

Piliavin, I., Sosin, M., Westerfelt, A. H. and Matseuda, R. L. (1993) 'The duration of homeless careers: An exploratory study', *Social Service Review*, 67(4), pp. 576–598.

Pinkerton, J. (2006) 'Reframing practice as family support', in Dolan, P., Canavan, J. and Pinkerton, J. (eds), *Family Support as Reflexive Practice*, London, Jessica Kingsley Publishers.

Pinkerton, J. and Dolan, P. (2007) 'Family support, social capital, resilience and adolescent coping', *Child and Family Social Work*, 12, pp. 219–228.

Stojanovic, D., Weitzman, B. C., Shinn, M., Labay, L. E. and Williams, N. P. (1999) 'Tracing the path out of homelessness: The housing patterns of families after exiting shelter', *Journal of Community Psychology*, 27(2), pp. 199–208.

Wong, Y. L. I. and Piliavin, I. (1997) 'A dynamic analysis of homeless domicile transitions', *Social Problems*, 44(3), pp. 408–423.

14

Aftercare not afterthought: Supporting the transition to adulthood for children in care

Ann Doyle, Paula Mayock and Kenneth Burns

Introduction

A core message arising from recent research on children and young people who grow up in substitute care is that leaving care represents a crucial moment in their lives. While both pre- and in-care experiences impact on young people in a wide variety of ways and may have consequences that last well into adulthood, the leaving care experience is increasingly recognised as having both short and long-term ramifications for young people. This recognition is linked to broader concerns about outcomes for care leavers and the considerable challenges they confront as they make the transition to adulthood. It is against this backdrop that this chapter considers aftercare provision for children and young people with care experience in the Irish context. The discussion draws on international research on care experiences and outcomes, as well as a far more limited body of literature on children in care in Ireland.

The chapter starts by discussing some key aspects of the transition from adolescence to adulthood, highlighting the unique challenges that care leavers face at the point of moving from care to independent living. This is followed by a review of the Irish and international literature on outcomes for children in care. The focus then shifts to present an overview of the legislation governing the provision of aftercare services to young people in care in Ireland. This discussion highlights weaknesses within the existing legislative framework guiding the provision and delivery of aftercare services while also acknowledging developments within policy and practice arenas, particularly over the past decade. The issue of aftercare planning is then considered before moving to discuss conditions and realities within the broader arena of child protection and welfare that constrain social work practice in relation to the provision of aftercare services. We conclude that aftercare provision for care leavers in Ireland is currently inconsistent to an unacceptable level and argue that the existing legislation governing aftercare provision requires amendment.

The transition from adolescence to adulthood

There is an increasing amount of research focusing on the transition to adulthood, a stage in the lifecycle where young people face demanding decisions in the domains of education, relationships, career, employment and housing (Aassve et al., 2006). The transition to adulthood presents challenges for all adolescents and, in more recent times, is judged to have become more protracted, making the journey to adulthood more challenging than for previous generations of youth (Arnett, 2000; Bynner et al., 2002; Coles, 1995; Furlong and Cartmel, 1997). This development is linked to changes in the youth labour market, the extension of training and educational provision, and a reduction in young people's ability to access universal benefit entitlements. For example, with increasing levels of participation in higher education, young people are dependent on the financial support of their parents for longer than was previously the case. The effect has been that all young people remain dependent on their families for financial, emotional and practical support for longer periods (Jones, 2002).[1] Yet, there is great diversity in these extended pathways to adulthood, with some adolescents and young adults far more vulnerable than others and less well equipped to successfully navigate the journey to adulthood. Thus, while modern-day youth transitions have come to be characterised as involving greater discontinuity and risk and as posing problems for all young people (Furlong et al., 2003), it can be 'a minefield for vulnerable populations' (Osgood et al., 2005, p. 3). For marginalised youth in particular, the transition to adulthood is even more fractured and complex (Coles and Craig, 1999; MacDonald et al., 2005).

Young care leavers are not a homogenous group but there are many who experience multiple levels of disadvantage, often leaving care with low educational attainment, poor social and emotional maturity, and lacking the ongoing supports necessary to ensure their successful inclusion within their communities and wider society (Kelleher et al., 2000; Courtney et al., 2001; Youth Homelessness Monitoring

Committee, 2004; Dixon and Stein, 2005; Courtney and Dworsky, 2006). Young people leave care to live independently, an average of six years earlier than their counterparts in the general population (Social Services Inspectorate, 2001a). Thus, for young care leavers the transitional period from youth to adulthood is less graduated and characterised by less support (Cashmore and Paxman, 2006). For many leaving care, as Stein (2006) puts it, 'there is the expectation of instant adulthood':

> Care leavers are expected to undertake their journey to adulthood, from restricted to full citizenship, far younger and in far less time than their peers, leading to their journey to adulthood being both accelerated and compressed. (Stein, 2006, p. 274)

Leaving home is typically a transition that unfolds with the continued support (material, social, emotional and financial) of family and friends and is a process that is not necessarily linear. Young people may, for example, leave home and return at a later stage because of changed circumstances or financial strain. However, young people who grow up in care may have limited contact with their families and, at the point of leaving care, their relationships with family members may be tenuous rather than supportive (Biehal and Wade, 1996; Sinclair et al., 2005), making the transition to independent living difficult, stressful and challenging. Many, for example, do not have the stability of a relationship with a parent or caregiver to provide them with a sound support base as they embark on a range of complex transitions. Thus, young care leavers may find themselves quite isolated and with no guarantee of financial support, particularly during times of crisis. This leaves them partly or solely dependent on social welfare supports and on the support of professionals and civil society organisations to enable them to make the transition to independence.

There is strong evidence internationally that many care leavers feel unprepared for the transition to independent living (Cook, 1994; English et al., 1994; Centrepoint, 2006). In the Irish context, evidence of young people's lack of readiness at the point of leaving care is mainly anecdotal. However, a small-scale study of care leavers in the Health Service Executive South (HSE South) found that a large number felt unprepared for the transition to adult life and that they had inadequate support and advice in relation to skills, training and employment. Many also felt poorly equipped to deal with the changes associated with leaving care and with the stress of having to live and cope independently (Doyle, 2001). Below is a sample of the accounts of care leavers who participated in the study:

> I don't think I was supported enough when I left care; I never saw a
> social worker, I was always lonely and I got in with the wrong crowd. I
> am presently awaiting a drug treatment programme.

> I would have liked to discuss the problems I have with relationships, and
> get help with problem solving. No one prepared me for life outside
> care. (Doyle, 2001, p. 38)

Young care leavers are not typically afforded the 'luxury' of a gradual
transition to adulthood and many are unlikely to have the safety net of
family support at the point of moving out of care. Unlike other young
people who can revert to the family home, they cannot return to
the child welfare system after the age of 18 years if they experience
difficulties or find they are unable to cope with the demands of
independent living.

Outcomes for care leavers

Research consistently demonstrates that young care leavers face
specific challenges and that many experience a cluster of problems
both when they are in care and after they transition out of the care
system (Stein, 2006). The difficulties care leavers experience may
relate to their early life histories and also to their in-care experiences.
For example, a large number are likely to continue to struggle with
negative or traumatic experiences, which may include physical, sexual
or emotional abuse or neglect. They may also continue to cope with
feelings of grief and loss associated with their separation from their
families of origin.

Many will also have experienced inadequacies while in state care,
including multiple placements and/or poor quality caregivers that
impact negatively on their well-being. Placement instability, resulting
in multiple care placements, is a distinctive feature of many care
careers and one that leads to fractured and dislocated experiences.
The disruption caused by placement moves are well documented both
in the international and Irish literature (Broad, 2005; Mayock and
Carr, 2008; Hyde and Kammerer, 2009). When a child or young
person experiences multiple placements, he or she enters successive
periods of instability and disruption. Multiple placements impact
negatively on a young person's education, resulting in numerous
disruptions to their schooling, which in turn may limit their ability to
secure employment. Aldgate *et al.* (1992) note that a key factor in
educational attainment is placement stability, arguing that educational success is higher where the young person has continuity of care

and schooling. Poor placement experiences can also generate feelings of failure and rejection, and can lead to the young person feeling more disconnected. Cashmore and Paxman's (2006) five-year longitudinal study found that young people who had had one placement lasting for 75 per cent of their time in care were more positive about their experience, were less mobile, and had better outcomes twelve months after they left care. Instability for young people in care can also be linked to the frequent changeover of social workers (Doyle, 2001).

Research consistently indicates that care leavers are over-represented in many sub-groups of social disadvantage, including the homeless and prison populations, persons with mental health and/or drug and alcohol problems, and learning disabled service users (Kelleher et al., 2000; Courtney and Dworsky, 2006; Stanley, 2007). Research into the post-care careers of samples of care leavers has also highlighted their over-representation among the unemployed (Broad, 1999; Pinkerton and McCrea, 1999; Wade and Dixon, 2006). Outcomes for care leavers are poorly researched in the Irish context, with Kelleher et al.'s (2000) research providing the only comprehensive published study on this topic (Gilligan, 2008). This national study of care leavers found that the vast majority came from backgrounds of poverty and social disadvantage and that a large percentage had experienced emotional trauma related to factors such as violence in the home, sexual abuse, alcohol and drug addiction in the home, and loss of a parent through separation. Twenty-five per cent of all young people in the study were considered to have been inappropriately placed, many more had experienced placement breakdown and, for 55 per cent of the sample, leaving care was precipitated by a crisis. The study identified the absence of guidelines, policy or dedicated budget for aftercare and resettlement as one of the major failings in the child care system (Kelleher et al., 2000, p. 19).

Research in the Irish context has repeatedly highlighted the link between homelessness and a history of state care. For example, the Southern Health Board's *Review of Adequacy of Child Care and Family Support Services* (1996) indicated that 35 per cent of young people presenting as homeless were previously in care. Kelleher et al. (2000) found that 33 per cent of respondents had experienced homelessness within the first six months, rising to 66 per cent within two years. More recently, Mayock and Carr's (2008) qualitative study of youth homelessness in Cork found that 20 respondents in their sample of 37 young people (54%) had a care history and identified a history of state care as a significant pathways into homelessness. A Dublin-based study similarly found that a large proportion (40%) of homeless young people reported a history of state care (Mayock and O'Sullivan, 2007).

Overall, the available research evidence strongly indicates a high risk of social exclusion for young people leaving the care system. Nonetheless, it is important to recognise that many care leavers display considerable resilience in overcoming adversity. Resilience is closely associated with young people's pre- and in-care experiences and with the support they receive. Particular factors that appear to contribute to resilience include: stable and good quality placements, positive educational experiences, ongoing professional and informal support with living skills and career planning, and supportive social experiences and relationships (Gilligan, 2001). According to Stein (2008, p. 42), the promotion of resilience requires 'more comprehensive responses across the life course', including 'opportunities for more gradual transitions from care' and 'ongoing support to those young people who need it'. One of the difficulties is that the predominant focus of social work practice tends to be on entry to care with much less attention to exit (Maunders et al., 1999). This finding is mirrored in the Health Information and Quality Authority's (2009) national review of children in care which found that insufficient attention was placed on planning and preparation for leaving care; some of the young adults who participated in the review expressed anxiety concerning the lack of planning for their aftercare. Furthermore, the support of social workers and other professionals tends to decline in the period after leaving care (Biehal et al., 1995; Doyle, 2001).

Aftercare provision in the Republic of Ireland

Children enter the care system when it is recognised by agencies of the state that they are in need of protection and ongoing care. In April 2009, there were 5,589 children in the care of the state. Of these, 376 were in residential or hostel accommodation and 180 were living in dedicated hostels for separated children seeking asylum (Health Service Executive, 2009). The vast majority (90%) were in foster care and of those living with foster families, two-thirds were placed with families previously unknown to them and one-third were in the care of a relative or neighbour with whom they had a previous relationship. These figures reflect a more general trend, starting in the early 1980s, towards a reduction in the placement of children in residential care and an increase in the numbers placed in foster care (O'Sullivan, 1996; O'Sullivan and Breen, 2008).

The Child Care Act 1991 and the Children Act 2001, which replaced the Children Act 1908 and the Health Acts 1953 and 1957, provide the statutory framework for child protection, welfare and youth justice provision in Ireland. Section 45 of the Child Care Act 1991 states that a health board *may* assist a person leaving its care up to the age of 21 years or until he or she has completed their education or training. According to Section 45(b), a Health Board may assist in one or more of the following ways:

a   by causing him to be visited or assisted;
b   by arranging for the completion of his education and by contributing towards his maintenance while he is completing his education;
c   by placing him in a suitable trade, calling or business and paying such fee or sum as may be requisite for that purpose;
d   by arranging hostel or other forms of accommodation for him;
e   by co-operating with housing authorities by planning accommodation for children leaving care on reaching the age of 18 years.

Section 45 thus empowers health boards (now the Health Service Executive) to provide aftercare support for children in their care. However, this provision in legislation is enabling rather than obligatory (Kelleher *et al.*, 2000), thereby providing a weak legislative basis for leaving care provision. With no mandatory requirement to provide aftercare, the type, nature and quality of aftercare provision is effectively left to the discretion of each individual HSE area. The weaknesses inherent in legislation also mean that aftercare provision lacks coherence and is inconsistent throughout the country. According to the Social Services Inspectorate (2001a, p. 3), 'Aftercare support tends to be provided by committed individual practitioners, rather than as the product of clear, strategic service planning.' Furthermore, inspection findings since 2002 have repeatedly highlighted inconsistency in care planning and leaving care and aftercare policies and procedures in residential care settings (Social Services Inspectorate, 2001b, 2002, 2003, 2004, 2005; Health Information and Quality Authority, 2009).

It is worth noting that the issue of deficits in leaving and aftercare provision for young people is by no means new. The *Report on the Reformatory and Industrial Schools System* (1970), more commonly known as the Kennedy Report, explicitly referenced deficiencies in this area. Similarly, the *Task Force on Child Care Services* (1980), established in 1974 to make recommendations for legislative and administrative reform of services 'for deprived children and children at risk' (1980, p. 1), noted the challenges facing young people leaving state care. The legacy of these deficits is echoed more recently in the recommendations of *The Report of the Commission to Inquire into Child Abuse* (better known as the Ryan Report),[2] published in May 2009. Shortly after its publication, the Office of the Minister for Children and Youth Affairs published an implementation plan which again noted the continued absence of standardised aftercare provision:

> Aftercare services are not provided consistently to all children across the State. Some HSE areas have dedicated aftercare workers, but most do not. Some areas provide aftercare services only to young people who have been in their care for a specific length of time; for others, support is offered only in the immediate period leaving the care placement. In some instances, the resources offered are based on the child's willingness to accept the aftercare resource at the time of leaving care. (Office of the Minister for Children and Youth Affairs, 2009, p. 48)

The implementation plan explicitly acknowledges the crucial role of aftercare, stressing that: 'It should not be seen as a discretionary service or as a once-off event' (2009, p. 48). In response to the Ryan Report recommendation that children 'should have access to support services', it states: 'The HSE will ensure the provision of aftercare services for children leaving care in all instances where the professional judgement of the allocated social worker determines it is required' (2009, p. 49).

Acknowledgement of the integral nature of aftercare provision is also present in both national and regional policy documents published over the past decade, in particular. For example, in relation to preparation for leaving care, the 2001 *National Standards for Children's Residential Centres* states that 'two years prior to a young person reaching the legal age of leaving care the care plan will outline the preparation and support in place for the young person', further noting that: 'Young people up to a minimum age of 21 should be supported, as they request, by the aftercare service' (Department of Health and Children, 2001a, pp. 20–21). Similarly, objective 4 of the 2001 *Youth Homelessness Strategy* states: 'Aftercare is an integral part of the care process, it is not an optional extra' (Department of Health and Children, 2001b, p. 27). Guidelines on the development of leaving and aftercare policy issued subsequently to health boards by the *Youth Homelessness Monitoring Committee* place a strong emphasis on the need for effective leaving and aftercare policies, outlining specific steps to be taken by all health boards when developing their aftercare policies (Youth Homelessness Monitoring Committee, 2004).

A regional *Policy on Leaving Care* developed a short time later by a sub-group of the Youth Homelessness Forum,[3] was adopted as policy by the then Eastern Regional Health Authority (ERHA)[4] in May 2004 (ERHA, 2004). This document set out a model of leaving care service provision that stressed the crucial role of planning, partnership, and active participation on the part of young people, as well as the importance of regular review and evaluation. Using this document as 'a key source of direction', in 2006, the HSE published a *Model for the Delivery of Leaving Care and Aftercare Services* in HSE North West Dublin, North Central Dublin and North Dublin (Health Service Executive, 2006, p. 4), with the stated aim of helping to achieve 'the delivery of appropriate preparation, leaving and aftercare services' (Health Service Executive, 2006, p. 6). The most recent policy statement on aftercare comes from the Health Information and Quality Authority, which sets standards for health and social care providers in Ireland, which in its review of foster care in one HSE area, advised that social workers should 'ensure that all children aged 16 and over have an aftercare plan and are adequately supported in leaving foster care' (Health Information and Quality Authority, 2010, p. x).

There has clearly been considerable investment, particularly in recent years, in the development of quite detailed guidelines on aftercare provision. Nonetheless, these policies and guidelines pertain only to particular regions. A *National Policy and Procedures for Aftercare Provision* was completed in early February 2011 and once it is approved by the HSE and The Department of Children and Youth Affairs, may go some way towards ensuring standardised service provision and practice nationally.

Recent years have seen mounting pressure and lobbying from the non-governmental organisation (NGO) sector in particular for an amendment to Section 45 of the Child Care Act 1991, which would place a legal obligation on the HSE to provide aftercare support.[5] A newly established consortium of NGOs, health and social care practitioners and academics, *Action for Aftercare*, actively lobbied for an amendment to the Child Care (Amendment) Bill 2009.[6] This amendment was not accepted into the draft legislation and, in any event, the Bill was not enacted before the dissolution of the 30th Dáil on 1 February 2011. Just a year previously (February 2010) the Assistant Director for Children and Families in the HSE had publicly articulated the view that the legislation on aftercare needed to be amended to reflect the state's role and responsibilities as a parent for children in its care (Smyth, 2010). However, in August 2010, the then Minister for Children and Youth Affairs, Barry Andrews, announced, following consideration of the legal provision with regard to aftercare services, that an amendment was not necessary since aftercare is already provided for in Section 45 of the Child Care Act 1991.

Aftercare: preparation, planning and models of provision

There is clearly greater acknowledgement than previously in the Irish context that young people leaving the care system do not receive adequate preparation and support. On leaving care, the lack of adequate preparation, coupled with the early age at which care leavers are expected to assume adult responsibilities mean that loneliness, isolation, unemployment, poverty, homelessness and 'drift', are likely to feature significantly in the later lives of many with a history of state care (Kelleher et al., 2000; Mayock and O'Sullivan, 2007; Mayock and Carr, 2008). This situation is not unique to Ireland, with research findings in other jurisdictions highlighting that preparation for leaving care tends to be variable, often poorly structured, and overly focused on practical rather than psycho-social skills (Biehal et al., 1995; Maunders et al., 1999; Stein and Wade, 2000).

Outcome studies evaluating specialist leaving care services have shown that they can have a positive impact on lives of care leavers. For example, research by Wade and Dixon (2006) provides evidence of an association between stability in accommodation and enhanced sense of well-being. Leaving care services can help young people in furthering their social networks, developing relationships and building self-esteem (Biehal et al., 1995). A significant association has also been found between preparation before leaving care and coping (Dixon and Stein, 2005). Saunders and Broad (1997) argue that good preparation for leaving care provides the young person with opportunities for planning, problem-solving and the learning of new competencies. Finally, research suggests young people who experience planned transitions from care and who leave care at an older age are likely to do better (Stein, 2002).

Meaningful preparation and planning for the transition out of care needs to encompass a range of supports aimed at enabling the young person to reach his or her full potential. Crucial in terms of conceptualising and providing preparation and support is the recognition that leaving care is a *process* rather than a single event.

> Leaving care is formally defined as the cessation of legal responsibility by the state for young people living in out-of-home care. But, in practice, leaving care is a major life event and process that involves transitioning from dependence on state accommodation and supports to so-called self-sufficiency. (Mendes and Moslehuddin, 2006, p. 111)

Just as the transition to adulthood takes place over a period of time, usually with the support of family, friends and other support systems, leaving care requires preparation over an extended period. This work needs to be viewed as a core part of a young person's care placement and planning should begin early in their care career, ideally when children and young people enter care (Maunders *et al.*, 1999; Stein and Wade, 2000). There are a number of models of practice highlighted in international literature that offer guidance to professionals. Maunders *et al.* (1999), for example, recommend a three-component model of support designed to minimise transition problems:

1 *Preparation*: based on a high quality, stable system of care with quality case planning and a flexible support continuum.
2 *Transition*: provision of appropriate information to young people about their past and options for the future, effective support (including financial) for developing life skills and establishing personal and social networks including the involvement of suitable mentors.
3 *Aftercare*: continuing access to support and contact with care agencies (with support continuing to at least until age 25).

One advantage of Maunders *et al.*'s (1999) model is that it recognises the graduated nature of the transition out of care. It also recognises the care experience itself as impacting on the post-care experience as well as highlighting young people's need for ongoing support until the age of 25. Young people leaving care will, of course, differ in their circumstances, including their age at entry to out-of-home care, how many placements they have had, where and with whom they are living at the time of discharge, and what sources of support they have and need (Cashmore and Paxman, 1996), highlighting the need for a comprehensive assessment of need prior to leaving care.

Both the regional *Policy on Leaving Care* (ERHA, 2004) and the *Model for the Delivery of Leaving Care and Aftercare Services* (Health Service Executive, 2006) stress that aftercare preparation and planning need to be seen as a through-care process 'beginning from reception into care' (ERHA, 2004, p. 10). Both of these documents outline models of provision and delivery of aftercare services that place a strong emphasis on assessment of need (incorporating the young person's material and psycho-social needs) and preparation for leaving care. The *Model for the Delivery of Leaving Care and Aftercare Services* in particular stresses the need for 'a comprehensive multi-disciplinary, multi-agency approach involving health, care, welfare, education, training and accommodation' (Health Service Executive, 2006, p. 6). Thus, many of the existing published guidelines on aftercare provision in Ireland bear the hallmarks of international best practice in the field. Significantly, however, policy and practice differ both within and between HSE regions. In any case, the nature and scope of aftercare provision is contingent on the allocation of resources within individual Health Service Executive regions.

Child protection and welfare social work in a changing climate: the importance of a renewed focus on relationship-based work

There is ample evidence that child protection and welfare teams are under-resourced in terms of adequate staffing levels and access to sufficient resources such as alternative care placements (see Chapter 1; Health Service Executive, 2008). What makes practice even more difficult, particularly during the current economic downturn, is the imperative to providing 'more for less', in essence 'increased output', in a climate of dwindling financial resources. Notwithstanding these difficulties, social work will always face challenges in promoting the welfare of its clients and never is this more obvious than for those who have a statutory responsibility for children in care. Moreover, on a positive note, despite difficulties with the [in]solvency of the Irish economy, the HSE has been active in filling posts in child protection and welfare that were left 'vacant' following the 2006–9 recruitment embargo. The HSE filled the new child protection and welfare social work posts promised by the government in response to criticisms of the system contained in the Ryan Report.

Research studies on what helps young people in care to transition successfully from care to independence repeatedly highlight the seminal importance of the quality of their relationships with professionals and carers. Practitioners increasingly find themselves engaged in crisis-driven practice, with increasingly high caseloads, and more demanding administrative tasks, which results in them being distanced from the meaningful face-to-face contact with service users. In such a practice environment, the important slow, patient and time-intensive relationship building work is not always prioritised or may be 'contracted' out.

One of the ways for social workers to challenge the creeping managerial ethos is to individually and collectively attempt to refocus attention on what social workers are trained to do: to analyse and be critical of policy and how it disadvantages service users, and to re-engage with core relationship building and engagement skills – to prioritise time to maximise opportunities to undertake direct face-to-face contacts with children and young people. Stein and Wade (2000, p. 3) argue that 'the planning and review process prior to a young person leaving care is the foundation upon which good aftercare support can be built', which in turn will facilitate better outcomes for care leavers. This can occur best when the social worker has a relationship with the young person and the importance of this relationship should not be underestimated. In a study by Happer *et al.* (2006), which looked at the successful outcomes for a sample of 30 care leavers, a number of key findings related to the quality and nature of the relationship between the young person and their social worker. Young people who participated in the study argued that outcomes were best for them when:

- The social worker had the ability to express warmth, was caring and demonstrated their interest in the young person's welfare, thus promoting positive engagement.
- There was a continuity of social work staff. This was seen as an essential ingredient to relationship development. Young people argued that it was difficult to build relationships and trust when there were frequent changes of social worker.
- The manner in which the social worker behaved towards them was very important; overall, participants recognised the difficulties and pressures experienced by the social worker, but they felt let down when they experienced rudeness or disrespect.
- Reliability was another key factor, for example, arriving on time for appointments (or advance notice that appointment time was changed), and an ability to follow through on agreed tasks, for example, 'doing what was promised'.

A further key practice message from this research was that where professionals provided encouragement and support and had high expectations about what was possible for the young person's future, it improved the young person's capacity to make positive decisions about their lives.

Concluding comments

> Children in state care are not in the same position as other children
> because they do not have a parent to advocate on their behalf or to find
> ways to ensure their needs are met and that the disadvantage they have
> experienced is counterbalanced with opportunities. No child should
> leave the long-term care system without the ability to earn a living, live
> independently and form wholesome relationships. The State has a duty
> to ensure this as far as possible. (Office of the Minister for Children and
> Youth Affairs, 2009, p. 14)

There is no denying the challenges involved in seeking to develop and
deliver effective services that provide quality leaving care and
aftercare provision. The past decade has seen a gradual accumulation
of support for aftercare provision among policy makers and practitioners in Ireland. This represents a positive shift and signals a clear
recognition of the aftercare needs of young care leavers, not simply at
the point of leaving but from the point of entering the care system.
The range of policy directives and practice guidelines published in
support of aftercare signals a commitment to change and helps to put
aftercare provision on a more solid footing (ERHA, 2004; Health
Service Executive, 2006). Further to this, there is undoubtedly no
shortage of professional commitment to the development of aftercare
provision.

Media coverage and public debate about poor outcomes for these
children may give the impression that the care system is failing *all*
children (see Chapter 8). However, there are many children and
young adults who do well in the care system and have good outcomes.
There is a need for more Irish and international research to learn
from these positive experiences and to counter overtly negative public
and media portrayals of the lives and outcomes for children in care
and in aftercare. Nonetheless, the available evidence suggests that in
Ireland, the provision of leaving care and after care services varies
across, and within, HSE areas. It is important that all children leaving
care (and those who have left the care system) receive the necessary
supports irrespective of where they live. To this end, primary legislation, the Child Care Act 1991, should be strengthened to make
Section 45 a regulatory and binding article. In the absence of a legal
requirement to provide aftercare services and supports, efforts to
strengthen service provision will remain discretionary. This situation
also significantly reduces the chances of aftercare provision receiving
the requisite resources to ensure comprehensive national coverage. As
a consequence, many young care leavers are likely to continue to have

their needs unmet, representing a failure to protect the welfare and rights of some of the most vulnerable children and young people in society.

Acknowledgements and correspondence

The authors would like to thank Nicola Carr, School of Sociology, Social Policy and Social Work, Queen's University Belfast, for her helpful comments on an earlier draft of this chapter. Please forward all correspondence to Ann Doyle at ann.doyle1@hse.ie.

Notes

1   The average age for leaving home is between 24 and 29 years across Europe (Iacovou, 2004).
2   The *Commission to Inquire into Child Abuse* was established in 2000 to investigate allegations of abuse in children's residential institutions and care settings. The Commission heard evidence through two separate committees – the Investigation Committee and the Confidential Committee. The chairperson of the Commission, Mr Justice Ryan, a High Court judge, was also chairperson of the Investigation Committee. The Commission's Report consists of five volumes, totalling approximately 2,500 pages, and is known collectively as the Ryan Report (see Chapter 2 for further background and details of this Report).
3   A Forum on Youth Homelessness was established in February 1999 with the objective of strategically addressing deficits in service provision and ensuring 'that services on offer are effective and responsive to the needs of young homeless people' (Forum on Youth Homelessness, 2000, p. 5). The Forum drew attention to absence of a legal obligation to provide services to young people once they reach the age of 18 years, pointing out that 'people do not become completely transformed on the morning of a particular birthday' (Forum on Youth Homelessness, 2000, p. 6).
4   In January 2005, the Health Service Executive (HSE) replaced the existing structure of regional health boards, the Eastern Regional Health Authority (EHRA) and a number of other different agencies and organisations.
5   For example, Focus Ireland have been actively advocating for an amendment to Section 45 which would place a duty of care on the HSE whereby support to those who need it becomes an *obligation* and not merely an *option* (see, for example, Focus Ireland, 2010). Empowering People in Care (EPiC) formerly the Irish Association for Young People in Care (IAYPIC) advocates at a local and national level for the rights of children in and with care experience (see www.epiconline.ie).
6   The Child Care (Amendment) Bill 2009 amends existing legislation in relation to secure or special care orders and also makes a number of other amendments to the Child Care Act 1991. The Bill additionally provides for the dissolution of the Children Acts Advisory Board (see Carr, 2010, for an overview and critique of this Bill).

References

Aassve, A., Iacovou, M. and Mencarini, L. (2006) 'Youth poverty and the transition to adulthood in Europe', *Demographic Research*, 15, pp. 21–49.

Aldgate, J., Colton, M., Ghate, D. and Heath, A. (1992) 'Educational attainment and stability in long-term foster care', *Children and Society*, 6, pp. 91–103.

Arnett, J. J. (2000) 'Emerging adulthood: A theory of development from the late teens through the twenties', *American Psychologist*, 55, pp. 469–480.

Biehal, N., Clayden, J., Stein, M. and Wade, J. (1995) *Moving On: Young People and Leaving Care Schemes*, London, HMSO.

Biehal, N. and Wade, J. (1996) 'Looking back, looking forward: Care leavers, families and change', *Children and Youth Services Review*, 18, pp. 425–445.

Broad, B. (1999) 'Young people leaving care: Moving towards "joined up" solutions', *Children & Society*, 13, pp. 81–93.

Broad, B. (2005) 'Young people leaving care: Implementing the Child (Leaving Care) Act 2000', *Children & Society*, 19, pp. 371–384.

Burns, K. and Lynch, D. (eds) (2008) *Child Protection and Welfare Social Work: Contemporary Themes and Practice Perspectives*, Dublin, A. & A. Farmar.

Bynner, J., Elias, P., McKnight, A., Pan, H. and Pierre, G. (2002) *Young People's Changing Routes to Independence*, York, Joseph Rowntree.

Carr, N. (2010) 'Child Care (Amendment) Bill, 2009: An attempt to arbitrate on a system's logic', *Irish Journal of Family Law*, 13, pp. 63–69.

Cashmore, J. and Paxman, M. (2006) 'Predicting after-care outcomes: The importance of 'felt' security', *Child & Family Social Work*, 11, pp. 232–241.

Centrepoint (2006) *A Place to Call Home: Care Leavers' Experience of Finding Suitable Accommodation*, London, Centrepoint.

Coles, B. (1995) *Youth and Social Policy*, London, UCL Press.

Coles, B. and Craig, G. (1999) 'Excluded youth and the growth of begging', in H. Dean (ed), *Begging Questions: Street Level Economic Activity and Social Policy Failure*, Bristol, The Policy Press.

Commission of Inquiry into the Reformatory and Industrial School System (1970) *Report on the Reformatory and Industrial Schools System (Kennedy Report)*, Dublin, Stationery Office.

Cook, R. J. (1994) 'Are we helping foster are youth prepare for their future?', *Children and Youth Services Review*, 16, pp. 213–229.

Courtney, M. and Dworsky, A. (2006) 'Early outcomes for young adults transitioning from out-of-home care in the USA, *Child & Family Social Work*, 11, pp. 209–219.

Courtney, M. E., Piliavan, I., Grogan-Kayor, A. and Nesmith, A. (2001)

'Foster youth transitions to adulthood: A longitudinal view of youth leaving care', *Child Welfare*, 6, pp. 685–717.

Department of Health and Children (2001a) *National Standards for Children's Residential Centres*, Dublin, Department of Health and Children.

Department of Health and Children (2001b) *Youth Homelessness Strategy*, Dublin, Stationery Office.Dixon, J. and Stein, M. (2005) *Leaving Care, Throughcare and Aftercare in Scotland*, London, Jessica Kingsley Publishers.

Doyle, A. (2001) 'A Proposal for the Development of an Aftercare Service for the Southern Health Board', (unpublished report), Cork, Southern Health Board.

Eastern Regional Health Authority (EHRA) (2004) *Policy on Leaving Care (Leaving Care Sub-group of the Youth Homeless Forum)*, Dublin, Eastern Regional Health Authority.

English, D. J., Kouidou-Giles, S. and Plocke, M. (1994) 'Readiness for independence: A study of youth in foster care', *Children and Youth Services Review*, 16, pp. 147–158.

Focus Ireland (2010) *Focus Ireland Calls on all TDs to give rights to young people Leaving State Care as Child Care (Amendment) Bill Goes Though Oireachtas* (online). Available from: http://focusireland.posterous .com/focus-ireland-calls-on-all-tds-to-give-rights (accessed 21 May 2010).

Forum on Youth Homelessness (2000) *Report of the Forum on Youth Homelessness*, Dublin, Northern Area Health Board.

Furlong, A. and Cartmel, F. (1997) *Young People and Social Change*, Buckingham, Open University Press.

Furlong, A., Cartmel, F., Biggart, A., Sweeting, H. and West, P. (2003) *Youth Transitions: Patterns of Vulnerability and Processes of Social Inclusion*, Edinburgh, The Stationery Office.

Gilligan, R. (2001) *Promoting Resilience*, London, British Agencies for Adoption and Fostering.

Gilligan, R. (2008) 'Ireland', in Stein, M. and Munro, E. (eds) *Young People's Transitions from Care to Adulthood: International Research and Practice*, London and Philadelphia, Jessica Kingsley Publishers.

Happer, H., McCreadie, J. and Aldgate, J. (2006) *Celebrating Success: What Helps Looked After Children Succeed*, Edinburgh, Social Work Inspection Agency.

Health Information and Quality Authority (2009) *National Children in Care Inspection Report 2008*, Dublin, Health Information and Quality Authority.

Health Information and Quality Authority (2010) *Inspection of the HSE Fostering Service in HSE Dublin North Area* (Online), Cork, HIQA.

Available from: www.hiqa.ie/publications.asp (accessed 14 July 2010).

Health Service Executive (2006) *Model for the Delivery of Leaving Care and Aftercare Service in HSE North West Dublin, North Central Dublin and North Dublin*, Dublin, Health Service Executive.

Health Service Executive (2008) *HSE South Review of Adequacy of Child and Family Services 2005* (online), Dublin, Health Service Executive. Available from: www.hse.ie/eng/Publications/Children_and_Young _People/Review_of_Adequacy_of_Child_and_Family_Services_2005 .html (accessed 21 April 2008).

Health Service Executive (2009) *HSE Child Welfare and Protection Social Work Departments Business Processes. Report of the NCCIS Business Process Standardisation Project October 2009*, Dublin, Health Service Executive.

Hyde, J. and Kammerer, N. (2009) 'Adolescents' perspectives on placement moves and congregate settings: Complex and cumulative instabilities in out-of-home care', *Children and Youth Services Review*, 31, pp. 265–273.

Iacovou, M. (2004) 'Patterns of family life', in Iacovou, M. and Berthoud, R. (eds), *Social Europe, Living Standards and Welfare States*, Cheltenham, Edward Elgar.

Jones, G. (2002) *The Youth Divide: Diverging Paths to Adulthood*, York, Joseph Rowntree Foundation.

Kelleher, P., Kelleher, C. and Corbett, M. (2000) *Left Out on Their Own: Young People Leaving Care in Ireland*, Dublin, Focus Ireland/Oak Tree Press.

MacDonald, R., Shildrick, T., Webster, C. and Simpson, D. (2005) 'Growing up in poor neighbourhoods: The significance of class and place in the extended transitions of 'socially excluded' young adults', *Sociology*, 39, pp. 873–891.

Maunders, D., Liddell, M., Liddell, M. and Green, S. (1999) *Young People Leaving Care and Protection*, National Youth Affairs Research Scheme, Hobart Tasmania, Australian Clearinghouse for Youth Studies.

Mayock, P. and Carr, N. (2008) *Not Just Homelessness ... A Study of 'Out of Home' Young People in Cork City*, Cork, Health Service Executive.

Mayock, P. and O'Sullivan, E. (2007) *Lives in Crisis: Homeless Young People in Dublin*, Dublin, The Liffey Press.

Mendes, P. and Moslehuddin, B. (2006) 'From dependence to interdependence: Towards better outcomes for young people leaving state care', *Child Abuse Review*, 15, pp. 110–126.

Office of the Minister for Children and Youth Affairs (2009) *Report of the Commission to Inquire into Child Abuse, 2009. Implementation Plan*, Dublin, Office of the Minister for Children and Youth Affairs, Department of Health and Children.

O'Sullivan, E. (1996) Adolescents leaving care or leaving home and child care provision in Ireland and the UK: A critical review', in Hill, M. and Aldgate, J. (eds) *Child Welfare Services: Developments in Law, Policy, Practice and Research*, London and Bristol Pennsylvania, Jessica Kingsley Publishers.

O'Sullivan, E. and Breen, J. (2008) 'Children in care in Ireland, 1970–2006', *Social Work Now*, 41 (December), pp. 28–34.

Osgood, D. W., Foster, E. M., Flanagan, C. and Ruth, G. R. (2005) 'Introduction: Why focus on the transition to adulthood for vulnerable populations?', in Osgood, D. W., Foster, E. M., Flanagan, C. and Ruth, G. R. (eds) *On Your Own Without a Net: The Transition to Adulthood for Vulnerable Populations*, Chicago, The University of Chicago Press.

Pinkerton, J. and McCrea, R. (1999) *Meeting the Challenge? Young People Leaving the Care in Northern Ireland*, Aldershot, Ashgate.

Ryan, S. (2009) *Report of the Commission to Inquire into Child Abuse* (Ryan Report), Dublin, The Stationery Office.

Saunders, L. and Broad, B. (1997) *The Health Needs of Young People Leaving Care*, Leicester, de Montford University.

Sinclair, I., Baker, C., Wilson, K. and Gibbs, I. (2005) *Foster Children: Where they go and How they get on*, London, Jessica Kingsley.

Social Services Inspectorate (2001a) *Social Services Inspectorate Practice Guidelines on: Leaving Care and Aftercare Support*. Available from: www.hiqa.ie/media/pdfs/sc_guidance_leaving_aftercare.pdf (accessed 29 July 2010).

Social Services Inspectorate (2001b) *Social Services Inspectorate Annual Report 2001*, Dublin, Social Services Inspectorate.

Social Services Inspectorate (2002) *Social Services Inspectorate Annual Report 2002*, Dublin, Social Services Inspectorate.

Social Services Inspectorate (2003) *Social Services Inspectorate Annual Report 2003*, Dublin, Social Services Inspectorate.

Social Services Inspectorate (2004) *Social Services Inspectorate Annual Report 2004*, Dublin, Social Services Inspectorate.

Social Services Inspectorate (2005) *Social Services Inspectorate Annual Report 2005*, Dublin, Social Services Inspectorate.

Smyth, J. (2010) '"I'm experiencing resistance", says new HSE children's director', *The Irish Times* (8 February).

Stanley, N. (2007) 'Young people's and carers' perspectives on mental health needs of looked-after adolescents', *Child & Family Social Work*, 12, pp. 258–267.

Stein, M. (2002) 'Young people leaving care: A research perspective' in Wheal, A. (ed.) *The RHP Companion to Leaving Care*, Dorset, Russell House Publishing.

Stein, M. (2006) 'Research review: Young people leaving care', *Child & Family Social Work*, 11, pp. 273–279.

Stein, M. (2008) 'Resilience and young people leaving care', *Child Care in Practice*, 14, pp. 35–44.

Stein, M. and Wade, J. (2000) *Helping Care Leavers: Problems and Strategic Responses*, London, Department of Health.

Youth Homelessness Monitoring Committee (2004) *Developing a Leaving and Aftercare Policy: Guidelines for Health Boards*. Available from: www.hiqa.ie/media/pdfs/sc_guidance_leaving_aftercare_policy.pdf (accessed 1 Aug 2010).

Wade, J. and Dixon, J. (2006) 'Making a home, finding a job: Investigating early housing and employment outcomes for young people leaving care', *Child & Family Social Work*, 11, pp. 199–208.

15

Moving beyond 'case-management': Social workers' perspectives on professional supervision in child protection and welfare

Kenneth Burns

Introduction

Child protection work is important and enjoyable work, which is also characterised by significant responsibilities: the work may often be with 'involuntary' service users, caseloads are sometimes high, and resources are often not sufficiently available to implement intervention plans (Stanley and Goddard, 2002; Mor Barak *et al.*, 2006; Burns, 2008, 2009). Social workers and other professionals undertaking this work require access to regular, high quality supervision. The essential role of supervision in child protection has been emphasised in child abuse inquires in Ireland (McGuinness, 1993; Western Health Board, 1996), in the United Kingdom (Lord Laming, 2003, 2009) and in Irish child protection policy (Office of the Minister for Children and Youth Affairs, 2010). The National Social Work Qualifications Board (NSWQB) (2005) argue that supervision is integral to service quality and public protection:

> Supervision is an essential and lifelong component of professional social work. For the protection of the public and promotion of quality service, social workers require access to formal supervision that is regular, consistent and of high quality.

The importance of supervision and its centrality to good practice and service provision is also highlighted in government policy, which states that 'social workers require ongoing training, support and supervision to deliver a safe and good quality service' (Office of the Minister for

Children and Youth Affairs, 2009, p. 42). In this and the previous quote, and often in the supervision literature, the word 'quality' is frequently used. In this chapter the use of the word quality when referring to supervision denotes regular supervision from a skilled and experienced supervisor that attends to all of the functions of supervision to facilitate improved outcomes for service users and to meet the needs of child protection workers, rather than a managerial/quality assurance connotation of the word.

Despite the acclaimed central role of supervision, anecdotal accounts from child protection and welfare social workers in the Republic of Ireland (hereafter, Ireland), some limited evidence in the Irish literature (see McGuinness, 1993; Buckley, 2002; Hanlon, 2008), and findings from the international literature (Dill and Bogo, 2009; Gibbs, 2009; Donnellan and Jack, 2010), suggest that there are difficulties with the quality and frequency of supervision provided to frontline practitioners in child protection and welfare.

This chapter begins by examining what supervision is and why supervision is important. I then explore the various functions of supervision by presenting Hawkins and Shohet's (2000) supervision model. This model is used as a framework to analyse the research data on supervision presented later in the chapter. A critique of research and policy in the area of supervision in child protection and welfare in Ireland is then presented. The second part of the chapter presents findings from a qualitative study that examined social workers' perspectives on professional supervision in child protection and welfare. The primary aim of the study was to examine the retention of social workers in child protection and welfare, and the research questions and interview guide reflected this core aim. However, within the job retention and social work literature, the role of supervision is often reported in study findings as one of the essential factors which contribute to the retention of social workers (Jacquet *et al.*, 2007; Chen and Scannapieco, 2010).

This chapter also highlights the dearth of published primary research studies on supervision in child protection and welfare, or indeed within most areas of social work in Ireland. While the literature on supervision has categorically demonstrated the key role of supervision in child protection to protect and promote the welfare of service users and workers (Gibbs, 2009; Mor Barak *et al.*, 2009), this chapter identifies the absence of substantive policy and guidance on the provision of supervision in the newly revised national child abuse guidelines (Office of the Minister for Children and Youth Affairs, 2010). I argue that the tendency reported in the international literature to provide 'unbalanced' and infrequent supervision which is focused on the *managerial* ('case management') function of supervision – examining the quality of the work and what needs to be 'done' on cases – appears to be replicated in child protection in Ireland. Organisational factors that contribute to this situation are analysed. In this chapter, the wide variety of methods of supervision such as reflective groups, peer or group supervision, as well as the more common one-to-one supervision with a line manager, are acknowledged. The chapter concludes with a discussion of the options available to workers who find that their experiences of supervision within their organisation is infrequent and/or does not address all of the functions of supervision.

What is professional supervision and why is supervision important?

In a definition by Ferguson (2005, cited in Davys and Beddoe, 2010, p. 10), which is employed in a recently published text, professional supervision is defined as:

> a process between someone called a supervisor and another referred to as the supervisee. It is usually aimed at enhancing the helping effectiveness of the person supervised. It may include acquisition of practical skills, mastery of theoretical or technical knowledge, personal development at the client/therapist interface and professional development.

However, in reviewing this literature, it is clear that there is no one accepted definition or preferred method of supervision. The quote above emphasises the traditional and most prevalent one-to-one supervision, despite developments in the area of group and peer supervision. Notwithstanding debates on definitions of supervision, the intricacy and complexity of the process of supervision could be a chapter on its own.

Supervision provides workers with a dedicated space for advice on cases, for support, and a place to progress the worker's professional development (Hawkins and Shohet, 2000). Supervision can 'contain' the child protection worker's anxieties and feelings (Wosket, 2001) generated by the complex, unpredictable and often intractable nature of child protection work which, if not addressed in supervision, can impact on a worker's thought processes and ability to think coherently (Ruch, 2007). Studies in child protection have consistently shown that professional supervision and support, and positive supervisory relationships – either with a supervisor or peers – can reduce the occupational stress experienced by social workers (Rushton and Nathan, 1996; Gibbs, 2001), contribute to employee retention (Jacquet *et al.*, 2007; Burns, 2009), positively affect morale and job satisfaction (Rycraft, 1994) and benefit service provision to users (Morrison, 2001; Department of Children Schools and Families, 2010). This link between the impact of supervision on the quality of services and care is also acknowledged in recommendation 12[1] of the *Report of the Commission to Inquire into Child Abuse, 2009. Implementation Plan* (Office of the Minister for Children and Youth Affairs, 2009).

For the employing agency, supervision is a process which facilitates an evaluation of service provision to 'clients', facilitates feedback to workers on their work; it is a way to manage workloads, and provides a means – through supervisors – for the organisation and management to acknowledge the workers' labour and to communicate that they and their work are valued.

Functions of supervision

The functions of supervision have been enumerated in a number of seminal texts on supervision (for example, Kadushin, 1992; Hughes and Pengelly, 1997; Hawkins and Shohet, 2000). In this chapter I employ Hawkins and Shohet's (2000) model, now in its third edition since its first publication in 1989, to describe the functions of supervision and use it as an organising framework to analyse the research data presented later. Hawkins and Shohet define the three core functions of supervision – educative, supportive and managerial – as follows:[2]

1. *The educative function* ... is about developing the skills, understanding and abilities of the supervisees. This is done through the reflection on and exploration of the supervisees' work with their clients.
2. *The supportive function* is a way of responding to how any workers engaged in intimate therapeutic work with clients are necessarily allowing themselves to be affected by the distress, pain and fragmentation of the client, and how they need time to become aware of how this has affected them and to deal with any reactions. This is essential if the worker is not to become over-full with emotions.
3. *The managerial aspect* of supervision provides the 'quality control' function in work with people. It is not only lack of training or experience that necessitates the need in us, as

workers, to have someone look with us at our work, but also our inevitable human failings, blind spots, areas of vulnerability from our own wounds and our prejudices that can affect the service we provide to clients.

In Table 15.1, the primary foci of supervision relating to the three categories of supervision are further described by Hawkins and Shohet (2000, p. 52):

Table 15.1 Primary foci of supervision

Purpose	Focus
To provide a regular space for the supervisees to reflect upon the *content* and *process* of their work	Educational
To develop understanding and skills within the work	Educational
To receive information and another perspective concerning one's work	Educational/supportive
To receive both content and process feedback	Educational/supportive
To be validated and supported both as a person and as a worker	Supportive
To ensure that as a person and as a worker one is not left to carry, unnecessarily, difficulties, problems and projections alone	Supportive
To have space to explore and express personal distress, restimulation, transference or counter-transference that may be brought up by the work	Supportive
To plan and utilise their *personal* and *professional* resources better	Managerial/supportive
To be proactive rather than reactive	Managerial/supportive
To ensure quality of work	Managerial

The reproduction of this text in useful inasmuch as it clearly describes what balanced, high quality supervision would look like. In this tripartite model, high quality supervision is a process whereby the needs of, interactions between, and potential conflicts between the worker, service user, supervisor and organisation are named, processed and addressed. The supervisor is constructed as a facilitator of learning whereby a reflective approach underpins aspects of the model; the supervisor is less so an expert providing didactic direction. The potential for distress arising from the work is a central component of this supervision model. The supervisor and supervisee are encouraged to attend to both the content and process of their work. The model also recognises the managerial functions of supervision in the allocation and rationing of scarce resources, the management of caseloads and monitoring practice standards.

   To attend successfully to these multifaceted and complex functions, supervisors require a considerable level of experience and knowledge of the work, regular training on supervision, to be in supervision themselves, have a manageable workload and sufficient time to dedicate to this critical role. Explicit in these descriptions is the cost that may be incurred by a party if a particular supervisory function is not attended to. For example, by attending to the supportive function, supervision provides a way for the worker to articulate, respond to and process how their emotional labour with clients has affected them, and not to become overwhelmed by their emotions (Hughes and Pengelly, 1997). Similarly, Davys and Beddoe (2010, p. 220) argue that 'to avoid becoming overwhelmed or wrung out by the emotional material which is brought by the supervisee to supervision', it is essential that supervisors are also contained through their own supervision process (see also Conclusion in Chapter 10). This is particularly salient in child protection work where research has shown that the work can be experienced by workers as stressful. Dill and Bogo (2009) argue that when supervision is attentive to and addresses each of the three inter-related functions of supervision, the service provided to users is more effective.

   It has been argued that the professional support and development functions of supervision within social work have been lacking, with too much focus on managerial surveillance (Gibbs, 2001; White and Harris, 2007). What policy and practice advice is there to guide supervision in child protection in Ireland, and what does Irish research say about the efficacy of supervision and compliance with these policies and guidelines?

Irish research and policy on supervision in child protection

Despite the importance and stated significance of supervision in child protection, a search of the leading peer-review research databases[3] did not return a single study that examined this issue in an Irish context. One study was identified which examined the introduction of reflective learning tools into hospital social work peer supervision groups (Dempsey *et al.*, 2008). A further search of the Children Acts Advisory Board's research databases[4] identified one chapter that reported on the findings a Postgraduate Diploma in Child Protection and Welfare thesis from a decade ago (Buckley, 2002). An additional review of the table of contents of Irish child protection and welfare books identified one other related chapter that examined a child protection and welfare team's experience of setting up a reflective practice group and the incorporation of reflective practice within individual supervision (Walsh, 2008). Within the profession's journal – *The Irish Social Worker* – were located an online study of social workers' supervision (Peet and Jennings, 2010) and the findings of a master's thesis, which examined the embedding of 'team-based performance management' model within social work supervision (Hanlon, 2008).

The online survey of 157 Irish Association of Social Workers members undertaken by Peet and Jennings (2010) found that nearly 60 per cent of social workers in the survey described their supervision as 'sporadic' (undefined term), 6 per cent were not in receipt of any supervision at all, and only 37 per cent had access to monthly supervision. Unfortunately, this exploratory paper did not further stratify the results for social workers in child protection and welfare. In Hanlon's (2008) study, respondents indicated that 'case-management activities' within supervision dominated, and that the high ratio of supervisors to supervisees and social workers' large caseloads were critical barriers in the provision of quality supervision. Overall, there is a very limited literature on supervision in Ireland and beyond what is cited here, there are no known comprehensive national research studies that examine supervision in child protection and welfare. However, the situation appears only marginally better in the international literature, where a review of literature on supervision by Collins-Camargo (2005, cited in Dill and Bogo, 2009, p. 90) found that there were few empirical studies on supervision in social work and there was 'little emphasis on supervision in child welfare'.

The supervision policy outlined in *Children First: National Guidelines for the Protection and Welfare of Children* (hereafter, *Children First* Guidelines) (Office of the Minister for Children and Youth Affairs, 2010, Section 6.1) comprises an exceptionally brief section which is limited in detail. In a separate section of the *Children First* Guidelines (5.11.1), the least ambiguous statement regarding supervision can be found: 'All practitioners must receive regular supervision from an appropriate line manager' (pp. 46–47), where 'regular supervision' is undefined. Some guidance on the frequency of supervision can be found in policy documents from the profession (National Social Work Qualifications Board, 2004; Irish Association of Social Workers, 2009) and a Health Service Executive (HSE) (2009) policy on supervision, which all define regular supervision as being once a month. The HSE policy recognises that newer workers will require more frequent supervision, whereas the NSWQB (2004, p. 27) induction framework is more explicit in stating that supervision should be weekly for workers 'who are taking up their first job or who are lacking in knowledge and skill in the area that they have been employed in ... [and] reduced to once a month by the end of the induction period'. Furthermore, the new *Code of Professional Conduct and Ethics for Social Workers Bye-Law* (CORU, 2011, p. 16) states that social workers 'should seek and engage in supervision in professional practice on an on-going and regular basis'. A recognition of the need to make special provision to support newly qualified social workers in child protection is also included in recommendation 50 of the government's Ryan Report implementation plan (which was to be implemented in January 2011 but, at the time of writing, is still outstanding), which states that 'The HSE will establish a mandatory year of limited caseload, supervision and support for newly-qualified social workers ...' (Office of the Minister for Children and Youth Affairs, 2009, p. 70).

Regarding the qualitative aspects of what supervision should address, section 6.1.3 of the *Children First* Guidelines offers the following guidance:

> It is essential that managers of all disciplines involved in child protec-
> tion work acknowledge the levels of actual or potential stress that may
> affect their staff and take steps to address any problems. These steps
> may include:
>   (i)   adequate and regular supervision of staff;
>   (ii) regular review of caseloads;
>   (iii) acknowledgement of positive achievement;
>   (iv) provision of opportunities for professional development, such
>   as training, staff rotation, special assignments;
>   (v)   development of inter-agency links;
>   (vi) putting in place the necessary arrangements and procedures to
>   ensure the safety and security of child welfare and protection
>   staff. (p. 54)

Within this section one can discern elements of the inter-related managerial (administrative), supportive and educative functions of supervision. However, the guidance provided in this section is far from comprehensive and therefore limited in its ability to guide practition-ers and supervisors. The new *Children First* Guidelines also recom-mends that the HSE should put in place a 'staff supervision and support policy' (p. 54). The *National Child and Family Services Staff Supervision Policy* (Health Service Executive, 2009), published before the revised *Children First* Guidelines, has many important characteris-tics including a directive to supervisors to 'ensure that there is equal emphasis on each of the four functions of supervision [Morrison]' (p. 7), but this policy is yet to be implemented. It is regrettable that a more comprehensive supervision policy was not incorporated within the *Children First* Guidelines document whereby staff supervision and support would have received greater prominence and recognition. Its inclusion may have facilitated greater uniformity of implementation under recommendation 20 of the Ryan implementation plan (p. 55) and benefited if the *Children First* Guidelines were placed on a statutory footing (see Shannon, 2010). Having analysed key research and policy on supervision in Ireland, the next section describes key aspects of the study's methodology prior to presenting the findings on social workers' experiences of supervision in child protection and welfare.

Methodology

Thirty-five participants who were working as social workers or senior social work practitioners in child protection and welfare in one HSE area were interviewed. Of these participants, 30 were women; 5 were senior social work practitioners; the median age on the day of interview was 33; all of the participants were professionally qualified social workers; 7 were born outside of the Republic of Ireland; the median practice experience of participants in child protection and welfare social work was 4 years (average = 6 years), and 27 (77%) of the participants had spent all of their professional career thus far working in child protection. To preserve anonymity, the HSE area and teams are not identified. Pseudonyms are used for all of the social workers quoted.

An informed consent process guided the collection of the data. Interviews were recorded and transcribed, and the data was coded using a qualitative data-analysis software programme (*Atlas 5.2*). The transcripts were analysed using a grounded theory method (Charmaz, 2006) and the findings are presented in the form of 'thick description' by reproducing quotes of verbatim data.

There were a number of limitations with this study. First, owing to resource limitations, only social workers from one HSE area were interviewed. Second, the study sample only included social workers and senior social work practitioners, therefore social work supervisors were not part of the study sample. Third, while copious amounts of rich data were collected on supervision in this study, it was not an exclusive study of supervision. Fourth, data on frequency of supervision is limited to a small number of social workers and caution should be exercised in generalising from this data.

Findings

In the interviews, several recurring and inter-related themes emerged regarding social workers' supervision. These themes included: frequency of supervision; the dominance of 'case-management' (managerial) type supervision; factors which impacted on effective supervision, and supervision and the induction of newly qualified and new workers in child protection and welfare.

Frequency of supervision

Despite organisational, professional and national policy guidance on the importance of regular supervision, participants on all teams described long periods where they had no structured supervision or had very short supervision sessions. Social workers in the study reported 'formal' supervision frequencies ranging from 60 per cent of participants who received supervision every 4–6 weeks; 20 per cent who received supervision bi-monthly; and 20 per cent who receive supervision every three months +, a figure that also includes one social worker who had not been supervised in the preceding six months prior to interview:

> Twice in seven months ... I had it more than the rest of the team ... They only had it once. (Jenna)

> The last time I had supervision ... [was] a few months ago maybe for half an hour. (Holly)

> Formal supervision would be maybe once every two to three months. (Nicole)

> I hadn't had supervision for about six months, partially because it hadn't happened between us, partially because I consciously decided to avoid it [identifying reason removed]. (Deborah)

The regularity of supervision varied within teams and between teams. However, about 60 per cent of social workers were receiving supervision on at least a 4–6 week basis and they often described their satisfaction with the approach to supervision:

> The amount now is probably absolutely correct for the position that I am in at the moment. It's monthly. (Caoimhe)

> I get regular basically every month say. Some people don't get supervision for three months. (Aoife)

> The supervision is, is outstanding and supportive and I think that's part of what keeps me going. (Shauna)

In the study, social workers differentiated between 'formal' or 'structured' supervision, which they defined as a dedicated time between 45 minutes and 2 hours with their supervisor, principally to discuss progress and to-do/action items on their cases (see next section), and 'informal' supervision which they described as frequent but short consultation times with their supervisor. For most social workers, even those who had limited access to 'formal' supervision, they described an open-door policy among most supervisors for frequent 'informal' consultations, which they found supportive and often described as a type of supervision:

> I mightn't have had supervision for a few months alright ... sitting down, that kind of supervision, [but] it doesn't mean that I wouldn't have consulted a lot ... so that's supervision too. (Shannon)

> Several months have passed now since I had my last supervision. That is compensated by the fact that in theory there is an open-door policy that you can go in and address your supervisor. (Clodagh)

When social workers did receive 'formal' supervision, to what extent did this supervision address the Hawkins and Shohet's functions of supervision and the good practice standards outlined in the *Children First* Guidelines?

Dominance of managerial function: 'We don't have supervision, we have case-management.'

A recurring feature of most social workers' interview transcripts was their use of the phrase 'case-management' to describe their supervision. The following is a small selection of illustrative quotes from social workers describing their supervision as case-management:

> Supervision is fine, but a lot of that is case-management. (Nicole)

> We don't have supervision, we have case-management. (Tara)

> My view of the supervision that is available is very negative. First of all, it's not supervision, it's case-management. (Denise)

What did social workers mean by describing their supervision as case-management? Case-management supervision was described as discussing what had happened and what needed to be done on social workers' cases: a dominance of the *managerial* function with an over-emphasis on administrative tasks. Social workers were very aware of the limitations of this managerial approach to supervision and the fact that the other educational and supportive functions of supervision were not being sufficiently addressed. Simon, Laura, Grace and Aoife explain:

> Supervision is seen as what are you doing on your cases and here are [more] new cases. (Simon)

> I feel that they are treating us like, more or less a number and that number should have 20.5 you know families in a case load, it's very much, there's nothing kind of, oh how are you and or how are you managing at the moment? (Laura)

> There is case management, but even case management is impossible. You don't even get enough of case management, there is absolutely no emotional, what I call emotional supervision available. (Grace)

> [The] quality is very good as far as direction and cases goes. Not very good personally, but brilliant professionally ... direction [is] excellent and I get an awful lot of informal supervision. [Supervision] is not about what, how a case made you feel, what happened to you, are you stressed out, no, it's not about anything like that. It's about what you haven't done. (Aoife)

In this and the previous section, social workers described their supervisors as very supportive in the sense of being available for regular short consultations and providing direction on cases on a day-to-day basis. However, they also described how their expectations of supervision and support through addressing the *supportive* function within supervision, whereby there is an acknowledgement of the impact on workers of child protection work, a containment of their anxieties, and an addressing of the emotions raised by this often difficult work were not being adequately met. Hawkins and Shohet (2006, p. 58) argue that 'not attending to these emotions soon leads to less than effective workers, who become either over-identified with their clients or defended against being further affected by them ... this in time leads to stress and ... "burn-out"'.

Barriers to effective supervision

Key themes within the data which social workers identified as impacting on the quality and frequency of their supervision included: the size of their caseloads, the size of their managers' caseloads, cultural issues within teams, and the skill and competence of their supervisor.

I previously reported that social workers in these teams were responsible for on average 40+ children each (Burns, 2008). Sophia and Hannah explain the impact of such high caseloads on supervision:

> I have 30 cases. I get supervision for an hour and a half once every six weeks. If I talked non-stop without drawing a breath you wouldn't ... I know you wouldn't go through the whole 30 cases – there is so much to talk about you know. (Sophia)

> I have 24 cases [families], which is a lot because they are big cases. I mean you sit in supervision at nine-thirty in the morning and by one o'clock, 'cause I talk a lot, you have gone through all the cases so there really isn't any time for you know [questions like]: how is that affecting you? (Hannah)

In Hannah's quote it is possible that the supervisor lacked the skills or awareness of the need to 'slow' the social worker down to explore what her needs were, set priorities for this and subsequent supervision sessions, and structure shorter more effective sessions. On the other hand, the quantity of work arising from social workers' large caseloads can mean that social workers prioritise the managerial (administrative) function at the 'cost' of getting their own professional needs met:

> I am in there for the ... the two hours or whatever it is, I ... I am looking to kind of get things sorted with ... with my cases, you know. And that's my priority when I am in there ... you kind of forget a little bit about your own needs ... we don't necessarily stand up for what we need ourselves as kind of professionals like. (Kelly)

Within Kelly's quote one can see elements of Morrison's (1997) Professional Accommodation Syndrome[5] where the social worker maintains secrecy by not speaking out about the impact of the work on them and does not articulate, or feels that she is not permitted within this team to articulate, what she needs from supervision. Social workers in the study reported that their team leaders (supervisors) were supervising up to 8 workers, which equates to approximately 320 children (8 x 40) for which supervisors had some level of overseeing. Grace in her interview is indicative of many social workers' accommodation of the constraints on their supervisors, owing to the large numbers of cases, and how she believes this can have a negative impact on the quality of supervision and decision making:

> There is no time. It is not even the managers' or supervisors' fault because they [are] managing seven to eight different, you know, different people at a time. You just can't do it. [The] supervision

process is so rushed, that like the poor supervisor has 20 or 30 other things in his or her mind and they will go along with what seems to come out first of their mind. Oh, we will do this, sure we have to go for a care order, we have to do this, but if you could take more time and to really assess the situation you would probably come up with a more feasible answer. (Grace)

Ava suggests that the culture within child protection social work inhibits addressing the emotional aspect of this work (supportive function):

> It's stressful because child protection is difficult work to do emotionally ... I think there is this sort of almost missionary zeal in child protection work where you think you know, God, I can't ... I can't spend time looking at ... having the luxury of looking at what I feel myself in this situation. Even though it might actually sort the whole fucking thing out, do you know. Because I may be going badly wrong with people and even contributing to the problem, or certainly at least not ... not helping, because of how I am approaching it, or how I am feeling about it, or how I am reacting to it. It's more important that we look at our feelings in child protection than any other area. But we can't let ourselves do it. I think we are not letting ourselves do it. (Ava)

Within this quote the social worker is critical of herself and her colleagues for contributing to an unhealthy culture that places barriers to their engagement with a more effective model of supervision where there is an emphasis and investment on all of the functions of supervision. However, a further analysis of this quote, again drawing on Morrison's Professional Accommodation Syndrome, emphasises that the team/agency culture is one where workers internalise the failures of their agency to provide appropriate supports and/or they are not 'allowed' to set the work context with reference to the [often] demanding nature of child protection work. Furthermore, there is a dilemma about telling the truth about their situation: the social worker might be constructed as not 'coping' or being unprofessional (accommodation and entrapment). Shannon suggests a further explanation as to why the supportive and educative functions of supervision are not addressed adequately:

> With the team leader now I haven't gone into the personal development [sic] sort of place with him. Whereas the one before that I started to do that. And then I suppose I got annoyed that ... I started to do that with somebody else, and you commit ... it's a kind of risk thing and it's a trust thing and also ... and you commit, and then the person disappears after three months. So I haven't ... I thought there is no point in

going back to there ... with this person just see how it goes for a while.
(Shannon)

In Shannon's and other interviews, social workers spoke about
trusting their supervisors and how this impacts on supervision,
whereas some social workers said that they go 'outside' to get the
'balance' of supervision that is not provided within the team. Social
workers further described how the educative function of supervision –
opportunities to examine the worker's skills, professional development, and effectiveness with service users – was often described as the
final quick item at the end of supervision, although it was mostly not
discussed at all.

Finally, some social workers questioned their supervisors' skills base
and the training needs of supervisors and supervisees in the area of
supervision training. For example, Sophia and Anna said:

> Is there a course for team leaders? I am not ... I am not knocking
> people at all, but I am just saying there is a lack of uniformity in the way
> supervision is approached by team leaders. (Sophia)

> I think they supervise too many people and I think they need more
> training and like I think it needs, they need to be [have] a lot more
> training for supervisors and maybe for the supervisee as well. (Anna)

It is interesting that Sophia – like Ava – prefaces her critical
comments, which may suggest a reticence in asking for the supervision
she needs, or a unwillingness or inability to be openly critical of her
supervisor and the quality of her supervision. These quotes suggest a
need to re-examine a practice with the HSE of promoting practitioners to management posts without providing them with adequate
training, supervision within their role, and the resources to effectively
carry out their responsibilities as supervisors. The skills, competencies
and responsibilities of line management are quite different to practice
and supervisors need to be inducted, mentored and trained into this
role: it cannot be assumed that a good practitioner will make a good
manager/supervisor.

Supervision and support for newly qualified social workers

Throughout the study, many social workers described very poor or
non-existent induction procedures for new staff when they first
entered child protection and welfare in this HSE area (see Burns,
2011). These interviews took place before the Ryan Report policy
recommendation 50, but after the publication of the NSWQB (2004)

induction framework. Notwithstanding these policies, there would still have been a recognition within teams – given the demands of this work – to 'protect' new and newly qualified staff. Caoimhe, a newly qualified graduate in her 20s, described how during her 'crucial' first six months in the job she was rarely supervised, and her quote, and the next quote from Mya, raises critical questions about the culture within some child protection teams:

> In my first week when I eventually had to get some guidance [from her team leader], I got 'short shrift', and I was to get on with it, that's what a social worker does. So, I thought to myself right, obviously I'm not going to get any support from you so I went elsewhere and I got it from my co-workers and more senior members of the team. Only for them, I probably would have walked out after the first week ... So, that was for a period of about 6 months, basically there was no support, there was no supervision, when I did have supervision it was more often than not cancelled, it was never rescheduled, six months of this. This is the most crucial phase of becoming a child protection social worker and I had nothing. When I did have it, the supervisor talked about themselves and twiddled with my cases on the computer. (Caoimhe)

Mya, a colleague of Caoimhe who now wants to stay, but for the first six to nine months regularly thought about leaving, described her 'induction' into child protection and welfare:

> There was virtually no induction. The induction, induction quote unquote that was there was just a joke ... off you go. It really was that. No exaggeration! And it's, it's extremely daunting ... I was crying going in to work. I was crying going home. I was having nightmares. I was, it was one of the worst times I think I've, I've experienced in my life in terms of stress levels ... When you're starting out in [name of social work department] is, is done on an *ad hoc* basis you know. There's no kind of consistency you know and it's almost a culture thing. I don't know if it's, it's, you know, sink or swim and if you're able to swim, then you're great and you can stay. (Mya)

Despite the absence of a formal induction system, social work colleagues appear to play a key role in inducting new colleagues. Claire, an experienced social worker when she started work in child protection, as with Mya's comment previously, found that in the absence of a formal induction process it was the support of her colleagues that encouraged her to stay:

> I wouldn't have survived if it wasn't for them [co-workers] as much as I've said I feel I'm a competent social worker. In, in that environment the, the newness of it and the difficulties that are involved, difficulties

that are involved with the high numbers ... I don't think I would have
lasted at all. (Claire)

There are a number of possible explanations that the organisation or
teams may put forward to explain this situation: high referral rates,
large caseloads, insufficient resources, high ratio of supervisors to
supervisees, an expectation that new graduates should be fully
'formed' professionals, and so on. Unfortunately, as supervisors and
senior managers were not interviewed, their perspectives on this and
other issues raised in this chapter were not collected and this chapter
therefore represents an incomplete depiction of supervision within
this HSE area.

Concluding comments

The data presented here suggest that this HSE area's compliance with
national and organisational policies on supervision is far from optimal
and that there is a considerable work to be undertaken if it is to meet
the practice principles outlined the *Children First* Guidelines and its
new staff supervision policy (Health Service Executive, 2009).
Moreover, the dominance of the managerial function of supervision,
often to the exclusion of the other functions of supervision, is cause
for concern, given the emphasis in policy, inquires and research on
supervision's centrality to good child protection and welfare practice
and service provision.

  Whatever the possible explanations for the supervision practices in
this HSE area, the impact of such practices are unacceptable and
place social workers under considerable, unnecessary strain and must
impact on the quality of service provided to users. As up to 6 out of
every 10 newly-qualified social workers begin their career in child
protection in Ireland (see Burns, 2009), the full and consistent implementation of recommendation 50 of the Ryan Report implementation
plan is of paramount importance.

  The research findings presented in this chapter and the stated
absence of any primary Irish research studies strongly suggest that a
national comprehensive research study on supervision in child protection and welfare is necessary. Regarding the findings associated with
social workers' perspectives on supervisor support, a study by Dill
(2007) which examined the impact of stress on child welfare supervisors highlights how supervisors are also at risk of burn-out and/or
compassion fatigue; this is a situation which would severely
undermine their capacity to provide support and supervision. Owing
to their daily contact with social workers, supervisors are best posi-

tioned to convey through their actions whether the organisation is supportive, values social workers' contributions and cares about their welfare. These points further highlight the importance of future studies including social work supervisors in their sample and how essential it is for the HSE to make provision for the supervision and support needs of supervisors (team leaders and principal social workers) in child protection and welfare.

While this chapter presents some critical perspectives from social workers regarding their experiences of supervision in child protection, there were also some grounds for optimism. Sixty per cent of these social workers were receiving some kind of supervision – if only case management – on at least a 4–6 week basis, and there were social workers who described satisfaction with the quality of their supervision. Since the completion of this study, there has been growing interest, and progress, on these child protection teams – often collectively with team management – to address perceived deficits in their supervision through locating reading materials to improve the quality of individual supervision and the setting up of peer supervision, reflective learning and/or case discussion groups. It would be interesting to return to these groups to examine whether they were able to address their stated goal of addressing deficits in their supervision or whether they replicated the dominant 'case-management' approach which characterised their individual supervision. However, despite the growing interest in these approaches to supervision, they are not provided for in the organisation's new supervision policy (Health Service Executive, 2009).

Other initiatives described earlier in the chapter to introduce reflective practice within individual and group supervision (Dempsey et al., 2008; Walsh, 2008) are important as the reflective approach emphasises the learning process in supervision and also addresses some of the limits to the tripartite model of supervision (Ruch, 2007; Davys and Beddoe, 2010). To address perceived deficits in their supervision identified by its members, the IASW set up a national social work supervision initiative whereby experienced supervisors make themselves available for 'outside' supervision to other members for a fee. This is also a welcome initiative with many positive aspects to commend it; however, there are also important reported issues with this type of 'outside' supervision that will need to be addressed in its roll-out (see Davys and Beddoe, 2010). Close attention to the progress of these initiatives may yield important learning and suggest options for individuals, groups and teams that wish to improve supervision practices in their area.

Acknowledgements

The author would like to acknowledge and thank Phil Mortell and Sally Ann Attale for their comments on earlier drafts of this chapter.

Notes

1   Recommendation 12: 'Management at all levels should be accountable for the quality of services and care', whereby a number of these responsibilities are listed, including that 'managers should be responsible for ... Ensuring ongoing supervision, support and advice for all staff' (Office of the Minister for Children and Youth Affairs, 2009, p. 40).

2   The labels for the three core functions of supervision (educative, supportive and managerial) in the 2000 edition of this text, which are adopted from Kadushin (1976), are preferred to the revised labels in their 2006 edition (resourcing, qualitative and developmental). The rationale for this decision is that the labels in the 2006 edition are likely to be less recognisable to social workers as they are a departure from the labels used in most social work texts on supervision.

3   Social Service Abstracts, ASSIA, Academic Search Complete, PsychInfo and CINAHL.

4   These research databases can be accessed through the CAAB website: http://caab.ie/Research/publications-database.aspx (see Chapter 12 for links to similar international resources).

5   In this model, Morrison, drawing on the work of Roland Summit's Child Sexual Abuse Accommodation Syndrome, argues that child protection workers can experience stress not just from the direct work with clients but also from how the employing agency responds 'to the strong, but normative feelings and fears which such work engenders. Normative anxieties become pathologised in such agency cultures, and solutions if restricted to the provision of counselling, serve to reinforce the same message that only "inadequate" workers complain' (Morrison, 1997, p. 19). The five stages of accommodation are: 1) secrecy, 2) helplessness, 3) accommodation and entrapment, 4) delayed or unconvincing disclosure, and 5) retraction.

References

Buckley, H. (2002) *Child Protection and Welfare: Innovations and Interventions*, Dublin, IPA.

Burns, K. (2008) '"Making a difference": Exploring job retention issues in child protection and welfare social work', in Burns, K. and Lynch, D. (eds), *Child Protection and Welfare Social Work: Contemporary Themes and Practice Perspectives*, Dublin, A. & A. Farmar.

Burns, K. (2009) *Job Retention and Turnover: A Study of Child Protection and Welfare Social Workers in Ireland* (PhD thesis), Cork, University College Cork.

Burns, K. (2011) '"Career preference", "transients" and "converts": A study of social workers' retention in child protection and welfare', *British Journal of Social Work*, 41, pp. 520–538.

Charmaz, K. (2006) *Constructing Grounded Theory: A Practical Guide Through Qualitative Analysis*, London, Sage.

Chen, S. Y. and Scannapieco, M. (2010) 'The influence of job satisfaction on child welfare worker's desire to stay: An examination of the interaction effect of self-efficacy and supportive supervision', *Children and Youth Services Review*, 32, pp. 482–486.

CORU (2011) *Code of Professional Conduct and Ethics for Social Workers Bye-Law*, Dublin, Coru.

Davys, A. and Beddoe, L. (2010) *Best Practice in Professional Supervision: A Guide for the Helping Professions*, London, Jessica Kingsley Publishers.

Dempsey, M., Murphy, M. and Halton, C. (2008) 'Introducing tools of reflective learning into peer supervision groups in a social work agency: An action research project', *Journal of Practice Teaching in Health & Social Work*, 8(2), pp. 25–43.

Department of Children Schools and Families (2010) *Working Together to Safeguard Children. A Guide to Inter-agency Working to Safeguard and Promote the Welfare of Children*, London, HM Government.

Dill, K. (2007) 'Impact of stressors on front-line child welfare supervisors', *The Clinical Supervisor*, 26(1/2), pp. 177–193.

Dill, K. and Bogo, M. (2009) 'Moving beyond the administrative: Supervisors' perspectives on clinical supervision in child welfare', *Journal of Public Child Welfare*, 3, pp. 87–105.

Donnellan, H. and Jack, G. (2010) *The Survival Guide for Newly Qualified Child and Family Social Workers. Hitting the Ground Running*, London, Jessica Kingsley Publishers.

Gibbs, J. (2009) 'Changing the cultural story in child protection: Learning from the insider's experience', 14, pp. 289–299.

Gibbs, J. A. (2001) 'Maintaining front-line workers in child protection: A case for refocusing supervision', *Child Abuse Review*, 10, pp. 323–335.

Hanlon, H. (2008) 'Performance embedded in professional supervision – The way forward for social work', *Irish Social Worker* (Winter), pp. 6–13.

Hawkins, P. and Shohet, R. (2000) *Supervision in the Helping Professions: An Individual, Group and Organizational Approach* (2nd edn), Buckingham, Open University Press.

Hawkins, P. and Shohet, R. (2006) *Supervision in the Helping Professions: An Individual, Group and Organizational Approach* (3rd edn), Milton Keynes, Open University Press.

Health Service Executive (2009) *National Child and Family Services Staff Supervision Policy* (April 2010 revision), Dublin, Health Service Executive.

Hughes, L. and Pengelly, P. (1997) *Staff Supervision in a Turbulent Environment: Managing Process and Task in Front-Line Supervision*, London, Jessica Kingsley Publishers.

Irish Association of Social Workers (2009) *CPD Folder and Policy Document* (online), Dublin. Available from: http://iasw.ie/index.php/cpd/193–continuous-professional-development-policy (accessed 14 August 2010).

Jacquet, S. E., Clark, S. J., Morazes, J. L. and Withers, R. (2007) 'The role of supervision in the retention of public child welfare workers', *Journal of Public Child Welfare*, 1(3), pp. 27–54.

Kadushin, A. (1992) *Supervision in Social Work* (3rd edn), New York, Columbia University Press.

Lord Laming (2003) *The Victoria Climbié Inquiry*, London, Stationery Office.

Lord Laming (2009) *The Protection of Children in England: A Progress Report*, London, Stationery Office.

McGuinness, C. (1993) *Kilkenny Incest Investigation: Report Presented to Mr. Brendan Howlin T.D. Minister for Health*, Dublin, Stationery Office.

Mor Barak, M. E., Levin, A., Nissly, J. A. and Lane, C. J. (2006) 'Why do they leave? Modelling child welfare workers' turnover intentions', *Children and Youth Services Review*, 28, pp. 548–577.

Mor Barak, M. E., Travis, D. J., Pyun, H. and Xie, B. (2009) 'The impact of supervision on worker outcomes: A meta-analysis', *Social Service Review*, 28(5), pp. 3–32.

Morrison, T. (1997) *Emotionally Competent Child Protection Organisations: Fallacy, Fiction or Necessity?* (online), Wellington, Social Work Now. Available from: www.cyf.govt.nz/documents/about-us/publications/social-work-now/social-work-now-06–april97.pdf (accessed 8 September 2010).

Morrison, T. (2001) *Staff Supervision in Social Care: Making a Real Difference for Staff and Service Users*, Brighton, Pavilion.

National Social Work Qualifications Board (2004) *Induction Framework for Newly Qualified and Non-Nationally Qualified Social Workers*, Dublin, National Social Work Qualifications Board.

National Social Work Qualifications Board (2005) *Supervision Policy Statement (28/2/05)* (online), Dublin, NSWQB. Available from: www.nswqb.ie/qualification/national.html (accessed 14 August 2010).

Office of the Minister for Children and Youth Affairs (2009) *Report of the Commission to Inquire into Child Abuse, 2009. Implementation Plan*, Dublin, Department of Health and Children.

Office of the Minister for Children and Youth Affairs (2010) *Children First: National Guidelines for the Protection and Welfare of Children* (2nd edn, Revision 2), Dublin, Stationery Office.

Peet, S. and Jennings, O. (2010) 'Examining social workers' views on supervision', *Irish Social Worker* (Summer), pp. 12–19.

Ruch, G. (2007) 'Reflective practice in contemporary child care social work: The role of containment', *British Journal of Social Work*, 37(4), pp. 659–680.

Rushton, A. and Nathan, J. (1996) 'The supervision of child protection work', *British Journal of Social Work*, 26, pp. 357–374.

Rycraft, J. R. (1994) 'The party isn't over: The agency role in the retention of public child welfare caseworkers', *Social Work*, 39(1), pp. 75–80.

Shannon, G. (2010) *Third Report of the Special Rapporteur on Child Protection. A Report Submitted to the Oireachtas 2009*, Dublin, Office of the Minister for Children and Youth Affairs.

Stanley, J. and Goddard, C. (2002) *In the Firing Line: Violence and Power in Child Protection Work*, West Sussex, Wiley.

Walsh, C. (2008) 'The critical role of reflection and process in child protection and welfare social work', in Burns, K. and Lynch, D. (eds) *Child Protection and Welfare Social Work: Contemporary Themes and Practice Perspectives*, Dublin, A. & A. Farmar.

Western Health Board (1996) *Kelly: A Child is Dead. Interim Report of the Joint Committee on the Family*, Dublin, Government Publications Office.

White, V. and Harris, J. (2007) 'Management', in Lymbery, M. and Postle, K. (eds), *Social Work: A Companion to Learning*, London, Sage.

Wosket, V. (2001) 'The cyclical model of supervision: A container for creativity and chaos', in Carroll, M. and Tholstrup, M. (eds), *Integrative Approaches to Supervision*, London, Jessica Kingsley Publishers.

Index

Lightning Source UK Ltd.
Milton Keynes UK
UKOW030030270313

208233UK00001B/1/P